ADOBE® PHOTOSHOP® CS4

CLASSROOM IN A BOOK®

The official training workbook from Adobe Systems

www.adobepress.com

Adobe

Adobe Photoshop CS4 Classroom in a Book

Adobe Press books are published by Peachpit, a division of Pearson Education located in Berkeley, California. For the latest on Adobe Press books, go to www.adobepress.com. To report errors, please send a note to errata@peachpit.com. For information on getting permission for reprints and excerpts, contact permissions@peachpit.com.

Printed and bound in the United States of America

ISBN-13: 978-0-321-57379-7

ISBN-10: 0-321-57379-X

9 8 7 6 5 4 3 2

WHAT'S ON THE DISC

Here is an overview of the contents of the Classroom in a Book disc

Lesson files ... and so much more

The *Adobe Photoshop CS4 Classroom in a Book* disc includes the lesson files that you'll need to complete the exercises in this book, as well as other content to help you learn more about Adobe Photoshop CS4 and use it with greater efficiency and ease. The diagram below represents the contents of the disc, which should help you locate the files you need.

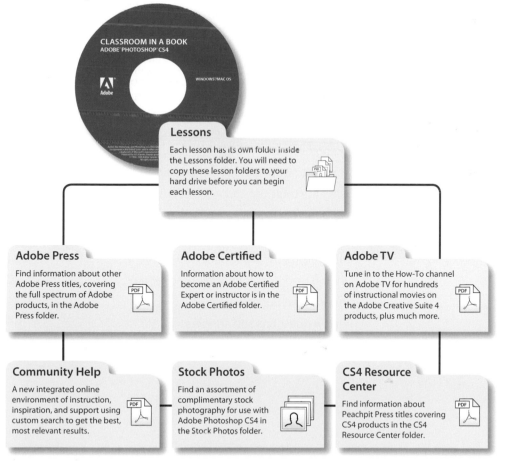

Lessons

Each lesson has its own folder inside the Lessons folder. You will need to copy these lesson folders to your hard drive before you can begin each lesson.

Adobe Press

Find information about other Adobe Press titles, covering the full spectrum of Adobe products, in the Adobe Press folder.

Adobe Certified

Information about how to become an Adobe Certified Expert or instructor is in the Adobe Certified folder.

Adobe TV

Tune in to the How-To channel on Adobe TV for hundreds of instructional movies on the Adobe Creative Suite 4 products, plus much more.

Community Help

A new integrated online environment of instruction, inspiration, and support using custom search to get the best, most relevant results.

Stock Photos

Find an assortment of complimentary stock photography for use with Adobe Photoshop CS4 in the Stock Photos folder.

CS4 Resource Center

Find information about Peachpit Press titles covering CS4 products in the CS4 Resource Center folder.

CONTENTS

GETTING STARTED

About Classroom in a Book. 1

What's new in this edition 2

What's in Photoshop Extended 2

Prerequisites. 3

Installing Adobe Photoshop. 3

Starting Adobe Photoshop. 4

Copying the Classroom in a Book files 4

Restoring default preferences 5

Additional resources 6

Adobe certification 7

1   GETTING TO KNOW THE WORK AREA

Lesson overview. 8

Starting to work in Adobe Photoshop 10

Using the tools 14

Using the options bar and other panels. 23

Undoing actions in Photoshop 26

Customizing the workspace. 34

Finding resources for using Photoshop 39

Checking for updates 39

Review questions and answers 45

2 BASIC PHOTO CORRECTIONS

Lesson overview 46

Strategy for retouching 48

Resolution and image size 49

Getting started 50

Straightening and cropping an image 52

Making automatic adjustments 53

Removing a color cast 56

Manually adjusting the tonal range. 57

Replacing colors in an image 59

Adjusting lightness with the Dodge tool 61

Adjusting saturation with the Sponge tool 62

Comparing automatic and manual results 63

Repairing areas with the Clone Stamp tool 64

Using the Spot Healing Brush tool 66

Using the Healing Brush and Patch tools 67

Applying the Unsharp Mask filter 71

Saving the image for four-color printing 72

Review questions and answers 74

3 WORKING WITH SELECTIONS

Lesson overview 76

About selecting and selection tools 78

Getting started 79

Using the Quick Selection tool 79

Moving a selected area 80

Manipulating selections. 81

Using the Magic Wand tool. 88

Selecting with the lasso tools 90

Rotating a selection. 91

Selecting with the Magnetic Lasso tool 92

Cropping an image and erasing within a selection 95

Refining the edge of a selection 96

Review questions and answers 103

4   LAYER BASICS

Lesson overview 104

About layers 106

Getting started 106

Using the Layers panel 107

Rearranging layers 112

Applying a gradient to a layer 119

Applying a layer style 121

Flattening and saving files 127

Review questions and answers 132

5   MASKS AND CHANNELS

Lesson overview 134

Working with masks and channels 136

Getting started 136

Creating a quick mask 137

Editing a mask 139

Viewing channels 147

Adjusting individual channels 149

Loading a mask as a selection 151

Applying filters to a mask 153

Applying effects using a gradient mask 154

Resizing the canvas 157

Removing the background from an image 158

Moving layers between documents 159

Colorizing with an adjustment layer 161

Grouping and clipping layers 163

Inverting a mask 164

Using type as a mask 166

Review questions and answers 170

6   CORRECTING AND ENHANCING DIGITAL PHOTOGRAPHS

Lesson overview 172

Getting started 174

About camera raw 177

Processing files in Camera Raw 177

Correcting digital photographs in Photoshop 189

Editing images with a vanishing-point perspective 196

Correcting image distortion 199

Adding depth of field 202

Creating a PDF image gallery 207

Review questions and answers 210

7 TYPOGRAPHIC DESIGN

Lesson overview 212

About type 214

Getting started 214

Creating a clipping mask from type 215

Creating a design element from type .220

Using interactive formatting controls .223

Warping point type 225

Designing a paragraph of type 226

Warping a layer 232

Review questions and answers 237

8 VECTOR DRAWING TECHNIQUES

Lesson overview 238

About bitmap images and vector graphics 240

About paths and the Pen tool 241

Getting started 241

Using paths with artwork 243

Creating vector objects for the background 252

Working with defined custom shapes .259

Importing a Smart Object 261

Review questions and answers 267

9 ADVANCED LAYERING

Lesson overview 268

Getting started 270

Clipping a layer to a shape 271

Setting up a Vanishing Point grid 273

Creating your own keyboard shortcuts 276

Placing imported artwork 277

Adding artwork in perspective 278

Adding a layer style 279

Placing the side panel artwork 280

Adding more artwork in perspective. 281

Adding an adjustment layer 282

Working with layer comps. 284

Managing layers 285

Flattening a layered image 287

Merging layers and layer groups 288

Stamping layers 288

Review questions and answers 290

10 ADVANCED COMPOSITING

Lesson overview 292

Getting started 294

Assembling a montage of images 295

Applying filters 303

Hand-coloring selections on a layer 306

Applying Smart Filters 312

Adding drop shadows and a border 315

Matching color schemes across images. 318

Automating a multistep task 319

Stitching a Panorama 324

Review questions and answers 329

11 PREPARING FILES FOR THE WEB

Lesson overview 330

Getting started 332

Selecting a web design workspace 334

Creating slices 336

Adding animation 342

Animating a layer style 346

Exporting HTML and images 349

Using the Zoomify feature 353

Creating a web gallery 354

Review questions and answers 360

12 WORKING WITH 3D IMAGES

Lesson overview 362

Getting started 364

Creating a 3D shape from a layer 364

Manipulating 3D objects 366

Using the 3D panel to adjust lighting and
surface texture 369

Merging two-dimensional layers onto 3D layers 373

Importing 3D files 374

Merging 3D layers to share the same 3D space 375

Adding a spot light 379

Painting on a 3D object 382

Adding 3D text 382

Creating a 3D postcard 383

Review questions and answers 390

13 WORKING WITH SCIENTIFIC IMAGES

Lesson overview 392

Getting started 394

Viewing and editing files in Adobe Bridge 394

Brightening and boosting color in an image 406

Creating a map border and work area .407

Making a custom border 410

Measuring objects and data 412

Exporting measurements 416

Measuring a cross-section 417

Measuring in perspective using the
Vanishing Point filter 419

Adding a legend 421

Creating a slide show 422

Review questions and answers 423

14 PRODUCING AND PRINTING CONSISTENT COLOR

Lesson overview 424

About color management. 426

Getting started 428

Specifying color-management settings. 428

Proofing an image 429

Identifying out-of-gamut colors 431

Adjusting an image and printing a proof. 432

Saving the image as a CMYK EPS file. .434

Printing 434

Review questions and answers 437

GETTING STARTED

Adobe® Photoshop® CS4, the benchmark for digital imaging excellence, provides strong performance, powerful image-editing features, and an intuitive interface. Adobe Camera Raw 5, included with Photoshop CS4, offers flexibility and control as you work with raw images, and now you can apply the same tools to TIFF and JPEG images, as well. Photoshop CS4 pushes the boundaries of digital image editing and helps you turn your dreams into designs more easily than ever before.

About Classroom in a Book

Adobe Photoshop CS4 Classroom in a Book® is part of the official training series for Adobe graphics and publishing software developed by experts at Adobe Systems. The lessons are designed to let you learn at your own pace. If you're new to Adobe Photoshop, you'll learn the fundamental concepts and features you'll need to master the program. And, if you've been using Adobe Photoshop for a while, you'll find that Classroom in a Book teaches many advanced features, including tips and techniques for using the latest version of the application and for preparing images for the web.

Although each lesson provides step-by-step instructions for creating a specific project, there's room for exploration and experimentation. You can follow the book from start to finish, or do only the lessons that match your interests and needs. Each lesson concludes with a review section summarizing what you've covered.

What's new in this edition

This edition covers many new features in Adobe Photoshop CS4, such as the Adjustments panel, making it easier than ever to add nondestructive adjustment layers; the application bar, which provides quick access to important settings; and the Masks panel, which gives you greater control over masks and channels. In addition, these lessons introduce you to enhancements to Camera Raw, the Clone Source panel, the Vibrance slider, and the ability to extend the depth of field in an image so that both foreground and background can be in clear focus,.

New exercises and lessons cover:

- Using the Clone Source panel and clone overlay to accurately copy pixels.
- Editing TIFF, JPEG, or raw image files in Camera Raw.
- Selecting, inverting, and otherwise manipulating masks using the Masks panel.
- Transforming 2D images into 3D objects.
- Manipulating, positioning, and painting on 3D objects.

This edition is also chock-full of extra information on Photoshop features and how best to work with this robust application. You'll learn about Adobe Photoshop Lightroom®—a toolbox for professional photographers that helps them manage, adjust, and present large volumes of digital photos. You'll also learn best practices for organizing, managing, and showcasing your photos, as well as how to optimize images for the web. And throughout this edition, look for tips and techniques from one of Adobe's own experts, Photoshop evangelist Julieanne Kost.

What's in Photoshop Extended

This edition of *Adobe Photoshop CS4 Classroom in a Book* works with many of the features in Adobe Photoshop CS4 Extended—a version with additional functions for professional, technical, and scientific users, intended for those creating special effects in video or in architectural, scientific, or engineering images.

Just some of the Photoshop Extended features include:

- The ability to import three-dimensional images and video, and edit individual frames or image sequence files by painting, cloning, retouching, or transforming them.
- Support for three-dimensional (3D) files including the U3D, 3DS, OBJ, KMZ, and Collada file formats, created by programs like Adobe Acrobat® 9 Professional, 3D Studio Max, Alias, Maya, and Google Earth. See Lesson 12, "Working with 3D Images," to learn about these features.

- Measurement and counting tools to measure any area, including an irregular area, defined with the Ruler tool or a selection tool. You can also compute the height, width, area, and perimeter, or track measurements of one or many images. See Lesson 13, "Working with Scientific Images," for more on how to use these features.

- Image stacks, stored as Smart Objects, that let you combine a group of images with a similar frame of reference, and then process the multiple images to produce a composite view, for example, to eliminate unwanted content or noise.

- Animation features that show the frame duration and animation properties for document layers in Timeline mode, and that let you navigate through frames, edit them, and adjust the frame duration for layers.

- Support for specialized file formats, such as DICOM—the most common standard for receiving medical scans; MATLAB, a high-level technical computing language and interactive environment for developing algorithms, visualizing and analyzing data, and computing numbers; and 32-bit high-resolution images, including a special HDR Color Picker and the capability to paint and layer these 32-bit HDR images.

Prerequisites

Before you begin to use *Adobe Photoshop CS4 Classroom in a Book*, you should have a working knowledge of your computer and its operating system. Make sure that you know how to use the mouse and standard menus and commands, and also how to open, save, and close files. If you need to review these techniques, see the documentation included with your Microsoft® Windows® or Apple® Mac® OS X documentation.

Installing Adobe Photoshop

Before you begin using *Adobe Photoshop CS4 Classroom in a Book*, make sure that your system is set up correctly and that you've installed the required software and hardware. You must purchase the Adobe Photoshop CS4 software separately. For system requirements and complete instructions on installing the software, see the Adobe Photoshop CS4 Read Me file on the application DVD or on the web at www.adobe.com/support/.

Photoshop and Bridge use the same installer. You must install these applications from the Adobe Photoshop CS4 application DVD onto your hard disk; you cannot run the programs from the DVD. Follow the onscreen instructions.

Make sure that your serial number is accessible before installing the application.

Starting Adobe Photoshop

You start Photoshop just as you do most software applications.

To start Adobe Photoshop in Windows:

Choose Start > All Programs > Adobe Photoshop CS4.

To start Adobe Photoshop in Mac OS:

Open the Applications/Adobe Photoshop CS4 folder, and double-click the Adobe Photoshop program icon.

Copying the Classroom in a Book files

The *Adobe Photoshop CS4 Classroom in a Book* CD includes folders containing all the electronic files for the lessons in the book. Each lesson has its own folder; you must copy the folders to your hard disk to complete the lessons. To save room on your disk, you can install only the folder necessary for each lesson as you need it, and remove it when you're done.

To install the lesson files, do the following:

1 Insert the *Adobe Photoshop CS4 Classroom in a Book* CD into your CD-ROM drive.

2 Browse the contents and locate the Lessons folder.

3 Do one of the following:

- To copy all the lesson files, drag the Lessons folder from the CD onto your hard disk.

- To copy only individual lesson files, first create a new folder on your hard disk and name it **Lessons**. Then, drag the lesson folder or folders that you want to copy from the CD into the Lessons folder on your hard disk.

● **Note:** As you complete each lesson, you will preserve the start files. In case you overwrite them, you can restore the original files by recopying the corresponding Lesson folder from the *Adobe Photoshop CS4 Classroom in a Book* CD to the Lessons folder on your hard drive.

Restoring default preferences

The preferences files store panel and command settings information. Each time you quit Adobe Photoshop, the positions of the panels and certain command settings are recorded in the respective preferences file. Any selections you make in the Preferences dialog box are also saved in the preferences file.

To ensure that you what you see onscreen matches the images and instructions in this book, you should restore the default preferences as you begin each lesson. If you prefer to preserve your preferences, be aware that the tools, panels, and other settings in Photoshop CS4 may not match those described in this book.

If you have custom-calibrated your monitor, save the calibration settings before you start work on this book. To save your monitor-calibration settings, follow the simple procedure described below.

To restore all preferences to default settings:

- Press and hold Alt+Control+Shift (Windows) or Option+Command+Shift (Mac OS) as you start Photoshop. You are prompted to delete the current settings.

- (Mac OS only) Open the Preferences folder in the Library folder, and drag the Adobe Photoshop CS Settings folder to the Trash. New Preferences files are created the next time you start Photoshop.

To save your current color settings:

1 Start Adobe Photoshop.

2 Choose Edit > Color Settings.

3 Note what is selected in the Settings menu:

- If it is anything other than Custom, write down the name of the settings file, and click OK to close the dialog box. You do not need to perform steps 4–6 of this procedure.

- If Custom is selected in the Settings menu, click Save (*not* OK).

The Save dialog box opens. The default location is the Settings folder, which is where you want to save your file. The default file extension is .csf (color settings file).

4 In the File Name field (Windows) or Save As field (Mac OS), type a descriptive name for your color settings, preserving the .csf file extension. Then click Save.

5 In the Color Settings Comment dialog box, type any descriptive text that will help you identify the color settings later, such as the date, specific settings, or your workgroup.

6 Click OK to close the Color Settings Comment dialog box, and again to close the Color Settings dialog box.

To restore your color settings:

1 Start Adobe Photoshop.

2 Choose Edit > Color Settings.

3 In the Settings menu in the Color Settings dialog box, select the settings file you noted or saved in the previous procedure and click OK.

Additional resources

Adobe Photoshop CS4 Classroom in a Book is not meant to replace documentation that comes with the program or to be a comprehensive reference for every feature in Photoshop CS4. Only the commands and options used in the lessons are explained in this book. For comprehensive information about program features, refer to any of these resources:

- Adobe Photoshop CS4 Community Help, which you can view by choosing Help > Photoshop Help. Community Help is an integrated online environment of instruction, inspiration, and support. It includes custom search of expert-selected, relevant content on and off Adobe.com. Community Help combines content from Adobe Help, Support, Design Center, Developer Connection, and Forums—along with great online community content so that users can easily find the best and most up-to-date resources. Access tutorials, technical support, online product help, videos, articles, tips and techniques, blogs, examples, and much more.

- Adobe Photoshop CS4 Product Support Center, where you can find and browse support and learning content on Adobe.com. Visit www.adobe.com/support/photoshop/.

- Adobe TV, where you will find programming on Adobe products, including a channel for professional photographers and a How To channel that contains hundreds of movies on Photoshop CS4 and other products across the Adobe Creative Suite 4 lineup. Visit http://tv.adobe.com/.

Also check out these useful links:

- The Photoshop CS4 product home page at www.adobe.com/products/photoshop/.

- Photoshop user forums at www.adobe.com/support/forums/ for peer-to-peer discussions of Adobe products.

- Photoshop Exchange at www.adobe.com/cfusion/exchange/ for extensions, functions, code, and more.

- Photoshop plug-ins at www.adobe.com/products/plugins/photoshop/.

Adobe certification

The Adobe Certified program is designed to help Adobe customers and trainers improve and promote their product-proficiency skills. There are four levels of certification:

- Adobe Certified Associate (ACA)
- Adobe Certified Expert (ACE)
- Adobe Certified Instructor (ACI)
- Adobe Authorized Training Center (AATC)

The Adobe Certified Associate (ACA) credential certifies that individuals have the entry-level skills to plan, design, build, and maintain effective communications using different forms of digital media.

The Adobe Certified Expert program is a way for expert users to upgrade their credentials. You can use Adobe certification as a catalyst for getting a raise, finding a job, or promoting your expertise.

If you are an ACE-level instructor, the Adobe Certified Instructor program takes your skills to the next level and gives you access to a wide range of Adobe resources.

Adobe Authorized Training Centers offer instructor-led courses and training on Adobe products, employing only Adobe Certified Instructors. A directory of AATCs is available at http://partners.adobe.com.

For information on the Adobe Certified program, visit www.adobe.com/support/certification/main.html.

1 GETTING TO KNOW THE WORK AREA

Lesson overview

In this lesson, you'll learn how to do the following:

- Open Adobe Photoshop files.

- Select and use some of the tools in the Tools panel.

- Set options for a selected tool using the options bar.

- Use various methods to zoom in and out on an image.

- Select, rearrange, and use panels.

- Choose commands in panel and context menus.

- Open and use a panel docked in the panel well.

- Undo actions to correct mistakes or to make different choices.

- Customize the workspace.

- Find topics in Photoshop Help.

 This lesson will take about 90 minutes to complete. Copy the Lesson01 folder into the Lessons folder that you created on your hard drive for these projects (or create it now), if you haven't already done so. As you work on this lesson, you'll preserve the start files. If you need to restore the start files, copy them from the *Adobe Photoshop CS4 Classroom in a Book* CD.

As you work with Adobe Photoshop, you'll discover that you can often accomplish the same task several ways. To make the best use of the extensive editing capabilities in Photoshop, you must first learn to navigate the work area.

Starting to work in Adobe Photoshop

The Adobe Photoshop work area includes menus, toolbars, and panels that give you quick access to a variety of tools and options for editing and adding elements to your image. You can also add commands and filters to the menus by installing third-party software known as *plug-in modules*.

Photoshop works with bitmapped, digitized images (that is, continuous-tone images that have been converted into a series of small squares, or picture elements, called *pixels*). You can also work with vector graphics, which are drawings made of smooth lines that retain their crispness when scaled. You can create original artwork in Photoshop, or you can import images into the program from many sources, such as:

- Photographs from a digital camera.

- Commercial CDs of digital images.

- Scans of photographs, transparencies, negatives, graphics, or other documents.

- Captured video images.

- Artwork created in drawing programs.

Starting Photoshop and opening a file

To begin, you'll start Adobe Photoshop and reset the default preferences.

1 On the desktop, double-click the Adobe Photoshop icon to start Adobe Photoshop and then immediately hold down Ctrl+Alt+Shift (Windows) or Command+Option+Shift (Mac OS) to reset the default settings.

If you don't see the Photoshop icon on your desktop, choose Start > All Programs > Adobe Photoshop CS4 (Windows) or look in either the Applications folder or the Dock (Mac OS).

2 When prompted, click Yes to confirm that you want to delete the Adobe Photoshop Settings file.

● **Note:** You won't typically need to reset defaults when you're working on your own projects. However, you'll reset the preferences before working on each lesson in this book to ensure that what you see onscreen matches the descriptions in the lessons. For more information, see "Restoring default preferences" on page 4.

The Photoshop work area appears as shown in the following illustration.

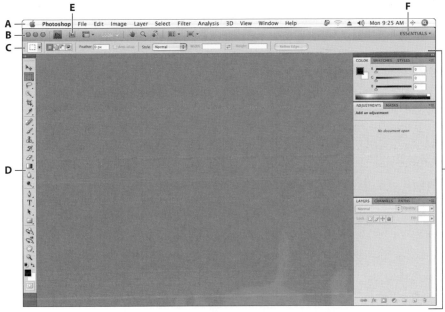

A. Menu bar
B. Application bar
C. Options bar
D. Tools panel
E. Adobe Bridge button
F. Workspaces menu
G. Floating panels

● **Note:** This illustration shows the Mac OS version of Photoshop. On Windows, the application bar and menu bar are on the same line. Otherwise, the arrangement is the same, but operating system styles may vary.

The default workspace in Photoshop consists of the application bar, menu bar, and options bar at the top of the screen, the Tools panel on the left, and several open panels in the panel dock on the right. When you have documents open, one or more image windows also appear, and you can display them at the same time using the new tabbed interface. The Photoshop user interface is very similar to the one in Adobe Illustrator®, Adobe InDesign®, and Adobe Flash®—so learning how to use the tools and panels in one application means that you'll know how to use them in the others.

There are a few differences between the Photoshop work area on Windows and that on Mac OS.

- On Windows, the menu bar is combined with the application bar, if your screen resolution makes it possible to fit them on the same line.

- On Mac OS, you can now work with an application frame, which contains the Photoshop application's windows and panels within a frame that is distinct from other applications you may have open; only the menu bar is outside the application frame. The application frame is disabled by default; to enable the application frame, choose Window > Application Frame. To use the new tabbed interface, you must have the application frame enabled. Additionally, you can enable and disable the application bar. This book assumes you are using the application bar.

On Mac OS, the application frame keeps the image, panels, and application bar together.

3   Choose File > Open, and navigate to the Lessons/Lesson01 folder that you copied to your hard drive from the *Adobe Photoshop CS4 Classroom in a Book* CD.

4   Select the 01A_End.psd file and click Open. Click OK if you see the Embedded Profile Mismatch dialog box.

The 01A_End.psd file opens in its own window, called the *image window*. The end files in this book show you what you are creating in the different projects. In this file, an image of a vintage car has been enhanced without overexposing the headlight.

5   Choose File > Close, or click the close button on the title bar of the image window. (Do not close Photoshop.)

Opening a file with Adobe Bridge

In this book, you'll work with different start files in each lesson. You may make copies of these files and save them under different names or locations, or you may work from the original start files and then copy them from the CD again if you want a fresh start. This lesson includes three start files.

In the previous exercise, you used the Open command to open a file. Now you'll open another file using Adobe Bridge, a visual file browser that helps take the guesswork out of finding the image file that you need.

1 Click the Launch Bridge button ( ) in the application bar. If you're prompted to enable the Photoshop extension in Bridge, click OK.

Note: You can also open Adobe Bridge by choosing File > Browse In Bridge.

Adobe Bridge opens, displaying a collection of panels, menus, and buttons.

2 From the Folders panel in the upper-left corner, browse to the Lessons folder you copied from the CD onto your hard disk. The Lessons folder appears in the Content panel.

3 Select the Lessons folder, and choose File > Add To Favorites. Adding files, folders, application icons, and other assets that you use often to the Favorites panel lets you access them quickly.

4 Select the Favorites tab to open the panel, and click the Lessons folder to open it. Then, in the Content panel, double-click the Lesson01 folder.

Thumbnail previews of the folder contents appear in the Content panel.

5 Double-click the 01A_Start.psd thumbnail in the Content panel to open the file, or select the thumbnail and choose File > Open.

The 01A_Start.psd image opens in Photoshop. Leave Bridge open; you'll use it to locate and open files later in this lesson.

Adobe Bridge is much more than a convenient visual interface for opening files. You'll have the chance to learn more about the many features and functions of Adobe Bridge in Lesson 13, "Working with Scientific Images."

Using the tools

Photoshop provides an integrated set of tools for producing sophisticated graphics for print, web, and mobile viewing. We could easily fill the entire book with details on the wealth of Photoshop tools and tool configurations. While that would certainly be a useful reference, it's not the goal of this book. Instead, you'll start gaining experience by configuring and using a few tools on a sample project. Every lesson will introduce you to more tools and ways to use them. By the time you finish all the lessons in this book, you'll have a solid foundation for further explorations of the Photoshop tool set.

Selecting and using a tool from the Tools panel

● **Note:** For a complete list of the tools in the Tools panel, see the Tools panel overview at the end of this lesson.

The Tools panel—the long, narrow panel on the far left side of the work area—contains selection tools, painting and editing tools, foreground- and background-color selection boxes, and viewing tools. In Photoshop Extended, it also includes 3D tools.

You'll start by using the Zoom tool, which appears in many other Adobe applications, including Illustrator, InDesign, and Acrobat.

1   Click the double-arrow button just above the Tools panel to toggle to a double-column view. Click the arrow again to return to a single-column Tools panel and use your screen space more efficiently.

2   Examine the status bar at the bottom of the work area (Windows) or image window (Mac OS), and notice the percentage listed on the far left. This represents the current enlargement view of the image, or zoom level.

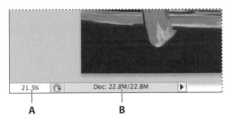

A. Zoom level B. Status bar

3   Move the pointer over the Tools panel and hover it over the magnifying-glass icon until a tool tip appears. The tool tip displays the tool's name (Zoom tool) and keyboard shortcut (Z).

4   Click the Zoom tool (🔍) in the Tools panel or press Z to select it.

5 Move the pointer over the image window. The pointer now looks like a tiny magnifying glass with a plus sign (+) in the center of the glass.

6 Click anywhere in the image window.

The image enlarges to a preset percentage level, which replaces the previous value in the status bar. The location you clicked when you used the Zoom tool is centered in the enlarged view. If you click again, the zoom advances to the next preset level, up to a maximum of 3200%.

7 Hold down the Alt key (Windows) or Option key (Mac OS) so that the Zoom tool pointer appears with a minus sign (-) in the center of the magnifying glass, and then click anywhere in the image. Then release the Alt or Option key.

Now the view zooms out to a lower preset magnification, so that you can see more of the image, but in less detail.

8 Using the Zoom tool, drag a rectangle to enclose the area of the image that includes the headlight.

The image enlarges so that the area you enclosed in your rectangle now fills the entire image window.

You have now used three methods with the Zoom tool to change the magnification in the image window: clicking, holding down a keyboard modifier while clicking, and dragging to define a magnification area. Many of the other tools in the Tools panel can be used with keyboard combinations, as well. You'll have opportunities to use these techniques in various lessons in this book.

● **Note:** You can use other methods to zoom in and out. For example, when the Zoom tool is selected, you can select the Zoom In or Zoom Out mode on the options bar. You can choose View > Zoom In or View > Zoom Out. Or, you can type a new percentage in the status bar and press Enter or Return.

Selecting and using a hidden tool

Photoshop has many tools you can use to edit image files, but you will probably work with only a few of them at a time. The Tools panel arranges some of the tools in groups, with only one tool shown for each group. The other tools in the group are hidden behind that tool.

A small triangle in the lower-right corner of a button is your clue that other tools are available but hidden under that tool.

1 Position the pointer over the second tool from the top in the Tools panel until the tool tip appears. The tool tip identifies the Rectangular Marquee tool (⬚) with the keyboard shortcut M. Select that tool.

2 Select the Elliptical Marquee tool (◯), which is hidden behind the Rectangular Marquee tool, using one of the following methods:

- Press and hold the mouse button over the Rectangular Marquee tool to open the pop-up list of hidden tools, and select the Elliptical Marquee tool.

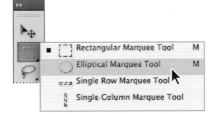

- Alt-click (Windows) or Option-click (Mac OS) the tool button in the Tools panel to cycle through the hidden marquee tools until the Elliptical Marquee tool is selected.

- Press Shift+M, which switches between the Rectangular and Elliptical Marquee tools.

3 Move the pointer over the image window, to the upper-left side of the headlight. When the Elliptical Marquee tool is selected, the pointer becomes cross hairs (+).

4 Drag the pointer down and to the right to draw an ellipse around the headlight, and then release the mouse button.

An animated dashed line indicates that the area inside it is *selected*. When you select an area, it becomes the only editable area of the image. The area outside the selection is protected.

5 Move the pointer inside your elliptical selection so that the pointer appears as an arrow with a small rectangle (⯑).

6 Drag the selection so that it is accurately centered over the headlight.

When you drag the selection, only the selection border moves, not pixels in the image. When you want to move the pixels in the image, you'll need to use a different technique. Youêll learn more about making different kinds of selections and moving the selection contents in Lesson 3, "Working with Selections."

Using keyboard combinations with tool actions

Many tools can operate under certain constraints. You usually activate these modes by holding down specific keyboard keys as you move the tool with the mouse. Some tools have modes that you choose in the options bar.

The next task is to make a fresh start at selecting the headlight. This time, you'll use a keyboard combination that constrains the elliptical selection to a circle that you'll draw from the center outward instead of from the outside inward.

1 Make sure that the Elliptical Marquee tool (◯) is still selected in the Tools panel, and deactivate the current selection by doing one of the following:

- In the image window, click anywhere outside the selected area.
- Choose Select > Deselect.
- Use the keyboard shortcut Ctrl+D (Windows) or Command+D (Mac OS).

2 Position the pointer in the center of the headlight.

3 Press Alt+Shift (Windows) or Option+Shift (Mac OS) and drag outward from the center of the headlight until the circle completely encloses the headlight. The Shift key constrains the ellipse to a perfect circle.

4 Carefully release first the mouse button and then the keyboard keys.

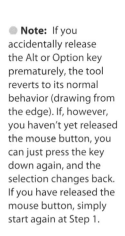

● **Note:** If you accidentally release the Alt or Option key prematurely, the tool reverts to its normal behavior (drawing from the edge). If, however, you haven't yet released the mouse button, you can just press the key down again, and the selection changes back. If you have released the mouse button, simply start again at Step 1.

If you are not satisfied with the selection circle, you can move it: Place the pointer inside the circle and drag, or click outside the selection circle to deselect it and then try again.

5 In the Tools panel, double-click the Zoom tool (🔍) to switch to 100% view. If the entire image doesn't fit in the image window, click the Fit Screen button in the options bar.

Notice that the selection remains active, even after you use the Zoom tool.

Applying a change to a selected area

Normally, you'd change the area within the selection. But in order to spotlight the headlight, you'll want to darken the rest of the image, not the area inside the current selection. To protect that area, you'll invert the selection, so that everything *but* the headlight is selected in the image.

1 Choose Select > Inverse.

Although the animated selection border around the headlight looks the same, notice that a similar border appears all around the edges of the image. Now the rest of the image is selected and can be edited, while the area within the circle is not selected. The unselected area (the headlight) cannot be changed while the selection is active.

A   B

A. Selected (editable) area
B. Unselected (protected) area

▶ **Tip:** The keyboard shortcut for this command, Ctrl+Shift+I (Windows) or Command+Shift+I (Mac OS) appears by the command name in the Select menu. In the future, you can just press that keyboard combination to invert a selection.

2 Click the Curves icon in the Adjustments panel to add a Curves adjustment layer. The Curves panel opens.

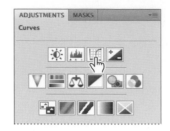

3 In the Curves panel, drag the control point in the upper-right corner of the graph straight across to the left until the Input value is approximately **204**. The Output value should remain 255.

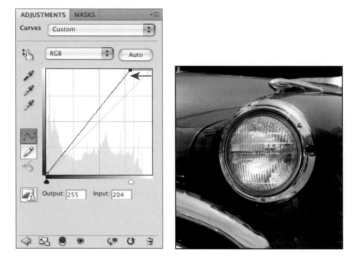

As you drag, highlights are brightened in the selected area of the image.

4 Adjust the Input value up or down until you are satisfied with the results.

5 In the Layers panel, examine the Curves adjustment layer. (If the Layers panel isn't open, click its tab or choose Window > Layers.)

Adjustment layers let you make changes to your image, such as adjusting the brightness of the highlights in this car, without affecting the actual pixels. Because you've used an adjustment layer, you can always return to the original image by hiding or deleting the adjustment layer—and you can edit the adjustment layer at any time. You'll learn more about adjustment layers in Lessons 5 and 9.

6 Do one of the following:

- If you want to save your changes, choose File > Save and then choose File > Close.

- If you want to revert to the unaltered version of the file, choose File > Close and click No or Don't Save when you are asked if you want to save your changes.

- To save your changes without affecting the original file, choose File > Save As, and then either rename the file or save it to a different folder on your computer, and click OK. Then choose File > Close.

You don't have to deselect, because closing the file cancels the selection.

Congratulations! You've just finished your first Photoshop project. Although a Curves adjustment layer is actually one of the more sophisticated methods of altering an image, it isn't difficult to use, as you have seen. You will learn more about making adjustments to images in many other lessons in this book. Lessons 2, 6, and 10, in particular, address techniques like those used in classic darkroom work, such as adjusting for exposure, retouching, and correcting colors.

Zooming and scrolling with the Navigator panel

The Navigator panel is another speedy way to make large changes in the zoom level, especially when the exact percentage of magnification is unimportant. It's also a great way to scroll around in an image, because the thumbnail shows you exactly what part of the image appears in the image window. To open the Navigator panel, choose Window > Navigator.

The slider under the image thumbnail in the Navigator panel enlarges the image when you drag it to the right (toward the large mountain icon) and reduces it when you drag to the left.

The red rectangular outline represents the area of the image that appears in the image window. When you zoom in far enough that the image window shows only part of the image, you can drag the red outline around the thumbnail area to see other areas of the image. This is also an excellent way to verify which part of an image you're working on when you work at very high zoom levels.

Using the options bar and other panels

You've already had some experience with the options bar. When you selected the Zoom tool in the previous project, you saw that the options bar contained options that change the view of the current image window. Now you will learn more about setting tool properties in the options bar, as well as using panels and panel menus.

Previewing and opening another file

The next project involves a promotional postcard for a community project. First, preview the end file to see what you're aiming to do.

1 Click the Launch Bridge button ([Br]) in the application bar to return to Bridge.

2 If the Lesson01 folder contents aren't displayed in the Content panel, navigate to the Lesson01 folder.

3 Select the 01B_End.psd file in the Content panel so that it appears in the Preview panel.

4 Examine the image and notice the text that is set against the sandy area across the lower part of the image.

5 Double-click the thumbnail for the 01B_Start.psd file to open it in Photoshop.

Setting tool properties in the options bar

With the 01B_Start.psd file open in Photoshop, you're ready to select the text properties and then to type your message.

1 In the Tools panel, select the Horizontal Type tool (T).

The buttons and menus in the options bar now relate to the Type tool.

2 In the options bar, select a font you like from the first pop-up menu. (We used Garamond, but you can use another font if you prefer.)

3 Specify **38** pt for the font size.

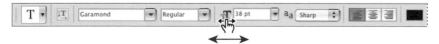

► **Tip:** You can place the pointer over the labels of most numeric settings in the tool options bar, in panels, and in dialog boxes in Photoshop, to display a "scrubby slider." Dragging the pointing-finger slider to the right increases the value; dragging to the left decreases the value. Alt-dragging (Windows) or Option-dragging (Mac OS) changes the values in smaller increments; Shift-dragging changes them in larger increments.

You can specify 38 points by typing directly in the font-size text box and pressing Enter or Return, or by scrubbing the font-size menu label. You can also choose a standard font size from the font-size pop-up menu.

4   Click once anywhere on the left side of the image and type **Monday is Beach Cleanup Day.**

The text appears with the font and font size that you selected.

● **Note:** Don't select the Move tool using the V keyboard shortcut, because you're in text-entry mode. Typing V will add the letter to your text in the image window.

5   In the Tools panel, select the Move tool (▶⊕). It's the first tool.

6   Position the Move tool pointer over the text you typed and drag the text onto the sand, centering it over the bench.

Using panels and panel menus

The text color in your image is the same as the Foreground Color swatch in the Tools panel, which is black by default. The text in the end-file example was a magenta that made the text stand out. You'll color the text by selecting it and then choosing another color.

1   In the Tools panel, select the Horizontal Type tool (T).

2 Drag the Horizontal Type tool across the text to select all the words. (Be sure to place the cursor immediately to the right of the text, then drag left to make the selection.)

3 In the Color panel group, click the Swatches tab to bring that panel forward.

4 Select any swatch. The color you select appears in three places: as the Foreground Color in the Tools panel, in the text color swatch in the options bar, and in the text you typed in the image window. (Select any other tool in the Tools panel to deselect the text so that you can see the color applied to it.)

● **Note:** When you move the pointer over the swatches, it temporarily changes into an eyedropper. Set the tip of the eyedropper on the swatch you want, and click to select it.

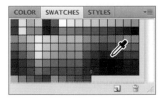

That's how easy it is to select a color, although there are other methods in Photoshop. However, you'll use a specific color for this project, and it's easier to find it if you change the Swatches panel display.

5 Select another tool in the Tools panel, such as the Move tool (▸₊) to deselect the Horizontal Type tool. Then, click the menu button (▾≡) on the Swatches panel to open the panel menu, and choose the Small List command.

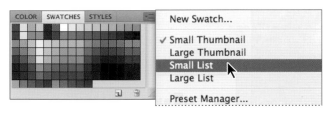

6 Select the Type tool and reselect the text, as you did in steps 1 and 2.

7 In the Swatches panel, scroll about halfway down the list to find the Light Violet Magenta swatch, and then select it.

Now the text appears in the lighter violet color.

8 Select the Hand tool (✋) to deselect the text. Then click the Default Foreground And Background Colors button in the Tools panel to make Black the foreground color.

Resetting the default colors does not change the color of the text, because the text is no longer selected.

9 You've finished the task, so close the file. You can either save it, close it without saving, or save it under a different name or location.

It's as simple as that—you've completed another project. Nice job!

Undoing actions in Photoshop

In a perfect world, you'd never make a mistake. You'd never click the wrong object. You'd always perfectly anticipate how specific actions would bring your design ideas to life exactly as you imagined them. In a perfect world, you'd never have to backtrack.

For the real world, Photoshop gives you the power to step back and undo actions so that you can try other options. The next project provides you with an opportunity to experiment freely, knowing that you can reverse the process.

This project also introduces you to layering, which is one of the fundamental and most powerful features in Photoshop. Photoshop features many kinds of layers, some of which contain images, text, or solid colors, and others that simply interact with layers below them. The file for this next project has both kinds of layers. You don't have to understand layers to complete this project successfully, so don't worry about that right now. You'll learn more about layers in Lesson 4, "Layer Basics," and Lesson 9, "Advanced Layering."

Undoing a single action

Even beginning computer users quickly come to appreciate the familiar Undo command. As you will do each time you start a new project, you'll begin by looking at the final result.

1   Click the Launch Bridge button (![Br]), and navigate to the Lessons/Lesson01 folder.

2   Select the 01C_End.psd file, press Shift, and select the 01C_Start.psd file. Both files appear in the Preview panel. In the start file, the tie is solid; in the end file, it is patterned.

3   Double-click the 01C_Start.psd file thumbnail to open it in Photoshop.

4   In the Layers panel, select the Tie Designs layer.

Notice the listings in the Layers panel. The Tie Designs layer is a clipping mask. A clipping mask works somewhat like a selection in that it restricts the area of the image that can be altered. With the clipping mask in place, you can paint a design over the tie without worrying about any stray brush strokes disturbing the rest of the image. You've selected the Tie Designs layer because it's the layer you'll be editing now.

5   In the Tools panel, select the Brush tool (![brush]), or press B to select it by its keyboard shortcut.

6 In the options bar, click the brush size to open the Brushes panel. Scroll down the list of brushes and select the Soft Round 65-pixel brush. (The name will appear as a tool tip if you hover the pointer over a brush.)

If you want to try a different brush, that's OK, but select a brush that's reasonably close to 65 pixels—preferably between 45 and 75 pixels.

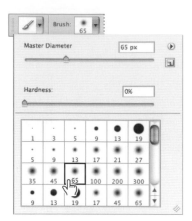

7 Move the pointer over the image so that it appears as a circle the same diameter as the brush. Then draw a stripe anywhere in the orange tie. You don't have to worry about staying within the lines, because the brush won't paint anything outside the tie clipping mask.

Oops! Your stripe may be very nice, but the design calls for dots, so you'll need to remove the painted stripe.

Illustration: Pamela Hobbs

● **Note:** You'll get more experience with clipping masks in Lesson 5, "Masks and Channels," Lesson 7, "Typographic Design," and Lesson 9, "Advanced Layering."

8 Choose Edit > Undo Brush Tool, or press Ctrl+Z (Windows) or Command+Z (Mac OS) to undo the Brush tool action.

The tie is again a solid orange color, with no stripe.

Undoing multiple actions

The Undo command reverses only one step. This is a practicality because Photoshop files can be very large, and maintaining multiple Undo steps can tie up a lot of memory, which tends to degrade performance. However, you can still step back through multiple actions using the History panel.

1 Using the same Brush tool settings, click once over the (unstriped) orange tie to create a soft dot.

2 Click several more times in different areas on the tie to create a pattern of dots.

3 Choose Windows > History to open the History panel. Then drag a corner of the History panel to resize it so that you can see more steps.

The History panel records the recent actions you've performed in the image. The current state is selected, at the bottom of the list.

4 Click an earlier action in the History panel, and examine the changes this causes in the image window: Several previous actions are undone.

5 In the image window, create a new dot on the tie with the Brush tool.

Notice that the History panel has removed the dimmed actions that had been listed after the selected history state and has added a new one.

6 Choose Edit > Undo Brush Tool or press Ctrl+Z (Windows) or Command+Z (Mac OS) to undo the dot you created in Step 5.

Now the History panel restores the earlier listing of dimmed actions.

7 Select the state at the bottom of the History panel list.

The image is restored to the condition it was in when you finished Step 2 of this exercise.

By default, the Photoshop History panel retains only the last 20 actions. This is also a compromise, striking a balance between flexibility and performance. You can change the number of levels in the History panel by choosing Edit > Preferences > Performance (Windows) or Photoshop > Preferences > Performance (Mac OS) and entering a different value for History States.

Using a context menu

Context menus are short menus that contain commands and options appropriate to specific elements in the work area. They are sometimes referred to as "right-click" or "shortcut" menus. Usually, the commands on a context menu are also available in some other area of the user interface, but using the context menu can save time.

1   If the Brush tool (✐) is not still selected in the Tools panel, select it now.

2   In the image window, right-click (Windows) or Control-click (Mac OS) anywhere in the image to open the Brush tool context menu.

Context menus vary with their context, of course, so what appears can be a menu of commands or a panel-like set of options, which is what happens in this case.

3   Select a finer brush, such as the Hard Round 9-pixel brush. You may need to scroll up or down the list in the context menu to find the right brush.

4   In the image window, use the selected brush to create smaller dots on the tie.

5   As it suits you, use the Undo command and the History panel to backtrack through your painting actions to correct mistakes or make different choices.

● **Note:** Clicking anywhere in the work area closes the context menu. If the tie area is hidden behind the Brush tool context menu, click another area or double-click your selection in the context menu to close it.

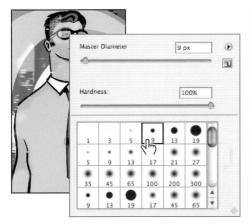

When you finish making changes to your tie design, give yourself a pat on the back because you've finished another project. You can choose File > Save if you want to save your results, choose File > Save As if you want to save it in another location or with a different name, or close the file without saving.

More about panels and panel locations

Photoshop panels are powerful and varied. Rarely would you need to see all panels simultaneously. That's why they're in panel groups and why the default configurations leave some panels unopened.

The complete list of panels appears in the Window menu, with check marks by the names of the panels that are open at the front of their panel groups. You can open a closed panel or close an open one by selecting the panel name in the Window menu.

You can hide all panels at once—including the options bar and Tools panel—by pressing the Tab key. To reopen them, press Tab again.

You already used the panel dock when you opened the Swatches panel. You can drag panels to or from the panel dock. This is convenient for bulky panels or ones that you use only occasionally but want to keep handy.

Other actions that you can use to arrange panels include the following:

- To move an entire panel group, drag the title bar to another location in the work area.

- To move a panel to another group, drag the panel tab into that panel group so that a blue highlight appears inside the group, and then release the mouse button.

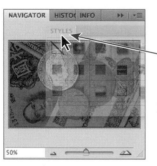
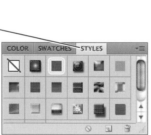

- To dock a panel or panel group, drag the title bar or panel tab onto the top of the dock.

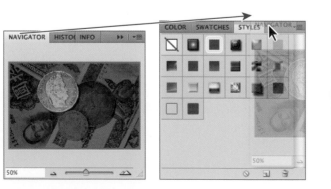

- To undock a panel or panel group so that it becomes a floating panel or panel group, drag its title bar or panel tab away from the dock.

Expanding and collapsing panels

You can also resize panels to use screen space more efficiently and to see fewer or more panel options, either by dragging or clicking to toggle between preset sizes:

- To collapse open panels to icons, click the double arrows in the title bar of the dock or panel group. To expand a panel, click its icon or the double arrow.

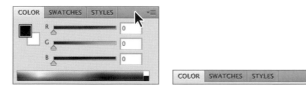

- To change the height of a panel, drag its lower right corner.

- To change the width of the dock, position the pointer on the left edge of the dock until it becomes a double-headed arrow, and then drag to the left to widen the dock, or to the right to narrow it.

- To resize a floating panel, move the pointer over the right, left, or bottom edge of the panel until it becomes a double-headed arrow, and then drag the edge in or out. You can also pull the bottom-right corner in or out.

- To collapse a panel group so that only the dock header bar and tabs are visible, double-click a panel tab or panel title bar. Double-click again to restore it to the expanded view. You can open the panel menu even when the panel is collapsed.

● **Note:** You can collapse, but not resize, the Color, Character, and Paragraph panels.

Notice that the tabs for the panels in the panel group and the button for the panel menu remain visible after you collapse a panel.

Special notes about the Tools panel and options bar

The Tools panel and the options bar share some characteristics with the other panels:

- You can drag the Tools panel by its title bar to a different location in the work area. You can move the options bar to another location by dragging the grab bar at the far left end of the panel.

- You can hide the Tools panel and options bar.

However, some panel features are not available or do not apply to the Tools panel or options bar:

- You cannot group the Tools panel or options bar with other panels.

- You cannot resize the Tools panel or options bar.

- You cannot stack the Tools panel or options bar in the panel dock.

- The Tools panel and options bar do not have panel menus.

Customizing the workspace

● **Note:** If you closed 01C_Start.psd at the end of the previous exercise, open it—or open any other image file—to complete the following exercise.

It's great that Photoshop offers so many ways to control the display and location of the options bar and its many panels, but it can be time-consuming to drag panels around the screen so that you can see some panels for certain projects and other panels for other projects. That's why Photoshop lets you customize your workspace, controlling which panels, tools, and menus are available at any time. In fact, it comes with a few preset workspaces suitable for different types of workflows—tone and color correction, painting and retouching, and so on. You'll experiment with them.

1 Choose Window > Workspace > Color And Tone. If prompted, click Yes to apply the workspace.

If you've been experimenting with opening, closing, and moving panels, you'll notice that Photoshop closes some panels, opens others, and stacks them neatly in the dock along the right edge of the workspace.

2 Choose Window > Workspace > Typography. If prompted, click Yes to apply the workspace. Different panels are open in the dock.

3 Click the workspace switcher in the application bar, and choose Essentials. Photoshop returns to the default workspace.

You can choose workspaces from the Window menu or from the pop-up menu in the application bar.

For times when presets don't suit your purposes, you can customize the workspace to your specific needs. Say, for example, that you do lots of web design, but no digital video work. You can specify which menu items to display in the workspace.

4 Click the View menu and drag down to see the Pixel Aspect Ratio submenu.

This submenu includes several DV formats that many print and web designers don't need to use.

5 Choose Window > Workspace > Keyboard Shortcuts And Menus.

The Keyboard Shortcuts & Menus dialog box lets you control which application and panel menu commands are available, as well as create custom keyboard shortcuts for menus, panels, and tools. You can hide commands that you use infrequently, or highlight commonly used commands to make them easier to see.

6 Click the Menus tab in the Keyboard Shortcuts And Menus dialog box, and then choose Application Menus from the Menu For pop-up menu.

7 Expand the View menu commands by clicking the triangle next to View.

Photoshop displays the View menu commands and subcommands.

8 Scroll down to Pixel Aspect Ratio and click the eye icon to turn off visibility for all of the DV and video formats—there are seven of them, beginning with D1/DV NTSC (0.91) and ending with DVDPro HD 1080 (1.5). Photoshop will remove them from the menu for this workspace.

9 Now expand the Image menu commands.

10 Scroll down to the Image > Mode > RGB Color command, and click None in the Color column. Choose Red from the pop-up menu. Photoshop will highlight this command in red.

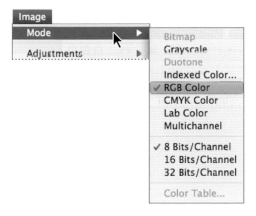

11 Click OK to close the Keyboard Shortcuts And Menus dialog box.

12 Choose Image > Mode. RGB Color is now highlighted in red.

13 Choose View > Pixel Aspect Ratio. The DV and video formats are no longer included in this submenu.

14 To save a workspace, choose Window > Workspace > Save Workspace. In the Save Workspace dialog box, give your workspace a name; select the Menus, Panel Locations, and Keyboard Shortcuts options; and then click Save.

The custom workspace you save will be listed in the Window > Workspace submenu and in the workspace switcher on the application bar.

For now, return to the default workspace configuration.

15 Choose Essentials from the Workspace pop-up menu on the application bar. Don't save the changes in the current workspace.

16 Return to Photoshop, and choose Help > Updates. In the Adobe Updater dialog box that appears, click the Preferences button.

17 In the Adobe Updater Preferences dialog box, select Automatically Check For Updates. Then, decide whether you want updates to be downloaded automatically, or whether you want to be alerted before updates are downloaded.

If you choose to not automatically check for updates every month, you can still manually go to the Adobe website (see the following page) to check for Photoshop updates.

18 Click OK to save your changes.

Congratulations again; you've finished Lesson 1.

Now that you're acquainted with the basics of the Photoshop work area, you can explore more about the Adobe Bridge visual file browser, or jump ahead and begin learning how to create and edit images. Once you know the basics, you can complete the *Adobe Photoshop CS4 Classroom in a Book* lessons either in sequential order, or according to the subject that most interests you.

Finding resources for using Photoshop

For complete and up-to-date information about using Photoshop panels, tools, and other application features, visit the Adobe website. Choose Help > Photoshop Help. You'll be connected to the Adobe Community Help website, where you can search Photoshop Help and support documents, as well as other websites relevant to Photoshop users. You can narrow your search results to view only Adobe Help and support documents, as well.

If you plan to work in Photoshop when you're not connected to the Internet, download the most current PDF version of Photoshop Help from www.adobe.com/go/documentation.

For additional resources, such as tips and techniques and the latest product information, check out the Adobe Community Help page at community.adobe.com/help/main.

● **Note:** If Photoshop detects that you are not connected to the Internet when you start the application, choosing Help > Photoshop Help opens the Help HTML pages installed with Photoshop. For more up-to-date information, view the Help files online or download the current PDF for reference.

Checking for updates

Adobe periodically provides updates to software. You can easily obtain these updates through Adobe Updater, as long as you have an active Internet connection.

1 In Photoshop, choose Help > Updates. The Adobe Updater automatically checks for updates available for your Adobe software.

2 In the Adobe Updater dialog box, select the updates you want to install, and then click Download And Install Updates to install them.

● **Note:** To set your preferences for future updates, click Preferences. Select how often you want Adobe Updater to check for updates, for which applications, and whether to download them automatically. Click OK to accept the new settings.

Tools panel overview

Photoshop CS4
Tools panel

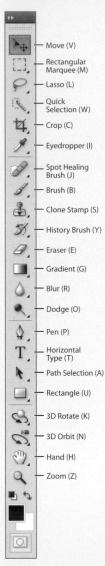

- Move (V)
- Rectangular Marquee (M)
- Lasso (L)
- Quick Selection (W)
- Crop (C)
- Eyedropper (I)
- Spot Healing Brush (J)
- Brush (B)
- Clone Stamp (S)
- History Brush (Y)
- Eraser (E)
- Gradient (G)
- Blur (R)
- Dodge (O)
- Pen (P)
- Horizontal Type (T)
- Path Selection (A)
- Rectangle (U)
- 3D Rotate (K)
- 3D Orbit (N)
- Hand (H)
- Zoom (Z)

The Move tool moves selections, layers, and guides.

The marquee tools make rectangular, elliptical, single row, and single column selections.

The lasso tools make free-hand, polygonal (straight-edged), and magnetic (snap-to) selections.

The Quick Selection tool lets you quickly "paint" a selection using an adjustable round brush tip.

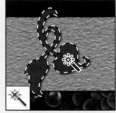

The Magic Wand tool selects similarly colored areas.

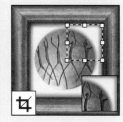

The Crop tool trims images.

The Eyedropper tool samples colors in an image.

The Color Sampler tool samples up to four areas of the image.

The Ruler tool measures distances, locations, and angles.

The Note tool makes notes that can be attached to an image.

The Count tool counts objects in an image.

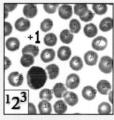

The Slice tool creates slices.

The Slice Select tool selects slices.

The Spot Healing Brush tool quickly removes blemishes and imperfections from photographs with a uniform background.

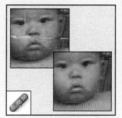

The Healing Brush tool paints with a sample or pattern to repair imperfections in an image.

The Patch tool repairs imperfections in a selected area of an image using a sample or pattern.

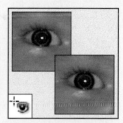

The Red Eye tool removes red-eye in flash photos with one click.

The Brush tool paints brush strokes.

The Pencil tool paints hard-edged strokes.

The Color Replacement tool substitutes one color for another.

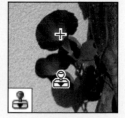

The Clone Stamp tool paints with a sample of an image.

Tools panel overview (continued)

The Pattern Stamp tool paints with a part of an image as a pattern.

The History Brush tool paints a copy of the selected state or snapshot into the current image window.

The Art History Brush tool paints stylized strokes that simulate the look of different paint styles, using a selected state or snapshot.

The Eraser tool erases pixels and restores parts of an image to a previously saved state.

The Background Eraser tool erases areas to transparency by dragging.

The Magic Eraser tool erases solid-colored areas to transparency with a single click.

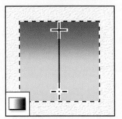

The Gradient tool creates straight-line, radial, angle, reflected, and diamond blends between colors.

The Paint Bucket tool fills similarly colored areas with the foreground color.

The Blur tool blurs hard edges in an image.

The Sharpen tool sharpens soft edges in an image.

The Smudge tool smudges data in an image.

The Dodge tool lightens areas in an image.

The Burn tool darkens areas in an image.

The Sponge tool changes the color saturation of an area.

The pen tools draw smooth-edged paths.

The type tools create type on an image

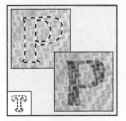

The type mask tools create a selection in the shape of type.

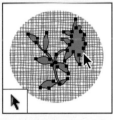

The path selection tools make shape or segment selections showing anchor points, direction lines, and direction points.

The shape tools and Line tool draw shapes and lines in a normal layer or shape layer.

The Custom Shape tool makes customized shapes selected from a custom shape list.

The Hand tool moves an image within its window.

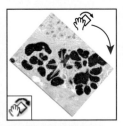

The Rotate View tool nondestructively rotates the canvas.

The Zoom tool magnifies and reduces the view of an image.

3D tools overview (Photoshop Extended)

The 3D Rotate tool rotates a 3D model around its x-axis or y-axis.

The 3D Roll tool rotates a 3D model around its z-axis.

The 3D Pan tool moves the model in the x or y direction.

The 3D Slide tool moves the 3D model along the z-axis, so that it appears closer or farther away.

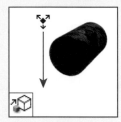

The 3D Scale tool resizes the 3D model.

The 3D Orbit tool orbits the camera in the x or y direction.

The 3D Roll View tool rotates the camera around the z-axis.

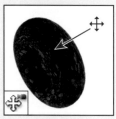

The 3D Pan View tool pans the camera in the x or y direction.

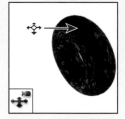

The 3D Walk View tool walks the camera.

The 3D Zoom tool changes the field of view closer or farther away.

Review questions

1 Describe two types of images you can open in Photoshop.

2 How do you open image files using Adobe Bridge?

3 How do you select tools in Photoshop?

4 Describe two ways to change your view of an image.

5 What are two ways to get more information about Photoshop?

Review answers

1 You can scan a photograph, transparency, negative, or graphic into the program; capture a digital video image; or import artwork created in a drawing program. You can also import digital photos.

2 Click the Launch Bridge button in the Photoshop application bar to jump to Bridge. Then, locate the image file you want to open, and double-click its thumbnail to open it in Photoshop.

3 Click a tool in the Tools panel, or press the tool's keyboard shortcut. A selected tool remains active until you select a different tool. To select a hidden tool, either use a keyboard shortcut to toggle through the tools, or hold down the mouse button on the tool in the Tools panel to open a pop-up menu of the hidden tools.

4 Choose commands from the View menu to zoom in or out of an image, or to fit it onscreen; or use the zoom tools and click or drag over an image to enlarge or reduce the view. You can also use keyboard shortcuts or the Navigator panel to control the display of an image.

5 The Photoshop Help system includes full information about Photoshop features plus keyboard shortcuts, task-based topics, and illustrations. Photoshop also includes a link to the Adobe Systems Photoshop web page for additional information on services, products, and tips pertaining to Photoshop.

2 BASIC PHOTO CORRECTIONS

Lesson overview

In this lesson, you'll learn how to do the following:

- Understand image resolution and size.

- Straighten and crop an image.

- Adjust the tonal range of an image.

- Remove a color cast from an image using Auto Color correction.

- Adjust the saturation and brightness of isolated areas of an image using the Sponge and Dodge tools.

- Use the Clone Stamp tool to eliminate an unwanted part of an image.

- Use the Spot Healing Brush tool to repair part of an image.

- Use Healing Brush and Patch tools to blend in corrections.

- Apply the Unsharp Mask filter to finish the photo-retouching process.

- Save an image file for use in a page-layout program.

 This lesson will take 45 minutes to an hour to complete. Copy the Lesson02 folder onto your hard drive if you haven't already done so. As you work on this lesson, you'll preserve the start files. If you need to restore the start files, copy them from the *Adobe Photoshop CS4 Classroom in a Book* CD.

This year's review of city parks by Jeff Brown

Once a Playground Movement grew, there was no stopping it. It began out of general concern in the 1920s about the wholesome use of leisure time. Led by the Playground and Recreation Association of America, the movement advocated community centers and recreational activities organized by labor unions and supported recreational programs in sports and the arts. The Laura Spelman Rockefeller Memorial Foundation helped fund the movement's efforts to organize community recreation, professionalize recreational work, and conduct surveys of parks, playgrounds, and recreational programs. City and state parks, small neighborhood greens, treeless school lots where youngsters could play ball, and community recreation centers were all viewed as appropriate spaces for leisure activity. The Playground and Recreation Association of America published Playground Magazine.
The PAA, which became the National Recreation Association in 1930, lobbied for municipal funding of supervised public playgrounds, developed training programs for "play leaders," provided professional consultation and coordination services to fledgling local recreation departments, and facilitated community surveys and playground campaigns. It also offered lectures and a publication service. The association's journal, Playground, was a source of practical advice, programming ideas, and playground theory. During the PAA's early years, funding from the Russell Sage Foundation helped the organization

URBAN PLAYGROUND

There's lots to do in the city with your kids!

Adobe Photoshop includes a variety of tools and commands for improving the quality of a photographic image. This lesson steps you through the process of acquiring, resizing, and retouching a photo intended for a print layout. The same basic workflow applies to web images.

Strategy for retouching

Adobe Photoshop provides a comprehensive set of color-correction tools for adjusting the color and tone of individual images. You can, for example, correct problems in color quality and tonal range created when a photograph was shot or an image was scanned, and you can correct problems in composition and sharpen the overall focus of the image.

Organizing an efficient sequence of tasks

Most retouching follows these eight general steps:

- Duplicating the original image or scan. (Always work in a copy of the image file so that you can recover the original later if necessary.)

- Checking the scan quality and making sure that the resolution is appropriate for the way you will use the image.

- Cropping the image to final size and orientation.

- Repairing flaws in scans of damaged photographs (such as rips, dust, or stains).

- Adjusting the overall contrast or tonal range of the image.

- Removing any color casts.

● **Note:** In Lesson 1, you used an adjustment layer, which gives you great flexibility to experiment with different correction settings without risking damage to the original image.

- Adjusting the color and tone in specific parts of the image to bring out highlights, midtones, shadows, and desaturated colors.

- Sharpening the overall focus of the image.

Usually, you should complete these processes in the order listed. Otherwise, the results of one process may cause unintended changes to other aspects of the image, making it necessary for you to redo some of your work.

Adjusting your process for different intended uses

The retouching techniques you apply to an image depend in part on how you will use the image. Whether an image is intended for black-and-white publication on newsprint or for full-color Internet distribution affects everything from the resolution of the initial scan to the type of tonal range and color correction that the image requires. Photoshop supports the CMYK color mode for preparing an image to be printed using process colors, as well as RGB and other color modes for web and mobile authoring.

To illustrate one application of retouching techniques, this lesson takes you through the steps of correcting a photograph intended for four-color print publication.

For more information about CMYK and RGB color modes, see Lesson 14, "Producing and Printing Consistent Color."

Resolution and image size

The first step in retouching a photograph in Photoshop is to make sure that the image has an appropriate resolution. The term *resolution* refers to the number of small squares known as *pixels* that describe an image and establish its detail. Resolution is determined by *pixel dimensions*, or the number of pixels along the width and height of an image.

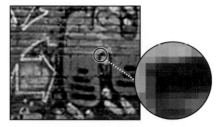

Pixels in a photographic image

In computer graphics, there are different types of resolution:

The number of pixels per unit of length in an image is called the *image resolution*, usually measured in pixels per inch (ppi). An image with a high resolution has more pixels (and therefore a larger file size) than an image of the same dimensions with a low resolution. Images in Photoshop can vary from high resolution (300 ppi or higher) to low resolution (72 ppi or 96 ppi).

The number of pixels per unit of length on a monitor is the *monitor resolution*, also usually measured in pixels per inch (ppi). Image pixels are translated directly into monitor pixels. In Photoshop, if the image resolution is higher than the monitor resolution, the image appears larger onscreen than its specified print dimensions. For example, when you display a 1-x-1-inch, 144-ppi image on a 72-ppi monitor, the image fills a 2-x-2-inch area of the screen.

4 x 6 inches at 72 ppi; file size 364.5 KB   100% onscreen view   4 x 6 inches at 200 ppi; file size 2.75 MB   100% onscreen view

> **Note:** It is important to understand what "100% view" means when you work onscreen. At 100%, one image pixel = one monitor pixel. Unless the resolution of your image is exactly the same as the resolution of the monitor, the image size (in inches, for example) onscreen may be larger or smaller than the image size will be when printed.

The number of ink dots per inch (dpi) produced by a platesetter or laser printer is the *printer*, or *output*, *resolution*. Of course, higher-resolution printers combined with higher-resolution images generally produce the best quality. The appropriate resolution for a printed image is determined both by the printer resolution and by the *screen frequency*, or lines per inch (lpi), of the halftone screens used to reproduce images.

● Note: To determine
the image resolution for
the photograph in this
lesson, we followed the
computer-graphics rule
of thumb for color or
grayscale images that
are intended for print
on large commercial
printers: scan at a
resolution 1.5 to 2 times
the screen frequency
used by the printer.
Because the magazine
in which the image will
be printed uses a screen
frequency of 133 lpi, the
image was scanned at
200 ppi (133 x 1.5).

Keep in mind that the higher the image resolution, the larger the file size, and the longer the file takes to download from the web.

For more information on resolution and image size, see Photoshop Help.

Getting started

The image you'll work on in this lesson is a scanned photograph. You'll prepare the image to be placed in an Adobe InDesign layout for a fictitious magazine. The final image size in the print layout will be 3.5 x 2.5 inches.

You'll start the lesson by comparing the original scan to the finished image.

1 Start Photoshop and then immediately hold down Ctrl+Alt+Shift (Windows) or Command+Option+Shift (Mac OS) to restore the default preferences. (See "Restoring default preferences" on page 4.)

2 When prompted, click Yes to confirm that you want to reset preferences.

3 Click the Launch Bridge button (Br) in the application bar to open Adobe Bridge.

4 In the Favorites panel in the upper-left corner of Bridge, click the Lessons folder. Then, in the Content panel, double-click the Lesson02 folder to see its contents.

5 Compare the 02Start.psd and 02End.psd files. To enlarge the thumbnails in the Content panel, drag the Thumbnail slider at the bottom of the Bridge window to the right.

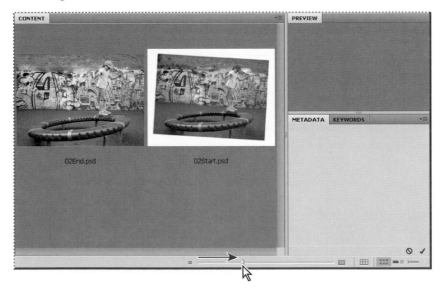

In the 02Start.psd file, notice that the image is crooked, the colors are relatively dull, and the image has a red color cast. The dimensions are also larger than needed for the requirements of the magazine. You will fix all of these problems in this lesson, starting with straightening and cropping the image.

6 Double-click the 02Start.psd thumbnail to open the file in Photoshop. If necessary, click OK to dismiss the embedded profile mismatch warning.

7 In Photoshop, choose File > Save As, rename the file **02Working.psd**, and click Save to save it in the Lesson02 folder.

8 If the Photoshop Format Options dialog box opens, deselect Maximize Compatibility, and click OK.

Remember, when you're making permanent corrections to an image file, it's always wise to work on a copy rather than on the original. Then, if something goes horribly wrong, at least you'll be able to start over on a fresh copy of the original image.

Julieanne Kost is an official Adobe Photoshop evangelist.

Tool tips from the Photoshop evangelist

The Crop tool rocks!

Here are two little-known but great ways to use the Crop tool (C) more effectively:

- Use the Crop tool to add canvas to any image. With the image open in Photoshop, drag a marquee with the Crop tool. After you release the mouse, drag the handles outside the image area. When you apply the crop (by pressing Enter or Return), the transparent area will be added to the canvas.

- Use the dimensions of one image to crop another. Open both images in Photoshop, and make the image with the desired crop dimensions active. Select the Crop tool, and click the Front Image button in the tool options bar. This enters the image's height, width, and resolution in the respective fields in the options bar. Switch to the image that you want to crop, and drag with the Crop tool. The tool constrains the aspect ratio as you drag, and when you release and apply the crop, the image will be resized to the desired height, width, and resolution.

Straightening and cropping an image

You'll use the Crop tool to trim and scale the photograph for this lesson so that it fits the space designed for it. You can use either the Crop tool or the Crop command to crop an image. Both methods permanently delete all the pixels outside the crop selection area.

1   In the Tools panel, select the Crop tool (⊟). Then, in the options bar (at the top of the work area), enter the dimensions (in inches) of the finished image. For Width, type **3.5 in,** and for Height type **2.5 in**.

2   Draw a crop marquee around the image. Don't worry about which part of the image is included, because you'll adjust the marquee in a moment.

As you drag, the marquee retains the same proportion as the dimensions you specified for the target size (3.5 x 2.5 inches).

When you release the mouse button, a *cropping shield* covers the area outside the cropping selection, and the options bar displays choices about the cropping shield.

3   In the options bar, make sure that the Perspective check box is *not* selected.

4   In the image window, move the pointer outside the crop marquee so that it appears as a curved double arrow (↱). Drag clockwise to rotate the marquee until it matches the angle of the picture.

5   Place the pointer inside the crop marquee, and drag the marquee until it contains the portion of the picture you want shown to produce an artistically pleasing result. If you need to adjust the size of the marquee, drag one of the corner handles. You can also press the arrow keys to adjust the marquee in 1-pixel increments.

6   Press Enter or Return. The image is now cropped, and the cropped image now fills the image window, straightened, sized, and cropped according to your specifications.

▶ **Tip:** You can choose Image > Trim to discard a border area around the edge of the image, based on transparency or edge color.

7   Choose File > Save to save your work.

Making automatic adjustments

Photoshop contains a number of highly effective automatic features that fix many pictures with very little effort on your part. These may be all you need for certain types of jobs. However, when you want more control, you can dig down into some of the more technical features and options available in Photoshop.

First, you'll try the automatic adjustments to brighten the colors in the lesson image file. Then, you'll make adjustments using manual controls on another copy of the image.

1 If you didn't save your work after you cropped the image in the previous exercise, choose File > Save now.

2 Now, to save a copy of the image, choose File > Save As, rename the cropped file **02Auto.psd**, and click Save.

If the Photoshop Format Options dialog box opens, deselect Maximize Compatibility, and click OK.

3 Choose Image > Auto Color. The color cast is gone.

Original

Result

About the Auto Color and Auto correction commands

The Auto Color command adjusts the contrast and color of an image by searching the actual image rather than the channel histograms for shadows, midtones, and highlights. It neutralizes the midtones and clips the white and black pixels based on the values set in the Auto Color Correction Options dialog box.

The Auto Color Correction Options dialog box lets you automatically adjust the overall tonal range of an image, specify clipping percentages, and assign color values to shadows, midtones, and highlights. You can apply the settings during a single use of the Levels or Curves dialog boxes, or you can save the settings for future use with the Levels, Auto Levels, Auto Contrast, Auto Color, and Curves commands.

To open the Auto Color Correction Options dialog box, click Options in the Levels dialog box or in the Curves dialog box, or choose Auto Options from the Levels or Curves panel menu.

4 Choose Image > Adjustments > Shadows/Highlights.

5 In the Shadows/Highlights dialog box, drag the Highlights and Shadows sliders until you think the image looks good. Make sure that Preview is selected so that you can see the changes applied to the image window as you work.

6 Click OK to close the dialog box, and then choose File > Save.

About the Auto Contrast command

You can also adjust the contrast (highlights and shadows) and the overall mix of colors in an image automatically by choosing Image > Auto Contrast. Adjusting the contrast maps the darkest and lightest pixels in the image to black and white. This remapping causes the highlights to appear lighter and the shadows to appear darker and can improve the appearance of many photographic or continuous-tone images. (The Auto Contrast command does not improve flat-color images.)

The Auto Contrast command clips white and black pixels by 0.5%—that is, it ignores the first 0.5% of either extreme when identifying the lightest and darkest pixels in the image. This clipping of color values ensures that white and black values are representative areas of the image content rather than extreme pixel values.

For this project, you won't use the Auto Contrast feature, but you may want to use it in your own projects.

7 Close the 02Auto.psd file. Then choose File > Open Recent > 02Working.psd to open that image file. Click OK if you see the embedded profile mismatch dialog box.

Removing a color cast

● **Note:** To see a color cast in an image on your monitor, you need a 24-bit monitor (one that can display millions of colors). On monitors that can display only 256 colors (8 bits), a color cast is difficult, if not impossible, to detect.

Some images contain color casts (imbalanced colors), which may be created when the image is scanned or which may have existed in the original image. This photograph of the playground has a red cast. You'll use a Color Balance adjustment layer to correct this.

1   Click the Color Balance button in the Adjustments panel.

2   In the Color Balance panel, select Midtones for the Tone, and select Preserve Luminosity at the bottom of the panel.

3   Shift the sliders to balance the color in the image. We moved the top slider to -90, the middle slider to +18, and the bottom slider to +6.

The red color cast is gone.

4   Click the Return To Adjustment List button (◁) in the Adjustments panel.

5   Choose File > Save. If the Photoshop Format Options dialog box opens, deselect Maximize Compatibility, and click OK.

Manually adjusting the tonal range

The tonal range of an image represents the amount of *contrast*, or detail, in the image and is determined by the image's distribution of pixels, ranging from the darkest pixels (black) to the lightest pixels (white). You'll now correct the photograph's contrast using a Levels adjustment layer.

In this task, you'll use a graph in the Levels panel that represents the range of values (dark and light) in the image. This graph has controls that adjust the shadows, highlights, and midtones (or gamma) of the image. You'll also refer to the Histogram panel, which displays this information for you. Unless you're aiming for a special effect, the ideal histogram extends across the full width of the graph, and the middle portion has fairly uniform peaks and valleys, representing adequate pixel data in the midtones.

1 Choose Window > Histogram to open the Histogram panel. Then choose Expanded View from the Histogram panel menu.

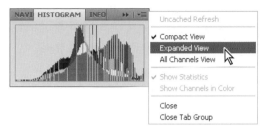

2 In the Histogram panel, choose RGB from the Channel menu.

3 Position the Histogram panel so that you can see it, the Adjustments panel, and the image window.

4 Click the Levels button in the Adjustments panel to open the Levels panel. Photoshop adds a Levels adjustment layer to the Layers panel.

In the Levels panel, the left (black) triangle below the histogram represents the shadows, the middle (gray) triangle represents the midtones, or *gamma*, and the right (white) triangle represents the highlights. If your image had colors across the entire brightness range, the graph would extend across the full width of the histogram. Notice that at this point, the graphs in the Levels panel and the Histogram panel are identical.

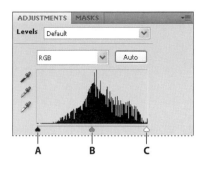

A. Shadows
B. Midtones, or gamma
C. Highlights

5 In the Levels panel, drag the left triangle to the right to the point where the histogram indicates that the darkest colors begin.

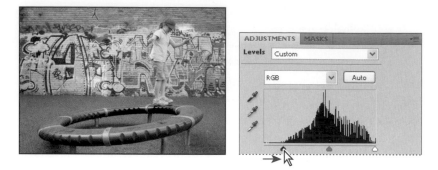

As you drag, the first Input Levels value (beneath the histogram graph in the Levels panel) changes and so does the image itself. In the Histogram panel, the left portion of the graph now stretches to the edge of the frame. This indicates that the darkest shadow values have shifted closer to black.

6 Drag the white triangle to the left to the point where the histogram indicates that the lightest colors begin. Again, notice the changes in the third Input Levels value, in the image itself, and in the Histogram panel graph.

7 Drag the middle (gray) triangle to the right to darken the midtones.

Watch the changes in the image window and in the Histogram panel graph to determine how far to drag the middle triangle.

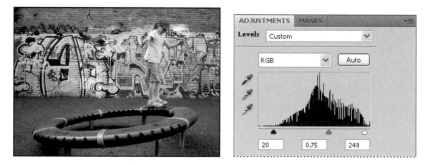

8 When the image looks good to you (we used Input Levels values of 20, 0.75, and 249), click the Return To Adjustment List button at the bottom of the Levels panel.

9 Close the Histogram panel

10 Choose File > Save.

Replacing colors in an image

With the Replace Color command, you can create temporary *masks* based on specific colors and then replace these colors. (A mask isolates an area of an image so that changes affect just the selected area and not the rest of the image.) The Replace Color dialog box contains options for adjusting the hue, saturation, and lightness components of the selection: *hue* is color, *saturation* is the purity of the color, and *lightness* is how much white or black is in the image.

You'll use the Replace Color command to change the color of the child's cap in the image of the playground.

1   Zoom in to see the child's cap clearly.

2   In the Layers panel, select the Background layer. The cap is on the Background layer.

3   Select the Rectangular Marquee tool (⬚), and draw a selection border around the child's cap. Don't worry about making a perfect selection, but be sure to include all of the cap, and try not to include the child's mouth.

4   Choose Image > Adjustments > Replace Color.

The Replace Color dialog box opens, and by default, the Selection area displays a black representation of the current selection.

The Replace Color dialog box contains three eyedroppers. The first, the Eyedropper tool, selects a color; the second adds a color to the sample; the third removes a color from the sample.

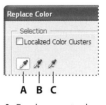

A. Eyedropper tool
B. Add To Sample eyedropper
C. Subtract From Sample eyedropper

5 Select Localized Color Clusters. Then, using the Eyedropper tool (🖋), click anywhere in the cap in the image window to sample that color.

6 Then, use the Add To Sample eyedropper (🖋) to sample other areas of the cap until the entire cap is selected and highlighted in the mask display in the Replace Color dialog box.

7 Drag the Fuzziness slider down to **35** to decrease the tolerance level slightly.

Fuzziness controls the degree to which related colors are included in the mask.

8 If the mask display includes any white areas that are not part of the cap, get rid of those now: Select the Subtract From Sample eyedropper (🖋). Then, click those areas in either the image window or in the Replace Color mask display to remove those stray pixels. (It's fine if a few remain in the selection.)

9 In the Replacement area of the Replace Color dialog box, drag the Hue slider to **+129**, the Saturation slider to **-76**, and the Lightness slider to **+10**.

As you change the values, the color of the cap changes in hue, saturation, and lightness. The cap becomes green.

10 Click OK to apply the changes.

11 Choose Select > Deselect, and then choose File > Save.

Adjusting lightness with the Dodge tool

You'll use the Dodge tool next to bring out the shadows and reduce the shininess of the playground equipment in the image. The Dodge tool is based on a traditional photographer's method of holding back light during an exposure to lighten an area of the image.

1 Zoom out or scroll down in the image window to see the play structure the girl is standing on.

2 In the Tools panel, select the Dodge tool (🔍), and click the Default Foreground and Background Colors button, so that black is the foreground color and white is the background color.

3 In the options bar, do the following:

- In the Brush pop-up panel, select a feathered brush, such as Soft Round 21 pixels, and then drag the Maste Diameter slider up to **30** px. Click outside the panel to close it.

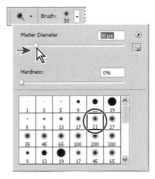

- Choose Shadows from the Range menu.
- Set Exposure to **100%**.

4 Using horizontal strokes, drag the Dodge tool over the playground equipment near the girl to remove the shininess so that it more closely matches the rest of the object.

Original   Result

You don't always need to use horizontal strokes with the Dodge tool, but they work well with this particular image. If you make a mistake or don't like the results, choose Edit > Undo and try again until you are satisfied.

5 Choose File > Save.

Adjusting saturation with the Sponge tool

When you change the saturation of a color, you adjust its strength or purity. The Sponge tool is useful for making subtle saturation changes to specific areas of an image. You'll use the Sponge tool to saturate the color of the graffiti.

1 Zoom out or scroll to see the colorful graffiti, if you need to.

2 Select the Sponge tool (⬤), hidden under the Dodge tool (🔍).

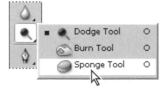

3 In the options bar, do the following:

- In the Brush pop-up panel, select a large, feathered brush, such as Soft Round 100 pixels, and then move the Master Diameter slider to **150** px.

- Choose Saturate from the Mode menu.

- For Flow, enter **40%**. The Flow value determines the intensity of the saturation effect.

4 Drag the sponge back and forth over the graffiti to increase its saturation. The more you drag over an area, the more saturated the color becomes. Be careful not to oversaturate the graffiti.

5 Select the Move tool to ensure you don't accidentally add saturation elsewhere.

6 Save your work.

Comparing automatic and manual results

Near the beginning of this lesson, you adjusted the lesson image using only automatic color and value controls. In the working copy of the image, you've applied manual adjustments to get specific results. Now it's time to compare the two.

1 Choose File > Open Recent > 02Auto.psd, if it is available. If necessary, click OK to dismiss the embedded profile mismatch warning.

2 Click the Arrange Documents button (▦) in the application bar to see the display options for multiple open files.

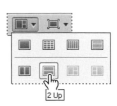

3 Select the 2 Up option to display both images, one above the other.

4 If necessary, change the zoom for each to 75% or lower, so that you can see the full image.

5 Visually compare the two results.

02Working.psd   02Auto.psd

6 Close the 02Auto.psd file.

If you're using Windows, or the application frame is enabled in Mac OS, the 02Working.psd canvas expands to fill the application window. If you're not using the application frame in Mac OS, click the Arrange Documents button in the application bar, and choose the Consolidate All option so that you can see your image clearly.

The automatic commands may be all some designers ever need. For others with more sensitive visual requirements, manual adjustments are the way to go. For each project, you can balance the time savings of using automatic commands with the precise control of manual adjustments.

Repairing areas with the Clone Stamp tool

The Clone Stamp tool uses pixels from one area of an image to replace the pixels in another part of the image. Using this tool, you can not only remove unwanted objects from your images, but you can also fill in missing areas in photographs you scan from damaged originals.

You'll start by replacing a bright white area of the wall, a hot spot, with cloned bricks from another area of the picture.

1 In the Layers panel, make sure the Background layer is selected. This is the layer you want to work with when you clone the bricks.

2 Select the Clone Stamp tool (🖌) in the Tools panel.

3 In the options bar, open the Brush Preset pop-up menu and select a brush with a soft edge, such as Soft Round 21. Then, make sure that the Aligned option is selected.

4 Choose Window > Clone Source to open the Clone Source panel. The Clone Source panel gives you greater control over the area you're cloning from (in this case, the bricks).

5 Select Show Overlay and Clipped in the Clone Source panel. Then, make sure Opacity is set to **100%**. The overlay lets you see what you're cloning before you stamp it.

6 Move the Clone Stamp tool over the darker bricks just to the right of the hot spot on the wall. (You may want to zoom in to see the area better.)

7 Alt-click (Windows) or Option-click (Mac OS) to start sampling that part of the image. (When you press Alt or Option, the pointer appears as target cross hairs.)

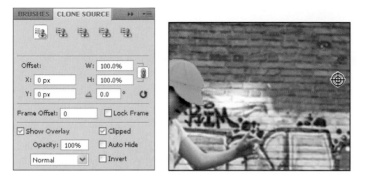

8 Starting at the area just to the right of the girl's hat, drag the Clone Stamp tool to the right, over the hot spot on the bricks. The clone overlay lets you see what will appear there. This is particularly useful for keeping the bricks in a straight line.

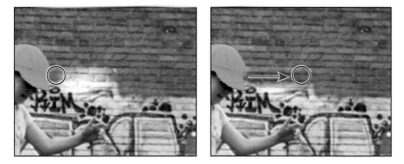

9 Release the mouse button and move the pointer to another area in the hot spot, and then start dragging again.

Each time you click the Clone Stamp tool, it begins again with a new source point, in the same relationship to the tool as the first stroke you made. That is, if you begin painting further right, it samples from bricks that are further right than the original source point. That's because Aligned is selected in the options bar.

● **Note:** When the Aligned option is not selected, each time you make a stroke, you begin sampling from the same source point, regardless of where you place the tool.

10 Continue cloning the bricks until the entire hot spot is filled in.

If necessary to help make the bricks appear to blend in naturally with the rest of the image, you can adjust your cloning by resetting the sample area (as you did in Step 7) and recloning. Or, you can try deselecting the Aligned option and cloning again.

11 When you are satisfied with the appearance of the bricks, close the Clone Source panel, and choose File > Save.

Using the Spot Healing Brush tool

The next task to be done is to clean up some dark spots in the wall. You could do this with the Clone Stamp tool, but instead you'll use another technique. You'll use the Spot Healing Brush to clean up the wall.

Painting with the Spot Healing Brush

The Spot Healing Brush tool quickly removes blemishes and other imperfections from photos. It works similarly to the Healing Brush tool (which you'll use later in this lesson): it paints with sampled pixels from an image or pattern and matches the texture, lighting, transparency, and shading of the sampled pixels to the pixels being healed. But unlike the Healing Brush, the Spot Healing Brush doesn't require you to specify a sample spot. It automatically samples from around the retouched area.

The Spot Healing Brush is excellent for retouching blemishes in portraits, but it will also work nicely in this image in the dark area of the wall, because the wall has a uniform, muted appearance to the right of the dark areas

1 Zoom in or scroll to see the dark areas on the upper-left corner of the image.

2 In the Tools panel, select the Spot Healing Brush tool (✐).

3 In the options bar, open the Brush pop-up panel, and specify a **100%** hard brush that is about **40** px in diameter.

4 In the image window, drag the Spot Healing Brush from right to left across the dark spots in the upper-right corner of the image. You can use as many or as few strokes as you like; paint until you are satisfied with the results. As you drag, the stroke at first appears black, but when you release the mouse, the painted area is "healed."

5 Choose File > Save.

Using the Healing Brush and Patch tools

The Healing Brush and Patch tools go one step beyond the capabilities of the Clone Stamp and Spot Healing Brush tools. Using their ability to simultaneously apply and blend pixels from area to area, they open the door to natural-looking touch-ups in areas that are not uniform in color or texture.

In this project, you'll touch up the brick wall, removing the large crack and the black graffiti above the colorful graffiti. Because the wall varies in color, texture, and lighting, it would be challenging to successfully use the Clone Stamp tool to touch up these areas. Fortunately, the Healing Brush and Patch tools make this process easy.

Using the Healing Brush to remove flaws

Your first goal for this image is to remove the crack in the brick wall.

1   Zoom into the area that contains the crack so that you can see it clearly, at about 200%.

2   In the Tools panel, select the Healing Brush tool (✐), hidden under the Spot Healing Brush tool (✐).

3   In the options bar, open the Brush pop-up panel, and set the brush diameter to **25** px. Click outside the pop-up panel to close it. Then, make sure the other settings in the options bar are set to the default values: Normal for Mode, Sampled for Source, and Aligned deselected.

4   Hold down Alt (Windows) or Option (Mac OS) and click the area to the left of the crack in the wall. Then release the Alt or Option key.

5   Click directly over the crack, and paint a short stroke.

Notice that as you paint, the area the brush covers temporarily looks as if it isn't making a good color match with the underlying image. However, when you release the mouse button, the brush stroke blends in nicely with the rest of the brick surface.

6   Continue using short strokes to paint over the crack, starting at the top and moving down until the crack is gone.

7   Zoom out to 150%, and choose File > Save.

Using the Patch tool

The Patch tool combines the selection behavior of the Lasso tool with the color-blending properties of the Healing Brush tool. With the Patch tool, you can select an area that you want to use as the source (area to be fixed) or destination (area used to do the fixing). Then, you drag the Patch tool marquee to another part of the image. When you release the mouse button, the Patch tool does its job. The marquee remains active over the mended area, ready to be dragged again, either to another area that needs patching (if the Destination option is selected) or to another sampling site (if the Source option is selected).

You'll use the Patch tool to remove the black and white graffiti above the main colorful strip of graffiti on the wall.

1 In the Tools panel, select the Patch tool (◉), hidden under the Healing Brush tool (🖊️).

2 In the options bar, make sure that Source is selected.

3 Drag the Patch tool around a section of the black graffiti, and then release the mouse button.

4 Choose Select > Refine Edge. In the Refine Edge dialog box, enter the following values:

- Radius: **1.0**

- Contrast: **0**

- Smooth: **70**

- Feather: **1.5**

- Contract/Expand: **6**

5 Click OK.

The Refine Edge dialog box lets you modify your selection with more precision. In this case, using it creates a smoother transition to the clean bricks.

6 Drag the selection to a clean area of the bricks.

As you drag, the original selected area shows the same pixels as the lassoed selection you are dragging. When you release the mouse button, the color—but not the texture—readjusts to the original color scheme of the selection. In this case, the patch picks up some of the color from the graffiti below.

7 Drag a new selection around some of the other graffiti and then drag to a clean area of the bricks. The Refine Edge settings remain the same for each addiitonal patch. Continue to patch the image until all the black graffiti is removed to your satisfaction. You can also patch the holes in the brick just to left of the child's head.

8 Choose Select > Deselect.

9 Choose File > Save.

Applying the Unsharp Mask filter

The last task you may do when retouching a photo is to apply the Unsharp Mask filter. The Unsharp Mask filter adjusts the contrast of the edge detail and creates the illusion of a more focused image.

1 Choose Filter > Sharpen > Unsharp Mask.

2 In the Unsharp Mask dialog box, make sure that Preview is selected so you can see the effect of settings you adjust in the image window.

You can drag inside the preview window in the dialog box to see different parts of the image, or use the plus (⊞) and minus (⊟) buttons below the thumbnail to zoom in and out.

3 Drag the Amount slider to about **70%** to sharpen the image.

4 Drag the Radius slider to determine the number of pixels surrounding the edge pixels that will affect the sharpening. The higher the resolution, the higher the Radius setting should be. (We used the default value, 1.0 pixel.)

Tip: As you try different settings, toggle the Preview option on and off to see how your changes affect the image. Or, you can click and hold the mouse button on the preview window in the dialog box to temporarily toggle the filter off in the preview window. If your image is large, using the preview window can be more efficient, because only a small area is redrawn.

5 (Optional) Adjust the Threshold slider. This determines how different the sharpened pixels must be from the surrounding area before they are considered edge pixels and subsequently sharpened by the Unsharp Mask filter. The default Threshold value of 0 sharpens all pixels in the image. Try a different value, such as 2 or 3.

6 When you are satisfied with the results, click OK to apply the Unsharp Mask filter.

7 Choose File > Save.

Saving the image for four-color printing

Before you save a Photoshop file for use in a four-color publication, you must change the image to CMYK color mode. You'll use the Mode command to change the image color mode.

For more information about converting between color modes, see Photoshop Help.

1   Choose File > Save As, and save the file as 02_CMYK.psd. It's a good idea to save a copy of your original file before changing color modes, so that you can make changes in the original later, if necessary.

2   Choose Layer > Merge Visible.

Merging adjustment layers with the Background layer ensures that all the changes you made will be included in the CMYK image. If you change the color mode without merging layers, you'll lose the Levels adjustment layer.

3   Choose Image > Mode > CMYK Color. Click OK in the alert about the color management profile.

If you were preparing this image for a real publication, you'd want to confirm that you were using the appropriate CMYK profile. See Lesson 14, "Producing and Printing Consistent Color," to learn about color management.

4   If you use Adobe InDesign to create your publications, simply choose File > Save. InDesign can import native Photoshop (PSD) files, so there is no need to convert the image to TIFF format.

    If you are using another layout application, choose File > Save As, and then proceed to step 5 to save the image as a TIFF file.

5   In the Save As dialog box, choose TIFF from the Format menu.

6   Click Save.

7   In the TIFF Options dialog box, select your operating system for the Byte Order and click OK.

The image is now fully retouched, saved, and ready for placement in a page layout application.

For more information about file formats, see Photoshop Help.

You can combine Photoshop images with other elements in a layout application such as Adobe InDesign.

Review questions

1 What does *resolution* mean?

2 What does the Crop tool do?

3 How can you adjust the tonal range of an image?

4 What tools can you use to remove blemishes in an image?

5 What effect does the Unsharp Mask filter have on an image?

Review answers

1 The term *resolution* refers to the number of pixels that describe an image and establish its detail. The three different types are *image resolution, monitor resolution*—both of which are measured in pixels per inch (ppi)—and *printer,* or *output, resolution,* which is measured in ink dots per inch (dpi).

2 You can use the Crop tool to trim, scale, and straighten an image.

3 Use a Levels adjustment layer. You can use the black, white, and gray triangles below the Levels histogram to control the midpoint and where the darkest and lightest points in the image begin, thus extending its tonal range.

4 The Healing Brush, Spot Healing Brush, Patch, and Clone Stamp tools let you replace unwanted portions of an image with other areas of the image. The Clone Stamp tool copies the source area exactly; the Healing Brush and Patch tools blends the area with the surrounding pixels. The Spot Healing Brush tool doesn't require a source area at all; it "heals" areas to match the surrounding pixels.

5 The Unsharp Mask filter adjusts the contrast of the edge detail and creates the illusion of a more focused image.

3 WORKING WITH SELECTIONS

Lesson overview

In this lesson, you'll learn how to do the following:

- Make specific areas of an image active using selection tools.

- Reposition a selection marquee.

- Move and duplicate the contents of a selection.

- Use keyboard-mouse combinations that save time and hand motions.

- Deselect a selection.

- Constrain the movement of a selected area.

- Adjust the position of a selected area using the arrow keys.

- Add to and subtract from a selection.

- Rotate a selection.

- Use multiple selection tools to make a complex selection.

- Erase pixels within a selection.

 This lesson will take about an hour to complete. Copy the Lesson03 folder onto your hard drive if you haven't already done so. As you work on this lesson, you'll preserve the start files. If you need to restore the start files, copy them from the *Adobe Photoshop CS4 Classroom in a Book* CD.

Learning how to select areas of an image is of primary importance—you must first select what you want to affect. Once you've made a selection, only the area within the selection can be edited.

About selecting and selection tools

● **Note:** You'll learn how to select vector areas using the pen tools in Lesson 8, "Vector Drawing Techniques."

Making changes to an area within an image in Photoshop is a two-step process. You first select the part of an image you want to change with one of the selection tools. Then, you use another tool, filter, or other feature to make changes, such as moving the selected pixels to another location or applying a filter to the selected area. You can make selections based on size, shape, and color. The selection process limits changes to within the selected area. Other areas are unaffected.

The best selection tool for a specific area often depends on the characteristics of that area, such as shape or color. There are four types of selections:

Geometric selections The Rectangular Marquee tool ( ) selects a rectangular area in an image. The Elliptical Marquee tool ( ), which is hidden behind the Rectangular Marquee tool, selects elliptical areas. The Single Row Marquee tool ( ) and Single Column Marquee tool ( ) select either a 1-pixel-high row or a 1-pixel-wide column, respectively.

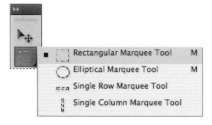

Freehand selections Drag the Lasso tool ( ) around an area to trace a freehand selection. Using the Polygonal Lasso tool ( ), click to set anchor points in straight-line segments around an area. The Magnetic Lasso tool ( ) works something like a combination of the other two lasso tools, and works best when good contrast exists between the area you want to select and its surroundings.

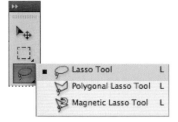

Edge-based selections The Quick Selection tool ( ) quickly "paints" a selection by automatically finding and following defined edges in the image.

Color-based selections The Magic Wand tool ( ) selects parts of an image based on the similarity in color of adjacent pixels. It is useful for selecting odd-shaped areas that share a specific range of colors.

Getting started

You'll start the lesson by viewing the finished lesson file and looking at the image you will create as you explore the selection tools in Photoshop.

1   Start Adobe Photoshop and then immediately hold down Ctrl+Alt+Shift (Windows) or Command+Option+Shift (Mac OS) to restore the default preferences. (See "Restoring default preferences" on page 4.)

2   When prompted, click Yes to confirm that you want to reset preferences.

3   Click the Launch Bridge button (Br) in the application bar to open Adobe Bridge.

4   In the Favorites panel, click the Lessons folder. Then, double-click the Lesson03 folder in the Content panel to see its contents.

5   Study the 03End.psd file. Move the thumbnail slider to the right if you want to see the image in more detail.

The project is a collage of objects, including a lettuce head, tomato, carrot, pepper, olives, cutting board, and "Salads" logo. The challenge in this lesson is to arrange these elements, which were scanned together on the single page you see in the 03Start.psd file. The ideal composition is up to you, so this lesson won't describe precise locations. There is no right or wrong position for any of the objects.

6   Double-click the 03Start.psd thumbnail to open the image file in Photoshop.

7   Choose File > Save As, rename the file **03Working.psd**, and click Save. By saving another version of the start file, you don't have to worry about overwriting the original.

Using the Quick Selection tool

The Quick Selection tool is one of the easiest ways to make a selection. You simply paint an area of an image, and the tool automatically finds the edges. You can add or subtract areas of the selection until you have exactly the area you want.

The image of the tomato in the 03Working.psd file has clearly defined edges, making it an ideal candidate for the Quick Selection tool. You'll select just the tomato, not the shadow or background behind it.

1 Select the Zoom tool in the Tools panel, and then zoom in so that you can see the tomato well.

2 Select the Quick Selection tool (✎) in the Tools panel.

3 Click on a red area near the outside edge of the tomato. The Quick Selection tool finds the full edge automatically, selecting the entire tomato.

Leave the selection active so that you can use it in the next exercise.

Moving a selected area

Once you've made a selection, any changes you make apply exclusively to the pixels within the selection. The rest of the image is not affected by those changes.

To move the selected area to another part of the composition, you use the Move tool. This image has only one layer, so the pixels you move will replace the pixels beneath them. This change is not permanent until you deselect the moved pixels, so you can try different locations for the selection you're moving before you make a commitment.

1 If the tomato is not still selected, repeat the previous exercise to select it.

2 Zoom out so you can see both the cutting board and the tomato.

3 Select the Move tool (⊹). Notice that the tomato remains selected.

4 Drag the selected area (the tomato) to the left area of the collage so that the tomato overlaps the lower-left edge of the cutting board.

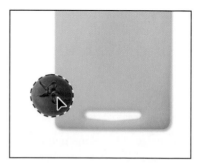

5 Choose Select > Deselect, and then choose File > Save.

In Photoshop, it's not easy to lose a selection. Unless a selection tool is active, clicking elsewhere in the image will not deselect the active area. To deliberately deselect a selection, you can choose Select > Deselect, press Ctrl+D (Windows) or Command+D (Mac OS), or click outside the selection with any selection tool to start a different selection.

Julieanne Kost is an official Adobe Photoshop evangelist.

Tool tips from the Photoshop evangelist

Move tool tip

If you're moving objects in a multilayer file with the Move tool and you suddenly need to select one of the layers, try this: With the Move tool selected, move the pointer over any area of an image and right-click (Windows) or Control-click (Mac OS). The layers that are under the pointer appear in the context menu. Choose the one you'd like to make active.

Manipulating selections

You can reposition selections as you create them, move them, and even duplicate them. In this section, you'll learn several ways to manipulate selections. Most of these methods work with any selection, but you'll use them here with the Elliptical Marquee tool, which lets you select ovals or perfect circles.

One of the best things about this section is the introduction of keyboard shortcuts that can save you time and arm motions.

Repositioning a selection marquee while creating it

Selecting ovals and circles can be tricky. It's not always obvious where you should start dragging, so sometimes the selection will be off-center, or the ratio of width to height won't match what you need. In this exercise, you'll learn techniques for managing those problems, including two important keyboard-mouse combinations that can make your Photoshop work much easier.

As you do this exercise, be very careful to follow the directions about keeping the mouse button or specific keyboard keys pressed. If you accidentally release the mouse button at the wrong time, simply start the exercise again from Step 1.

1 Select the Zoom tool (🔍), and click the bowl of olives on the lower-right side of the image window to zoom in to at least 100% view (use 200% view if the entire bowl of olives will still fit in the image window on your screen).

2 Select the Elliptical Marquee tool (○) hidden under the Rectangular Marquee tool.

3 Move the pointer over the olive bowl, and drag diagonally across the oval bowl to create a selection, but *do not release the mouse button*. It's OK if your selection does not match the bowl shape yet.

If you accidentally release the mouse button, draw the selection again. In most cases—including this one—the new selection replaces the previous one.

4 Still holding down the mouse button, press the spacebar and continue to drag the selection. Instead of resizing the selection, now you're moving it. Position it so that it more closely aligns with the bowl.

● **Note:** You do not have to include every pixel in the olive bowl, but the selection should be the shape of the bowl, and should contain the olives comfortably.

5 Carefully release the spacebar (but not the mouse button) and continue to drag, trying to make the size and shape of the selection match the oval olive bowl as closely as possible. If necessary, hold down the spacebar again and drag to move the selection marquee into position around the olive bowl.

Begin dragging a selection   Press the spacebar to move it   Complete the selection

6 When the selection border is positioned appropriately, release the mouse button.

7 Choose View > Zoom Out or use the slider in the Navigator panel to reduce the zoom view so that you can see all of the objects in the image window.

Leave the Elliptical Marquee tool and the selection active for the next exercise.

Moving selected pixels with a keyboard shortcut

Now, you'll use a keyboard to move the selected pixels onto the cutting board. The shortcut temporarily switches the active tool to the Move tool, so that you don't need to select it from the Tools panel.

1 If the olive bowl is not still selected, repeat the previous exercise to select it.

2 With the Elliptical Marquee tool (○) selected in the Tools panel, press Ctrl (Windows) or Command (Mac OS), and move the pointer within the selection. The pointer icon now includes a pair of scissors (✂) to indicate that the selection will be cut from its current location.

3   Drag the oval bowl onto the cutting board so that it overlaps the lower right edge of the cutting board. (You'll use another technique to nudge the oval bowl into the exact position in a minute.)

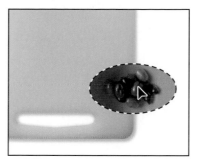

● **Note:** You can release the Ctrl or Command key after you start dragging, and the Move tool remains active. Photoshop reverts to the previously selected tool when you deselect, either by clicking outside the selection or using the Deselect command.

4   Release the mouse button but do not deselect the olive bowl.

Moving with the arrow keys

You can make minor adjustments to the position of selected pixels using the arrow keys. You can nudge the selection in increments of either 1 pixel or 10 pixels.

When a selection tool is active in the Tools panel, the arrow keys nudge the selection border, but not the contents. When the Move tool is active, the arrow keys move the selection border and its contents.

You'll use the arrow keys to nudge the olive bowl. Before you begin, make sure that the olive bowl is still selected in the image window.

1   Press the Up Arrow key (⬆) on your keyboard a few times to move the oval upward.

Notice that each time you press the arrow key, the olive bowl moves 1 pixel. Experiment by pressing the other arrow keys to see how they affect the selection.

2   Hold down the Shift key as you press an arrow key.

When you hold down the Shift key, the selection moves 10 pixels every time you press an arrow key.

Sometimes the border around a selected area can distract you as you make adjustments. You can hide the edges of a selection temporarily without actually deselecting, and then display the selection border once you've completed the adjustments.

3 Choose View > Show > Selection Edges or View > Extras to deselect it.

Either command hides the selection border around the olive bowl.

4 Use the arrow keys to nudge the olive bowl until it is positioned where you want it. Then choose View > Show > Selection Edges to reveal the selection border again.

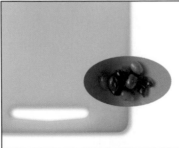

Hidden selection edges   Visible selection edges

5 Choose Select > Deselect, or press Ctrl+D (Windows) or Command+D (Mac OS).

6 Choose File > Save to save your work so far.

Selecting from a center point

In some cases, it's easier to make elliptical or rectangular selections by drawing a selection from the center point. You'll use this technique to select the salad graphic.

1 Select the Zoom tool (🔍), and zoom in on the salad graphic to a magnification of about 300%. Make sure that you can see the entire salad graphic in your image window.

2 Select the Elliptical Marquee tool (◯) in the Tools panel.

3 Move the pointer to the approximate center of the salad graphic.

4 Click and begin dragging. Then, without releasing the mouse button, press Alt (Windows) or Option (Mac OS) as you continue dragging the selection to the outer edge of the salad graphic.

The selection is centered over its starting point.

5 When you have the entire salad graphic selected, release the mouse button first and then release Alt or Option (and the Shift key if you used it). Do not deselect, because you'll use this selection in the next exercise.

▶ **Tip:** To select a perfect circle, press Shift as you drag. If you hold down Shift while dragging the Rectangular Marquee tool, you'll select a perfect square.

6 If necessary, reposition the selection border using one of the methods you learned earlier. If you accidentally released the Alt or Option key before you released the mouse button, try selecting the salad graphic again.

Moving and changing the pixels in a selection

Now you'll move the salad graphic to the upper-right corner of the cutting board. Then, you'll change its color for a dramatic effect.

Before you begin, make sure that the salad graphic is still selected. If it is not, reselect it by completing the previous exercise.

1 Choose View > Fit On Screen so that the entire image fits within the image window.

2 Select the Move tool (⯈₊) in the Tools panel.

3 Position the pointer within the salad graphic selection. The pointer becomes an arrow with a pair of scissors (⯈✂), which indicates that dragging the selection will cut it from its current location and move it to the new location.

4 Drag the salad graphic above the upper-right corner of the cutting board. If you want to adjust the position after you stop dragging, simply start dragging again. The salad graphic remains selected throughout the process.

5 Choose Image > Adjustments > Invert.

The colors making up the salad graphic are inverted so that now it is effectively a color negative of itself.

6 Leaving the salad graphic selected, choose File > Save to save your work.

Moving and duplicating a selection simultaneously

You can move and duplicate a selection at the same time. You'll make a copy of the salad graphic. If your salad graphic image is no longer selected, reselect it now, using the techniques you learned earlier.

1 With the Move tool (⤢) selected, press Alt (Windows) or Option (Mac OS) as you position the pointer inside the salad graphic selection. The pointer becomes a double arrow, which indicates that a duplicate will be made when you move the selection.

2 Continue holding down the Alt or Option key as you drag a duplicate of the salad graphic down and to the right. The salad graphics can overlap. Release the mouse button and the Alt or Option key, but do not deselect the duplicate salad graphic.

3 Choose Edit > Transform > Scale. A bounding box appears around the selection.

4 Press the Shift key as you drag one of the corner points to enlarge the salad graphic so that it becomes about 50% larger than the original. Then, press Enter or Return to commit the change and remove the transformation bounding box.

As you resize the object, the selection marquee resizes, too. The duplicate salad graphic remains selected. Pressing the Shift key as you resize the selection constrains the proportions so that the enlarged object is not distorted.

5 Hold down Alt+Shift (Windows) or Option+Shift (Mac OS), and drag a new copy of the second salad graphic down and to the right.

Pressing the Shift key as you move a selection constrains the movement horizontally or vertically in 45-degree increments.

6 Repeat steps 3 and 4 for the third salad graphic, making it about twice the size of the first one.

7 When you are satisfied with the size and position of the third salad graphic, press Enter or Return to confirm the scale, choose Select > Deselect, and then choose File > Save.

▶ **Tip:** Shortcut: Choose Edit > Transform > Again to duplicate the salad logo and enlarge it by twice as much as the last transformation.

For information on working with the center point in a transformation, see "Set or move the reference point for a transformation" in Photoshop Help.

Copying selections or layers

You can use the Move tool to copy selections as you drag them within or between images, or you can copy and move selections using the Copy, Copy Merged, Cut, and Paste commands. Dragging with the Move tool saves memory because the clipboard is not used as it is with the Copy, Copy Merged, Cut, and Paste commands.

Photoshop has several copy and paste commands:

- Copy copies the selected area on the active layer.
- Copy Merged creates a merged copy of all the visible layers in the selected area.
- Paste pastes a cut or copied selection into another part of the image or into another image as a new layer.
- Paste Into pastes a cut or copied selection inside another selection in the same or a different image. The source selection is pasted onto a new layer, and the destination selection border is converted into a layer mask.

Keep in mind that when a selection or layer is pasted between images with different resolutions, the pasted data retains its pixel dimensions. This can make the pasted portion appear out of proportion to the new image. Use the Image Size command to make the source and destination images the same resolution before copying and pasting.

Using the Magic Wand tool

The Magic Wand tool selects all the pixels of a particular color or color range. It's most successful for selecting an area of similar colors surrounded by areas of very different colors. As with many of the selection tools, after you make the initial selection, you can add or subtract areas of the selection.

The Tolerance option sets the sensitivity of the Magic Wand tool. This value limits or extends the range of pixel similarity. The default tolerance value of 32 selects the color you click plus 32 lighter and 32 darker tones of that color. You may need to adjust the tolerance level up or down depending on the color ranges and variations in the image.

If a multicolored area that you want to select is set against a differently colored background, it can be much easier to select the background than the area itself. In this procedure, you'll use the Rectangular Marquee tool to select a larger area, and then use the Magic Wand tool to subtract the background from the selection.

1 Select the Rectangular Marquee tool (⬚), hidden behind the Elliptical Marquee tool.

2 Drag a selection around the lettuce. Make sure that your selection is large enough so that a margin of white appears between the lettuce leaves and the edges of the marquee.

At this point, the lettuce and the white background area are selected. You'll subtract the white area from the selection so that only the lettuce remains in the selection.

3 Select the Magic Wand tool (✴), hidden under the Quick Selection tool (✎).

4 In the options bar, confirm that the Tolerance value is **32**. This value determines the range of colors the wand selects.

5 Select the Subtract From Selection button (⬓) in the options bar. A minus sign appears next to the wand in the pointer icon. Anything you select now will be subtracted from the initial selection.

6 Click in the white background area within the selection marquee.

The Magic Wand tool selected the entire background, subtracting it from the selection. Now all the white pixels are deselected, leaving the lettuce perfectly selected.

7 Select the Move tool (▸⊕), and drag the lettuce to the upper-left corner of the cutting board, placing it so that about a quarter of the lettuce overlaps the edge of the cutting board.

8 Choose Select > Deselect, and then save your work.

Selecting with the lasso tools

Photoshop includes three lasso tools: the Lasso tool, the Polygonal Lasso tool, and the Magnetic Lasso tool. You can use the Lasso tool to make selections that require both freehand and straight lines, using keyboard shortcuts to move back and forth between the Lasso tool and the Polygonal Lasso tool. You'll use the Lasso tool to select the carrot. It takes a bit of practice to alternate between straight-line and freehand selections—if you make a mistake while you're selecting the carrot, simply deselect and start again.

1 Select the Zoom tool (🔍), and click the carrot until the view enlarges to 100%. Make sure that you can see the entire carrot in the window.

2 Select the Lasso tool (♀). Starting at the lower-left section of the carrot, drag around the rounded end of the carrot, tracing the shape as accurately as possible. *Do not release the mouse button.*

3 Press the Alt (Windows) or Option (Mac OS) key, and then release the mouse button so that the lasso pointer changes to the polygonal lasso shape (♀). *Do not release the Alt or Option key.*

4 Begin clicking along the end of the carrot to place anchor points, following the contours of the carrot. Be sure to press the Alt or Option key throughout this process.

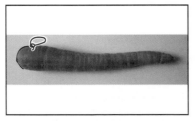
Drag with the Lasso tool

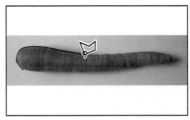
Click with the Polygonal Lasso tool

The selection border automatically stretches like a rubber band between anchor points.

5 When you reach the tip of the carrot, hold down the mouse button as you release the Alt or Option key. The pointer again appears as the lasso icon.

6 Carefully drag around the tip of the carrot, keeping the mouse button down.

7 When you finish tracing the tip and reach the lower side of the carrot, first press Alt or Option again, and then release the mouse button. Click along the lower side of the carrot with the Polygonal Lasso tool as you did on the top. Continue to trace the carrot until you arrive back at the starting point of your selection near the left end of the image.

8 Click at the start of the selection, and then release the Alt or Option key. The carrot is now entirely selected. Leave the carrot selected for the next exercise.

Rotating a selection

So far, you've moved, resized, duplicated, and inverted the color of selected areas. In this exercise, you'll see how easy it is to rotate a selected object.

Before you begin, make sure that the carrot is still selected.

1 Choose View > Fit On Screen to resize the image window to fit on your screen.

2 Press Ctrl (Windows) or Command (Mac OS) as you drag the carrot to the lower section of the cutting board. The pointer changes to the Move tool icon.

3 Choose Edit > Transform > Rotate. The carrot and selection marquee are enclosed in a bounding box.

4 Move the pointer outside the bounding box so that it becomes a curved, double-headed arrow (↱). Drag to rotate the carrot to a 45-degree angle. You can verify the angle in the Rotate box in the options bar. Press Enter or Return to commit the transformation changes.

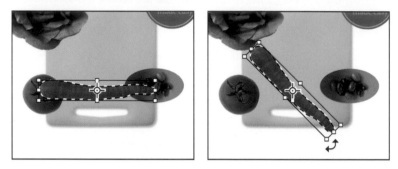

5 If necessary, select the Move tool (▸₊) and drag to reposition the carrot. When you're satisfied, choose Select > Deselect.

6 Choose File > Save.

Selecting with the Magnetic Lasso tool

You can use the Magnetic Lasso tool to make freehand selections of areas with high-contrast edges. When you draw with the Magnetic Lasso tool, the selection border automatically snaps to the edge between areas of contrast. You can also control the selection path by occasionally clicking the mouse to place anchor points in the selection border.

You'll use the Magnetic Lasso tool to select the yellow pepper so that you can move it to the center of the cutting board.

1 Select the Zoom tool (🔍), and click the pepper to zoom in to at least 100%.

2 Select the Magnetic Lasso tool (🧲), hidden under the Lasso tool (🔗).

3 Click once along the left edge of the yellow pepper, and then move the Magnetic Lasso tool along the edge of the pepper to trace its outline.

▶ **Tip:** In low-contrast areas, you may want to click to place your own fastening points. You can add as many as you need. To remove the most recent fastening point, press Delete, and then move the mouse back to the remaining fastening point and continue selecting.

 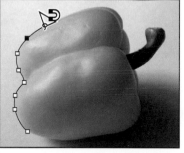

Even though you're not holding down the mouse button, the tool snaps to the edge of the pepper and automatically adds fastening points.

4 When you reach the left side of the pepper again, double-click to return the Magnetic Lasso tool to the starting point, closing the selection. Or, move the Magnetic Lasso tool over the starting point and click once.

5 Double-click the Hand tool (✋) to fit the image in the image window.

6 Select the Move tool (), and drag the pepper onto the cutting board.

7 Choose Select > Deselect, and then choose File > Save.

Softening the edges of a selection

To smooth the hard edges of a selection, you can apply anti-aliasing or feathering, or use the Refine Edge option.

Anti-aliasing smooths the jagged edges of a selection by softening the color transition between edge pixels and background pixels. Since only the edge pixels change, no detail is lost. Anti-aliasing is useful when cutting, copying, and pasting selections to create composite images.

Anti-aliasing is available for the Lasso, Polygonal Lasso, Magnetic Lasso, Elliptical Marquee, and Magic Wand tools. (Select the tool to display its options in the options bar.) To apply anti-aliasing, you must select it before making the selection. Once a selection is made, you cannot add anti-aliasing to it.

Feathering blurs edges by building a transition boundary between the selection and its surrounding pixels. This blurring can cause some loss of detail at the edge of the selection.

You can define feathering for the marquee and lasso tools as you use them, or you can add feathering to an existing selection. Feathering effects become apparent when you move, cut, or copy the selection.

Once you have a selection, you can use the Refine Edge option to smooth the outline, feather it, or contract or expand it. You'll use the Refine Edge option later in this lesson.

- To use anti-aliasing, select a lasso tool, or the Elliptical Marquee or Magic Wand tool, and select Anti-alias in the options bar.

- To define a feathered edge for a selection tool, select any of the lasso or marquee tools. Enter a Feather value in the options bar. This value defines the width of the feathered edge and can range from 1 to 250 pixels.

- To define a feathered edge for an existing selection, choose Select > Modify > Feather. Enter a value for the Feather Radius, and click OK.

Cropping an image and erasing within a selection

Now that your composition is in place, you'll crop the image to a final size and clean up some of the background scraps left behind when you moved selections. You can use either the Crop tool or the Crop command to crop an image.

1   Select the Crop tool (⊟), or press C to switch from the current tool to the Crop tool. Then, drag diagonally across the collage composition to select the area you want to keep. Photoshop dims the area outside the crop border.

2   Adjust the crop area, as necessary:

   • To reposition the crop border, position the pointer inside the cropping area and drag.

   • To resize the crop area, drag a handle.

3   When you are satisfied with the position of the crop area, press Enter or Return to crop the image.

The cropped image may include some scraps of the gray background from which you selected and removed shapes. You'll fix that next.

4 If a scrap of background gray protrudes into the composition, use a marquee selection tool or the Lasso tool (🔗) to select it. Be careful not to include any of the image that you want to keep.

5 Select the Eraser tool (✎) in the Tools panel, and then make sure that the foreground and background color swatches in the Tools panel are set to the defaults: black in the foreground and white in the background.

6 In the options bar, open the Brushes pop-up panel, and specify an **80**-pixel brush with **100%** hardness.

7 Drag the Eraser tool across the area you want to remove. You can erase quickly because the Eraser tool only affects the selected area.

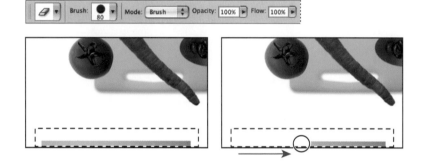

8 Repeat steps 4–7 to remove any other unwanted scraps of background.

9 Choose File > Save to save your work.

Refining the edge of a selection

Sometimes you'll get better results if you feather a selection edge to soften it, increase the edge's contrast, or expand or contract the edge to capture wisps of hair or other detail. The Refine Edge option improves the quality of a selection's edge, and it lets you see the edge more clearly by removing it from context and placing it against different backgrounds.

In this composition, the lettuce has more complicated edges than other elements. You'll select it and then fine-tune its edges.

1 Select the Quick Selection tool (✎), hidden beneath the Magic Wand tool (✳) in the Tools panel.

2 Drag from the upper-left corner of the composition across the lettuce to select it with part of the white background.

3 In the options bar, click the Subtract From Selection button (✎).

4 Click throughout the white portion of the selection, until only the lettuce is selected.

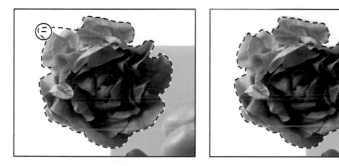

5 Click Refine Edge in the options bar.

The Refine Edge dialog box contains options to improve the selection edges by softening, feathering, or expanding them, or increasing their contrast. You can also view the selection edges as if masked or against various mattes, or backgrounds.

6 To prepare the edge for a drop shadow, set Contrast to **25**, Smooth to **9**, Feather to **2**, and Contract/Expand to **-49**.

7 Select the Zoom tool in the dialog box, and then drag a marquee around the lettuce head to zoom in on its edges.

You'll preview the shadow that you'll add to the lettuce against one of the mattes.

8 Click the center Black Matte button at the bottom of the dialog box. A black background appears under the selection and the selection edges disappear. You can click the other buttons to see the edges against different backgrounds.

9 Increase the Expand value to add more of a shadow around the lettuce edges. We used a value of 30%.

10 When you're satisfied with the adjustments, click OK.

You've gone to a lot of work to make and refine your selection. So that you don't lose it, you'll save it.

▶ **Tip:** You'll learn other ways to save selections in Lesson 5, "Masks and Channels."

11 Choose Edit > Copy, and then choose Edit > Paste to paste the selection on a new layer. In the Layers panel, double-click this new layer and rename it **Lettuce**.

Isolating and saving selections

You'll save selections of the other elements in the composition, as well. That way, your selections remain intact and easily available for editing.

1 In the Layers panel, select the Background layer.

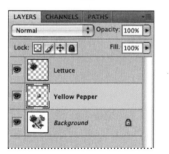

2 Zoom out or scroll across the image so that you can see the yellow pepper. Select the Background layer in the Layers panel. Then, use the Quick Selection tool (✎) to select the pepper, dragging carefully within its green stem. Remember that you can add or subtract from the selection using the buttons in the options bar.

► **Tip:** To add to the selection, press Shift as you click or drag. To subtract from the selection, press Alt or Option as you click or drag.

3 Choose Edit > Copy, and then choose Edit > Paste to paste a copy of the pepper onto a new layer. In the Layers panel, double-click the layer name and rename it **Yellow Pepper**.

4 Repeat steps 1 and 2 for the bowl of olives, carrot, tomato, and Salads logo: naming their new layers **Olives**, **Carrot, Tomato**, and **Logo**, respectively.

5 Choose File > Save.

It's good to save your selections on discrete layers—especially when you've spent time and effort creating them—so that you can easily retrieve them.

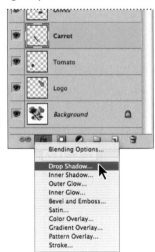

Creating a soft drop shadow

To complete your composition, you'll add a drop shadow behind the vegetables and logo. Adding the drop shadow is a simple matter of adding a layer effect.

1 In the Layers panel, select the Carrot layer.

2 At the bottom of the Layers panel, click the Add A Layer Style button (*fx*), and choose Drop Shadow from the pop-up menu.

3 In the Layer Styles dialog box, adjust the shadow settings to add a soft shadow. We used these values: Blend mode: Normal, Opacity: **60**%, Angle: **30**, Distance: **5** px, Spread **3**%, Size: **18** px. Then click OK.

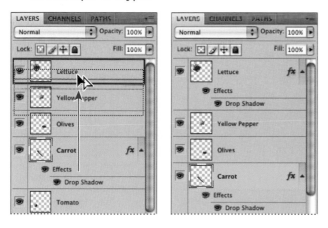

The carrot now has a soft drop shadow.

To replicate this shadow for the rest of the vegetables and the Salads logo, you'll simply copy the effect to their layers.

4 In the Layers panel, position the pointer on the Drop Shadow layer effect beneath the Carrot thumbnail (the pointer turns into a pointing hand).

5 Hold down Alt (Windows) or Option (Mac OS), and drag the effect up to the Lettuce layer to copy it.

There you have it! You've copied the drop shadow.

6 Repeat Step 5, Alt-dragging (Windows) or Option-dragging (Mac OS) the Drop Shadow effect onto each of the other layers except the Background layer.

● **Note:** To remove a layer effect, drag the effect icon to the Delete Layer button at the bottom of the Layers panel.

7 Choose File > Save to save your work.

You've used several different selection tools to move all the vegetables into place. The collage is complete!

Separating portions of an image onto different layers

To quickly create multiple images from one scan, use the Crop And Straighten Photos command. Images with a clearly delineated outline and a uniform background—such as the 03Start.psd file—work best. To try it, open the 03Start.psd file in the Lesson03 folder, and choose File > Automate > Crop And Straighten Photos. Photoshop automatically crops each image in the start file and creates individual Photoshop files for each. You can close each file without saving.

Original image

Result

Review questions

1 Once you've made a selection, what area of the image can be edited?

2 How do you add to and subtract from a selection?

3 How can you move a selection while you're drawing it?

4 When drawing a selection with the Lasso tool, how should you finish drawing the selection to ensure that it is the shape you want?

5 What does the Quick Selection tool do?

6 How does the Magic Wand tool determine which areas of an image to select? What is tolerance, and how does it affect a selection?

Review answers

1 Only the area within the selection can be edited.

2 To add to a selection, click the Add To Selection button in the options bar, and then click the area you want to add. To subtract from a selection, click the Subtract From Selection button in the options bar, and then click the area you want to subtract. You can also add to a selection by pressing Shift as you drag or click; to subtract, press Alt (Windows) or Option (Mac OS) as you drag or click.

3 Without releasing the mouse button, hold down the spacebar and drag to reposition the selection.

4 To make sure that the selection is the shape you want, end the selection by dragging across the starting point of the selection. If you start and stop the selection at different points, Photoshop draws a straight line between the start point of the selection and the end point of the selection.

5 The Quick Selection tool expands outward from where you click to automatically find and follow defined edges in the image.

6 The Magic Wand tool selects adjacent pixels based on their similarity in color. The Tolerance setting determines how many color tones the Magic Wand tool will select. The higher the tolerance setting, the more tones are selected.

4 LAYER BASICS

Lesson overview

In this lesson, you'll learn how to do the following:

- Organize artwork on layers.
- Create, view, hide, and select layers.
- Rearrange layers to change the stacking order of artwork in the image.
- Apply blending modes to layers.
- Resize and rotate layers.
- Apply a gradient to a layer.
- Apply a filter to a layer.
- Add text and layer effects to a layer.
- Save a copy of the file with the layers flattened.

 This lesson will take about an hour to complete. Copy the Lesson04 folder onto your hard drive if you haven't already done so. As you work on this lesson, you'll preserve the start files. If you need to restore the start files, copy them from the *Adobe Photoshop CS4 Classroom in a Book* CD.

Adobe Photoshop lets you isolate different parts of an image on *layers*. Each layer can then be edited as discrete artwork, allowing tremendous flexibility in composing and revising an image.

About layers

Every Photoshop file contains one or more *layers*. New files are generally created with a *background layer*, which contains a color or an image that shows through the transparent areas of subsequent layers. All new layers in an image are transparent until you add text or artwork (pixel values).

Working with layers is analogous to placing portions of a drawing on clear sheets of film, such as those viewed with an overhead projector: Individual sheets may be edited, repositioned, and deleted without affecting the other sheets. When the sheets are stacked, the entire composition is visible.

Getting started

You'll start the lesson by viewing an image of the final composition.

1   Start Photoshop and then immediately hold down Ctrl+Alt+Shift (Windows) or Command+Option+Shift (Mac OS) to restore the default preferences. (See "Restoring default preferences" on page 4.)

2   When prompted, click Yes to confirm that you want to reset preferences.

3   Click the Launch Bridge button (Br) in the application bar to open Adobe Bridge.

4   In the Favorites panel, click the Lessons folder. Then, double-click the Lesson04 folder in the Content panel, and view the 04End.psd file.

This layered composite represents a postcard. You will create it now, and in doing so, learn how to create, edit, and manage layers.

5   Double-click the 04Start.psd file to open it in Photoshop.

6   Choose File > Save As, rename the file **04Working.psd**, and click Save. Click OK if you see the Photoshop Format Options dialog box.

Saving another version of the start file frees you to make changes without worrying about overwriting the original.

Using the Layers panel

The Layers panel lists all the layers in an image, displaying the layer names and thumbnails of the content on each layer. You can use the Layers panel to hide, view, reposition, delete, rename, and merge layers. The layer thumbnails are automatically updated as you edit the layers.

1 If the Layers panel is not visible in the work area, choose Window > Layers.

The Layers panel lists five layers for the 04Working.psd file (from top to bottom): Postage, HAWAII, Flower, Pineapple, and Background.

2 Select the Background layer to make it active (if it is not already selected). Notice the layer thumbnail and the icons on the Background layer level:

- The lock icon (🔒) indicates that the layer is protected.

- The eye icon (👁) indicates that the layer is visible in the image window. If you click the eye, the image window no longer displays that layer.

The first task for this project is to add a photo of the beach to the postcard. First, you'll open the image in Photoshop.

> ▶ **Tip:** Use the context menu to hide or resize the layer thumbnail. Right-click (Windows) or Control-click (Mac OS) on a thumbnail in the Layers panel to open the context menu, and then select No Thumbnails, Small Thumbnails, Medium Thumbnails, or Large Thumbnails.

3 Click the Launch Bridge button () in the options bar. Double-click the Beach.psd file in the Lesson04 folder to open it in Photoshop.

The Layers panel changes to display the layer information for the active Beach.psd file. Notice that only one layer appears in the Beach.psd image: Layer 1, not Background. (For more information, see the sidebar, "About the background layer.")

About the background layer

When you create a new image with a white or colored background, the bottom layer in the Layers panel is named Background. An image can have only one background. You cannot change the stacking order of a background layer, its blending mode, or its opacity. You can, however, convert a background layer to a regular layer.

When you create a new image with transparent content, the image does not have a background layer. The bottom layer is not constrained like the background layer; you can move it anywhere in the Layers panel, and change its opacity and blending mode.

To convert a background layer into a regular layer:

1 Double-click the name Background in the Layers panel, or choose Layer > New > Layer From Background.

2 Rename the layer and set any other layer options.

3 Click OK.

To convert a regular layer into a background layer:

1 Select a layer in the Layers panel.

2 Choose Layer > New > Background From Layer.

● **Note:** To create a background layer from a regular layer, you must use the Background From Layer command; you cannot create a background layer simply by renaming a regular layer Background.

Renaming and copying a layer

To add content to an image and create a new layer for it simultaneously, drag an object or layer from one file into the image window of another file. Whether you drag from the image window of the original file or from its Layers panel, only the active layer is reproduced in the destination file.

You'll drag the Beach.psd image onto the 04Working.psd file. Before you begin, make sure that both the 04Working.psd and Beach.psd files are open, and that the Beach.psd file is active.

First, you will give Layer 1 a more descriptive name.

1   In the Layers panel, double-click the name Layer 1, type **Beach**, and then press Enter or Return. Keep the layer selected.

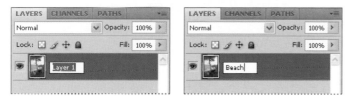

2   Click the Arrange Documents button (■)in the application bar, and then select one of the 2 Up layouts. Photoshop displays both of the open image files. Select the Beach.psd image so that it is the active file.

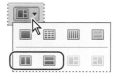

3   Select the Move tool (►⊕), and use it to drag the Beach.psd image onto the 04Working.psd image window.

The Beach layer now appears in the 04Working.psd file image window and its Layers panel, between the Background and Pineapple layers. Photoshop always adds new layers directly above the selected layer; you selected the Background layer earlier.

► **Tip:** If you hold
down Shift as you
drag an image from
one file into another,
the dragged image
automatically centers
itself in the target
image window.

4 Close the Beach.psd file without saving changes to it.

Viewing individual layers

The 04Working.psd file now contains six layers. Some of the layers are visible and some are hidden. The eye icon (👁) next to a layer thumbnail in the Layers panel indicates that the layer is visible.

1 Click the eye icon (👁) next to the Pineapple layer to hide the image of the pineapple.

You can hide or show a layer by clicking this icon or clicking in its column—also called the Show/Hide Visibility column.

2 Click again in the Show/Hide Visibility column to display the pineapple.

Adding a border to a layer

Now you'll add a white border around the Beach layer to create the impression that it is a photograph.

1   Select the Beach layer. (To select the layer, click the layer name in the Layers panel.)

The layer is highlighted, indicating that it is active. Changes you make in the image window affect the active layer.

2   To make the opaque areas on this layer more obvious, hide all layers except the Beach layer: press Alt (Windows) or Option (Mac OS) as you click the eye icon (👁) next to the Beach layer.

The white background and other objects in the image disappear, leaving only the beach image against a checkerboard background. The checkerboard indicates transparent areas of the active layer.

3   Choose Layer > Layer Style > Stroke.

The Layer Style dialog box opens. Now you will select the options for the white stroke around the beach image.

4 Specify the following settings:

- Size: **5** px

- Position: Inside

- Blend Mode: Normal

- Opacity: **100**%

- Color: White (Click the Color box, and select white in the Color Picker.)

5 Click OK. A white border appears around the beach photo.

Rearranging layers

The order in which the layers of an image are organized is called the *stacking order*. The stacking order determines how the image is viewed—you can change the order to make certain parts of the image appear in front of or behind other layers.

You'll rearrange the layers so that the beach image is in front of another image that is currently hidden in the file.

1   Make the Postage, HAWAII, Flower, Pineapple and Background layers visible by clicking the Show/Hide Visibility column next to their layer names.

The beach image is almost entirely blocked by images on other layers.

2   In the Layers panel, drag the Beach layer up so that it is positioned between the Pineapple and Flower layers—when you've positioned it correctly, you'll see a thick line between the layers in the panel—and then release the mouse button.

The Beach layer moves up one level in the stacking order, and the beach image appears on top of the pineapple and background images, but under the flower and "HAWAII."

▶ **Tip:** You can also control the stacking order of layered images by selecting them in the Layers panel and choosing Layer > Arrange, and then choosing Bring To Front, Bring Forward, Send To Back, or Send Backward.

Changing the opacity of a layer

You can reduce the opacity of any layer to let other layers show through it. In this case, the postmark is too dark on the flower. You'll edit the opacity of the Postage layer to let the flower and other images show through.

1   Select the Postage layer, and then click the arrow next to the Opacity box to display the Opacity slider. Drag the slider to **25%**. You can also type the value in the Opacity box or scrub the Opacity label.

The Postage layer becomes partially transparent, so you can see the other layers underneath. Notice that the change in opacity affects only the image area of the Postage layer. The Pineapple, Beach, Flower and HAWAII layers remain opaque.

2   Choose File > Save to save your work.

Duplicating a layer and changing the blending mode

You can also apply different blending modes to a layer. *Blending modes* affect how the color pixels in the image on one layer blend with pixels in the layers underneath. First you'll use blending modes to increase the intensity of the image on the Pineapple layer so that it doesn't look so dull. Then you'll change the blending mode on the Postage layer. (Currently, the blending mode for both layers is Normal.)

1   Click the eye icons next to the HAWAII, Flower, and Beach layers to hide them.

2   Right-click or Control-click the Pineapple layer, and choose Duplicate Layer from the context menu. (Make sure you click the layer name, not its thumbnail, or you'll see the wrong context menu.) Click OK in the Duplicate Layer dialog box.

A layer called "Pineapple copy" appears above the Pineapple layer in the Layers panel.

3 With the Pineapple copy layer selected, choose Overlay from the Blending Modes menu in the Layers panel.

The Overlay blending mode blends the Pineapple copy layer with the Pineapple layer beneath it to create a vibrant, more colorful pineapple with deeper shadows and brighter highlights.

4 Select the Postage layer, and choose Multiply from the Blending Modes menu. The Multiply blending mode multiplies the colors in the underlying layers with the color in the top layer. In this case, the postmark becomes a little stronger.

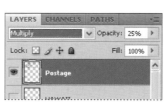

▶ **Tip:** For more about blending modes, including definitions and visual examples, see Photoshop Help.

5 Choose File > Save to save your work.

Resizing and rotating layers

You can resize and transform layers.

1 Click the Visibility column on the Beach layer to make it visible.

2 Select the Beach layer in the Layers panel, and then choose Edit > Free Transform. A Transform bounding box appears around the beach image. The bounding box has handles on each corner and each side.

First, you'll resize and angle the layer.

3 Press Shift as you drag a corner handle inward to scale the beach photo down by about 50%. (Watch the Width and Height percentages in the options bar.)

4 Then, with the bounding box still active, position the pointer just outside one of the corner handles until it becomes a curved double-arrow. Drag counter-clockwise to rotate the beach image approximately 15 degrees. You can also enter **15** in the Set Rotation box in the options bar.

5 Click the Commit Transform button (✔) in the options bar.

6 Make the Flower layer visible. Then, select the Move tool (➤₊), and drag the beach photo so that its corner is tucked neatly beneath the flower, as in the illustration.

7 Choose File > Save.

Using a filter to create artwork

Next, you'll create a new layer with no artwork on it. (Adding empty layers to a file is comparable to adding blank sheets of acetate to a stack of images.) You'll use this layer to add realistic-looking clouds to the sky with a Photoshop filter.

1   In the Layers panel, select the Background layer to make it active, and then click the New Layer button (▣) at the bottom of the Layers panel.

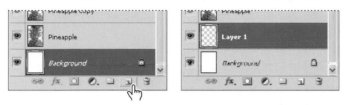

A new layer, named Layer 1, appears between the Background and Pineapple layers. The layer has no content, so it has no effect on the image window.

2   Double-click the name Layer 1, type **Clouds**, and press Enter or Return to rename the layer.

3   In the Tools panel, click the Foreground Color swatch, and select a sky blue color from the Color Picker, and click OK. We selected a color with the following values: R 48, G 138, and B 174. The Background Color remains white.

● **Note:** You can also create a new layer by choosing Layer > New > Layer, or by choosing New Layer from the Layers panel menu.

4 With the Clouds layer still active, choose Filter > Render > Clouds. Now, realistic-looking clouds appear behind the image.

5 Choose File > Save.

Adding text

Now, you're ready to create some type using the Horizontal Type tool, which places the text on its own type layer. You'll then edit the text and apply a special effect.

1 Make the HAWAII layer visible. You'll add text just below this layer, and apply special effects to both layers.

2 Choose Select > Deselect Layers, so that no layers are selected.

3 Click the Foreground Color swatch in the Tools panel, and then select a shade of grassy green in the Color Picker. Click OK to close the Color Picker.

4 In the Tools panel, select the Horizontal Type tool (T). Then, choose Window > Character to open the Character panel. Do the following in the Character panel:

- Select a serif font (we used Birch Std).

- Select a font style (we used Regular).

- Select a large font size (we used 36 points).

- Select Crisp from the Anti-aliasing menu (ªa).

- Select a large tracking value (≡) (we used 250).

- Click the All Caps button (TT).

- Click the Faux Bold button (T).

5 Click just below the "H" in the word *HAWAII*, and type **Island Paradise**. Then, click the Commit Any Current Edits button (✔) in the options bar.

● **Note:** If you make a mistake when you click to set the type, simply click away from the type and repeat Step 5.

The Layers panel now includes a layer named Island Paradise with a "T" thumbnail, indicating that it is a type layer. This layer is at the top of the layer stack.

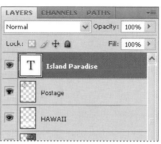

The text appears where you clicked, which probably isn't exactly where you want it to be positioned.

6 Select the Move tool (▸₊), and drag the "Island Paradise" text so that it is centered below HAWAII.

Applying a gradient to a layer

You can apply a color gradient to all or part of a layer. In this example, you'll apply a gradient to the HAWAII type to make it more colorful. First, you'll select the letters, and then you'll apply the gradient.

1 Select the HAWAII layer in the Layers panel to make it active.

2 Right-click or Control-click the thumbnail in the HAWAII layer, and choose Select Pixels. Everything on the HAWAII layer (the white lettering) is selected.

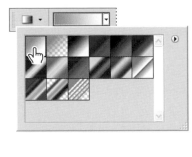

Now that you've selected the area to fill, you'll apply a gradient.

3 In the Tools panel, select the Gradient tool (▭).

4 Click the Foreground Color swatch in the Tools panel, select a bright color of orange in the Color Picker, and click OK. The Background Color should still be white.

5 In the options bar, make sure that Linear Gradient (▭) is selected.

6 In the options bar, click the arrow next to the Gradient Editor box to open the gradient picker. Select the Foreground To Background swatch (it's the first one), and then click anywhere outside the gradient picker to close it.

▶ **Tip:** To list the gradient options by name rather than by sample, click the gradient picker menu button, and choose either Small List or Large List. Or, hover the pointer over a thumbnail until a tool tip appears, showing the gradient name.

7 With the selection still active, drag the Gradient tool from the bottom to the top of the letters. If you want to be sure you drag straight up, press the Shift key as you drag.

The gradient extends across the type, starting with orange at the bottom and gradually blending to white at the top.

8 Choose Select > Deselect to deselect the HAWAII type.

9 Save your work so far.

Applying a layer style

You can enhance a layer by adding a shadow, stroke, satin sheen, or other special effect from a collection of automated and editable layer styles. These styles are easy to apply and link directly to the layer you specify.

Like layers, layer styles can be hidden by clicking eye icons (👁) in the Layers panel. Layer styles are nondestructive, so you can edit or remove them at any time. You can apply a copy of a layer style to a different layer by dragging the effect onto the destination layer.

Earlier, you used a layer style to add a stroke to the beach photo. Now, you'll add drop shadows to the text to make it stand out.

1   Select the Island Paradise layer, and then choose Layer > Layer Style > Drop Shadow.

2   In the Layer Style dialog box, make sure that the Preview option is selected, and then, if necessary, move the dialog box so that you can see the Island Paradise text in the image window.

3   In the Structure area, select Use Global Light and then specify the following settings:

- Blend Mode: Multiply
- Opacity: **75**%
- Angle: **78** degrees
- Distance: **5** px
- Spread: **30**%
- Size: **10** px

▶ **Tip:** You can also open the Layer Style dialog box by clicking the Add A Layer Style button at the bottom of the Layers panel and then choosing a layer style, such as Bevel And Emboss, from the pop-up menu.

Photoshop adds a drop shadow to the "Island Paradise" text in the image.

4   Click OK to accept the settings and close the Layer Style dialog box.

Photoshop nests the layer style in the Island Paradise layer. First, it lists Effects, and then the layer styles applied to the layer. An eye icon (👁) appears next to the effect category and next to each effect. To turn off an effect, click the eye icon. Click the visibility column again to restore the effect. To hide all layer styles, click the eye icon next to Effects. To collapse the list of effects, click the arrow next to the layer.

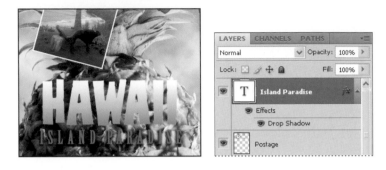

5 Before you continue, make sure that eye icons appear for both items nested in the Island Paradise layer.

6 Press Alt (Windows) or Option (Mac OS) and drag the Effects line down onto the HAWAII layer. The Drop Shadow layer style is applied to the HAWAII layer, using the same settings you applied to the Island Paradise layer.

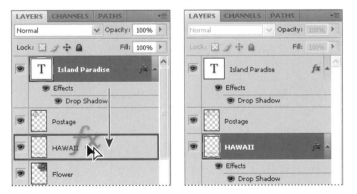

Now you'll add a green stroke around the word HAWAII.

7 Select the HAWAII layer in the Layers panel, click the Add A Layer Style button (𝑓𝑥) at the bottom of the panel, and choose Stroke from the pop-up menu.

8 In the Structure area of the Layer Styles dialog box, specify the following settings, and then click OK:

- Size: **4** px

- Position: Outside

- Blend Mode: Normal

- Opacity: **100**%

- Color: Green (select a color that goes well with the color you used for the "Island Paradise" text)

9 Click OK to apply the stroke.

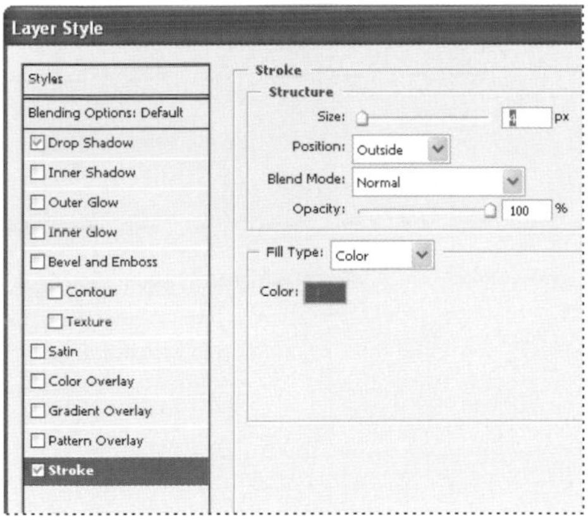

Now you'll add a drop shadow and a satin sheen to the flower.

10 Select the Flower layer, and choose Layer > Layer Style > Drop Shadow. Then change the following settings in the Structure area: Opacity: **60**%, Distance: **13** px, Spread: **9**%. Make sure Use Global Light is selected, and that the Blend Mode is Multiply. Do not click OK.

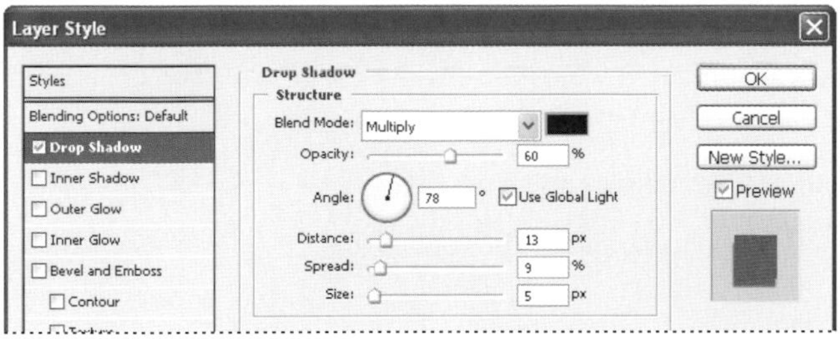

Note: While you have the Layer Style dialog box open, you can edit any style effect by clicking on its name to select it.

11 With the Layer Style dialog box still open, select the Satin effect on the left by clicking its name. Then, make sure Invert is selected, and apply the following settings:

- Color (next to Blend Mode): Fuchsia (choose a color that complements the flower color)

- Opacity: **20**%

- Distance: **22** px

12 Click OK to apply both layer styles.

Updating layer effects

Layer effects are automatically updated when you make changes to a layer. You can edit the text and watch how the layer effect tracks the change.

1 Select the Island Paradise layer in the Layers panel.

2 In the Tools panel, select the Horizontal Type tool (T).

3   In the options bar, set the font size to **32** points and press Enter or Return.

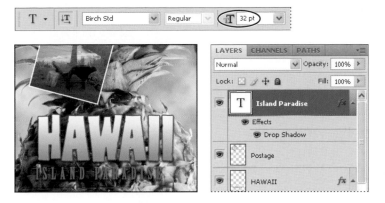

Although you didn't select the text by dragging the Type tool (as you would have to do in a word-processing program), "Island Paradise" now appears in 32-point type.

4   Using the Horizontal Type tool, click between "Island" and "Paradise," and type **of**.

As you edit the text, the layer styles are applied to the new text.

5   You don't actually need the word "of," so delete it.

6   Select the Move tool (🕂) and drag "Island Paradise" to center it beneath the word "HAWAII."

7   Choose File > Save.

● **Note:** You don't have to click the Commit Any Current Edits button after making any text edits, because choosing the Move tool has the same effect.

Adding a border

The Hawaii postcard is almost done. The elements are almost all arranged correctly in the composition. You'll finish up by positioning the postmark and then adding a white postcard border.

1 Select the Postage layer, and then use the Move tool (⊹) to drag it to the middle-right of the image, as in the following illustration.

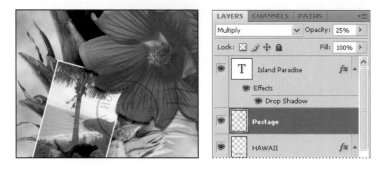

2 Select the Island Paradise layer in the Layers panel, and then click the Add Layer button (◻) at the bottom of the panel.

3 Choose Select > All.

4 Choose Select > Modify > Border. In the Border Selection dialog box, type **10** pixels for the Width, and click OK.

A 10-pixel border is selected around the entire image. Now, you'll fill it with white.

5 Select white for the Foreground Color, and then choose Edit > Fill.

6 In the Fill dialog box, make sure Foreground Color is selected, and click OK.

7 Choose Select > Deselect.

8 Double-click the Layer 1 name in the Layers panel, and rename the layer **Border**.

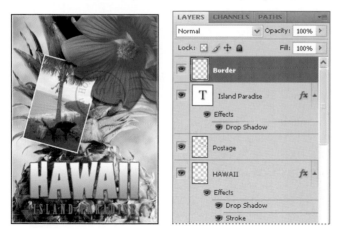

Flattening and saving files

When you finish editing all the layers in your image, you can merge or flatten layers to reduce the file size. Flattening combines all the layers into a single background layer. However, you cannot edit layers once you've flattened them, so you shouldn't flatten an image until you are certain that you're satisfied with all your design decisions. Rather than flattening your original PSD files, it's a good idea to save a copy of the file with its layers intact, in case you need to edit a layer later.

To appreciate what flattening does, notice the two numbers for the file size in the status bar at the bottom of the image window.

Note: Click the status bar pop-up menu arrow and choose Show > Document Sizes if the sizes do not appear in the status bar.

The first number represents what the file size would be if you flattened the image. The second number represents the file size without flattening. This lesson file, if flattened, would be about 2.29 MB, but the current file is actually much larger—about 26 MB. So flattening is well worth it in this case.

1 Select any tool but the Type tool (T), to be sure that you're not in text-editing mode. Then choose File > Save (if it is available) to be sure that all your changes have been saved in the file.

2 Choose Image > Duplicate.

3 In the Duplicate Image dialog box, name the file **04Flat.psd** and click OK.

4 Leave the 04Flat.psd file open, but close the 04Working.psd file.

5 Choose Flatten Image from the Layers panel menu. Only one layer, named Background, remains in the Layers panel.

Tip: If you want to flatten only some of the layers in a file, click the eye icons to hide the layers you don't want to flatten, and then choose Merge Visible from the Layers panel menu.

6 Choose File > Save. Even though you chose Save rather than Save As, the Save As dialog box appears.

7 Make sure that the location is the Lessons/Lesson04 folder, and then click Save to accept the default settings and save the flattened file.

You have saved two versions of the file: a one-layer, flattened copy as well as the original file, in which all the layers remain intact.

About layer comps

Layer comps provide one-click flexibility in switching between different views of a multilayered image file. A layer comp is simply a definition of the settings in the Layers panel. Once you've defined a layer comp, you can change as many settings as you please in the Layers panel and then create another layer comp to preserve that configuration of layer properties. Then, by switching from one layer comp to another, you can quickly review the two designs. The beauty of layer comps becomes apparent when you want to demonstrate a number of possible design arrangements, for example. When you've created a few layer comps, you can review the design variations without having to tediously select and deselect eye icons or change settings in the Layers panel.

Say, for example, that you are designing a brochure, and you're producing a version in English as well as in French. You might have the French text on one layer, and the English text on another in the same image file. To create two different layer comps, you would simply turn on visibility for the French layer and turn off visibility for the English layer, and then click the Create New Layer Comp button on the Layer Comps panel. Then, you'd do the inverse—turn on visibility for the English layer and turn off visibility for the French layer, and click the create New Layer Comp button—to create an English layer comp.

To view the different layer comps, you click the Apply Layer comp box for each comp to view them in turn. With a little imagination, you can appreciate how much time this saves for more complex variations. Layer comps can be an especially valuable feature when the design is in flux or when you need to create multiple versions of the same image file.

You've created a colorful, attractive postcard. This lesson only begins to explore the vast possibilities and the flexibility you gain when you master the art of using Photoshop layers. You'll get more experience and try out different techniques for layers in almost every chapter as you progress forward in the book, and especially in Lesson 9, "Advanced Layering."

Extra Credit

Take the blinking and bad poses out of an otherwise great family portrait with the Auto-Align Layers feature.

1   Open FamilyPhoto.psd in your Lesson04 folder.

2   In the Layers panel, turn Layer 2 on and off to see the two similar photos. When both layers are visible, Layer 2 shows the tall man in the center blinking, and the two girls in the lower left looking away. You'll align the two photos, and then use the Eraser tool to brush out the parts of the photo on Layer 2 that you want to improve.

3   Make both layers visible, and Shift-click to select them. Choose Edit > Auto-Align Layers; click OK to accept the default Auto position. Now click the eye icon next to Layer 2 off and on to see that the layers are perfectly aligned.

Now for the fun part! You'll brush out the photo where you want to improve it.

4   Select the Eraser tool in the Tools panel, and pick a soft, 45-pixel brush in the options bar. Select Layer 2, and start brushing in the center of the blinking-man's head to reveal the smiling face below.

5 Use the Eraser tool on the two girls looking away, revealing the image below, where they look into the camera.

You've created a natural family snapshot.

Review questions

1 What is the advantage of using layers?

2 When you create a new layer, where does it appear in the Layers panel stack?

3 How can you make artwork on one layer appear in front of artwork on another layer?

4 How can you apply a layer style?

5 When you've completed your artwork, what can you do to minimize the file size without changing the quality or dimensions?

Review answers

1 Layers let you move and edit different parts of an image as discrete objects. You can also hide individual layers as you work on other layers.

2 The new layer always appears immediately above the active layer.

3 You can make artwork on one layer appear in front of artwork on another layer by dragging layers up or down the stacking order in the Layers panel, or by using the Layer > Arrange subcommands—Bring to Front, Bring Forward, Send to Back, and Send Backward. However, you cannot change the layer position of a background layer.

4 Select the layer and then click the Add A Layer Style button in the Layers panel, or choose Layer > Layer Style > [style].

5 You can flatten the image, which merges all the layers onto a single background. It's a good idea to duplicate image files with layers intact before you flatten them, in case you have to make changes to a layer later.

5 MASKS AND CHANNELS

Lesson overview

In this lesson, you'll learn how to do the following:

- Refine a selection using a quick mask.

- Save a selection as a channel mask.

- View a mask using the Channels panel.

- Load a saved mask.

- Edit a mask using the Masks panel.

- Apply filters, effects, and blending modes to a mask.

- Move an image within a mask.

- Create a layer mask.

- Paint in a mask to modify a selection.

- Make an intricate selection using the Quick Selection tool.

- Create and use a gradient mask.

- Isolate a channel to make specific image corrections.

- Create a high-quality grayscale image by mixing channels.

 This lesson will take about 90 minutes to complete. Copy the Lesson05 folder onto your hard drive if you haven't already done so. As you work on this lesson, you'll preserve the start files. If you need to restore the start files, copy them from the *Adobe Photoshop CS4 Classroom in a Book* CD.

Zen Garden

Andrew Faulkner

Use masks to isolate and manipulate specific parts of an image. The cutout portion of a mask can be altered, but the area surrounding the cutout is protected from change. You can create a temporary mask to use once, or you can save masks for repeated use.

Working with masks and channels

Photoshop masks isolate and protect parts of an image, just as masking tape protects a window glass or trim from paint when a house is painted. When you create a mask based on a selection, the area you haven't selected is *masked,* or protected from editing. With masks, you can create and save time-consuming selections and then use them again. In addition, you can use masks for other complex editing tasks—for example, to apply color changes or filter effects to an image.

In Photoshop, you can make temporary masks, called *quick masks,* or you can create permanent masks and store them as special grayscale channels called *alpha channels.* Photoshop also uses channels to store an image's color information. Unlike layers, channels do not print. You use the Channels panel to view and work with alpha channels.

A key concept in masking is that black hides and white reveals. As in life, rarely is anything black and white. Shades of gray partially hide, depending on the gray levels (255 is the value for black, hiding artwork completely; 0 is the value for white, revealing artwork completely).

Getting started

First, you'll view the image that you'll create using masks and channels.

1   Start Photoshop and then immediately hold down Ctrl+Alt+Shift (Windows) or Command+Option+Shift (Mac OS) to restore the default preferences. (See "Restoring default preferences" on page 4.)

2   When prompted, click Yes to confirm that you want to reset preferences.

3   Click the Launch Bridge button (⊞) in the application bar to open Adobe Bridge.

4   Click the Favorites tab on the left side of the Bridge window. Select the Lessons folder, and then double-click the Lesson05 folder in the Content panel.

5   Study the 05End.psd file. To enlarge the thumbnail so that you can see it more clearly, move the thumbnail slider at the bottom of the Bridge window to the right.

In this lesson, you'll create the cover for a book titled *Zen Garden*. You will use masks to combine several photos—a Buddha statue, a Japanese temple, a bamboo fence—and embossed text into one image. You'll also make intricate selections of the ripped edges of paper that will serve as the composition's background. Your final touch will be to add type to the cover that reveals the paper texture.

6 Double-click the 05Start.psd thumbnail
   to open it in Photoshop.

Creating a quick mask

You'll use Quick Mask mode to convert a selection border into a temporary mask. Later, you will convert this temporary quick mask back into a selection border. Unless you save a quick mask as a more permanent alpha-channel mask, Photoshop discards the temporary mask once it is converted to a selection.

1 Choose File > Save As, rename the file **05Working.psd**, and click Save. Click OK
   if a compatibility warning appears.

Saving a working version of the file lets you return to the original if you need it.

You'll mask the Buddha statue so that you can separate it from its background and paste it in front of a new background.

2 In the Layers panel, select the Buddha
   layer.

3 Click the Edit In Quick Mask Mode
   button (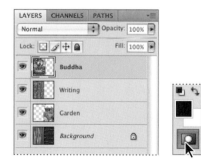) in the Tools panel. (By
   default, you have been working in
   Standard mode.)

In Quick Mask mode, a red overlay appears as you make a selection, masking the area outside the selection the way that a rubylith, or red acetate, masked images in traditional print shops. You can apply changes only to the unprotected area that is visible and selected. Notice, too, that the selected layer in the Layers panel appears gray, indicating you are in Quick Mask mode.

4   In the Tools panel, select the Brush tool (✎).

5   In the options bar, make sure that the mode is Normal. Open the Brush pop-up panel, and select a large hard brush with a diameter of **65** px. Click outside the panel to close it.

You'll use this large brush to rough out a mask, which you'll refine in the next exercise.

6   In the image, drag the Brush tool to mask the halo; the brush size should match the width of the halo. It's fine to paint a little over the halo edges. A red overlay appears wherever you paint, indicating the mask you're creating.

In Quick Mask mode, Photoshop automatically defaults to Grayscale mode, with a foreground color of black, and a background color of white. When using a painting or editing tool in Quick Mask mode, keep these principles in mind:

- Painting with black adds to the mask (the red overlay) and decreases the selected area.

- Painting with white erases the mask (the red overlay) and increases the selected area.

- Painting with gray partially adds to the mask.

7   Continue painting with the Brush tool to add the Buddha statue to the mask. Don't include the background.

Don't worry if you paint outside the outline of the statue. You'll fine-tune the mask in the next exercise.

8   In the Layers panel group, click the Channels tab to display the Channels panel.

In the Channels panel, the default color-information channels are listed—a full-color preview channel for the CMYK image and separate channels for cyan, magenta, yellow, and black.

The quick mask you just created appears as a new alpha channel, named Quick Mask. Remember, this channel is temporary: unless you save it as a selection or apply it as a mask, the quick mask will disappear as soon as you deselect.

Note: To hide and display individual color channels, click the eye icons in the Channels panel. When the CMYK channel is visible, so are all four individual channels.

Note: If you save and close a file while in Quick Mask mode, the quick mask will show in its own channel the next time you open the file. If, however, you save and close your file while in Standard mode, the quick mask will be gone the next time you open your file.

Editing a mask

You created a rough mask of the statue, but it overlaps the scenery. You'll use the Masks panel to convert the quick mask to a layer mask, and then to refine its edges. The advantage of editing your selection as a mask is that you can use almost any tool or filter to modify the mask. (You can even use selection tools.)

Converting a quick mask to a layer mask

Quick masks are temporary. They disappear as soon as you deselect. However, you can save a selection as an alpha-channel mask so that your time-consuming work won't be lost, and you can reuse the selection in this work session or a later one. You can even use alpha channels in other Photoshop image files.

To avoid confusing channels and layers, think of channels as containing an image's color and selection information; think of layers as containing painting and effects.

1 Click the Edit In Standard Mode button at the bottom of the Tools panel to exit Quick Mask mode. The quick mask becomes an active selection. You'll use that selection to refine the mask.

2 Click the Layers tab to display the Layers panel, and make sure the Buddha layer is still active.

3 Click the Masks tab to display the Masks panel. (The Masks panel is grouped with the Adjustments panel.) The Masks panel provides options for refining, inverting, and otherwise working with masks.

4 Click the Add A Pixel Mask button (⬛) in the Masks panel. Photoshop converts the active selection to a layer mask (pixel mask) on the Buddha layer.

5 Click the Channels tab to display the Channels panel. Notice that the Quick Mask channel is gone, but a Buddha Mask alpha channel has been added.

About alpha channels

If you work in Photoshop very long, you're bound to work with alpha channels. It's a good idea to know a few things about them:

- An image can contain up to 56 channels, including all color and alpha channels.

- All channels are 8-bit grayscale images, capable of displaying 256 levels of gray.

- You can specify a name, color, mask option, and opacity for each channel. (The opacity affects the preview of the channel, not the image.)

- All new channels have the same dimensions and number of pixels as the original image.

- You can edit the mask in an alpha channel using the painting tools, editing tools, and filters.

- You can convert alpha channels to spot-color channels.

Refining a mask

The Buddha statue is masked, but you still need to smooth out its edges. You'll invert the mask so that you can see the statue clearly as you work with the Quick Selection tool and tools in the Masks panel.

First, you'll hide the layers beneath the statue so that you can see it more clearly.

1 Click the Layers tab to display the Layers panel again. Then, click the eye icons (👁) next to the Writing, Garden, and Background layers to hide them. Everything but the greenery is transparent, represented by a checkerboard pattern.

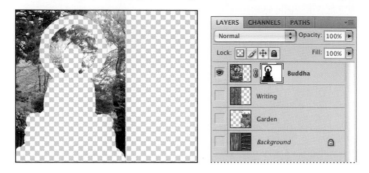

2 Make sure the Buddha layer is active in the Layers panel. Then, in the Masks panel, click Invert. Now the scenery is transparent and the statue is visible. Seeing the statue will make it easier for you to refine the mask with greater precision.

You're ready to add pixels to and subtract them from the mask. Remember that when you're painting with white, you're adding to the mask, and when you're painting with black, you're subtracting.

3 Zoom in to see the area you're working with more clearly. You'll probably need to scroll or pan across the image to work with different areas.

Julieanne Kost is an official Adobe Photoshop evangelist.

Tool tips from the Photoshop evangelist

Zoom tool shortcuts

Often when you are editing an image, you'll need to zoom in to work on a detail and then zoom out again to see the changes in context. Here are several keyboard shortcuts that make the zooming even faster and easier to do.

- Press Ctrl+spacebar (Windows) or Command+spacebar (Mac OS) to temporarily select the Zoom In tool from the keyboard. When you finish zooming, release the keys to return to the tool you were previously using.

- Press Alt+spacebar (Windows) or Option+spacebar (Mac OS) to temporarily select the Zoom Out tool from the keyboard. When you finish zooming, release the keys to return to the tool you were using.

- Double-click the Zoom tool in the Tools panel to return the image to 100% view.

- Press Alt (Windows) or Option (Mac OS) to change the Zoom In tool to the Zoom Out tool, and click the area of the image you want to reduce. Each Alt/Option-click reduces the image by the next preset increment.

- With any tool selected, press Ctrl+plus (Windows) or Command+plus (Mac OS) to zoom in, or press Ctrl+minus or Command+minus to zoom out.

4 Select the Quick Selection tool (🖌) from the Tools panel. In the options bar, select an 8-pixel, soft brush.

5 Use the edges of the statue to guide the selection.

- When you've selected an area you want to add to the mask (so that it is transparent), press Alt+Delete (Windows) or Option+Delete (Mac OS).

- To remove the selected area from the mask (so that it is visible), press Delete. Be sure to click the New Selection button in the options bar each time you're ready to make a new selection. (By default, the Add To Selection button is selected.)

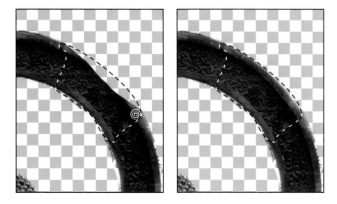

You may prefer to use other selection tools, such as the Magnetic Lasso tool. Use any selection tool, or simply the Brush tool to add and subtract from the mask. If you're using the Brush tool, press the X key on your keyboard to switch the foreground and background colors. You may need to change brush sizes as you work to refine the mask.

For help using the selection tools, see Lesson 3, "Working with Selections."

6 When you're satisfied that you've removed most of the greenery from the visible area, and that most of the statue is visible, choose Select > Deselect. Then, click the Mask Edge button in the Masks panel. The Refine Mask dialog box opens. You can soften or harden a mask edge or make other changes to the mask.

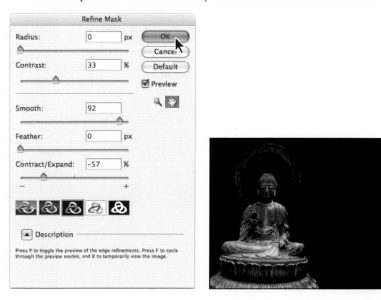

7 Adjust the options in the Refine Mask dialog box so that the mask fits more snugly around the edge of the statue. We set Radius to 0, Contrast to 33, Smooth to 92, Feather to 0, and Contract/Expand to -57. Click the Black Background button to preview the mask clearly. Click OK when the mask looks accurate.

8 In the Layers panel, make all the layers visible so you can see how the mask looks against them.

9 Zoom in and use a small, soft brush to touch up any final areas.

The greenery is masked, but your goal is to mask out the statue. You'll invert the mask now.

10 Click Invert in the Masks panel.

If you want to see the mask without any distractions, open the Channels panel, and then show the Buddha Mask channel and hide all the other channels. When you're done viewing the channel, show the other channels and hide the Buddha Mask channel.

11 Choose File > Save to save your work so far.

Masking tips and shortcuts

Mastering masks can help you work more efficiently in Photoshop. These tips will get you started.

- Masks are nondestructive, which means that you can edit the masks later without losing the pixels that they hide.

- When editing a mask, be aware of the color selected in the Tools panel. Black hides, white reveals, and shades of gray partially hide or reveal. The darker the gray, the more is hidden in the mask.

- To reveal a layer's content without masking effects, turn off the mask by Shift-clicking the layer mask thumbnail, or choose Layer > Layer Mask > Disable. A red X appears over the mask thumbnail in the Layers panel when the mask is disabled.

- To turn a layer mask back on, Shift-click the layer mask thumbnail with the red X in the Layers panel, or choose Layer > Layer Mask > Enable. If the mask doesn't show up in the Layers panel, choose Layer > Layer Mask > Reveal All to display it.

- Unlink layers and masks to move the two independently and shift the masks' boundaries separately from the layer. To unlink a layer or group from its layer mask or vector mask, click the link icon between the thumbnails in the Layers panel. To relink them, click the blank space between the two thumbnails.

- To convert a vector mask to a layer mask, select the layer containing the vector mask you want to convert, and choose Layer > Rasterize > Vector Mask. Note, however, that once you rasterize a vector mask, you can't change it back into a vector object.

- To modify a mask, use the Density and Feather sliders in the Masks panel. The Density slider determines the opacity of the mask: at 100%, the mask is fully in effect; at lower opacities, the contrast lessens; and at 0%, the mask has no effect. The Feather slider softens the edge of the mask.

Viewing channels

You're ready to assemble a background for the book cover, using a mask to hide unwanted elements. You'll start by looking at each channel in the image to determine which channel offers the most contrast for the mask you're about to create.

1   Drag the Layers tab out of the dock so that the Layers panel is a floating panel. Position the Layers panel next to the Channels panel, so that you can see both. If you can't see all of the contents of the Layers panel, drag its lower-right corner down until you can.

2   In the Layers panel, Alt-click (Windows) or Option-click (Mac OS) the eye
icon (👁) next to the Background layer to hide all of the other layers. Select the
Background layer.

3   In the Channels panel, select the CMYK channel so that all channels are visible.
Then, hide the Cyan channel. The eye icon next to the composite (CMYK)
channel disappears, too. Now, only the Magenta, Yellow, and Black channels are
visible.

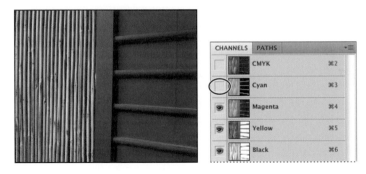

Note: To display
channels in their
respective colors (red,
green, and blue; or
cyan, magenta, yellow,
and black) select Show
Channels In Color in
the Interface category
of the Photoshop
Preferences dialog
box. For this lesson,
however, leave that
option deselected.

If you view a combination of channels, they appear in color, whether or not you are
viewing channels in color.

4   Hide the Magenta and Yellow channels. Only the Black channel remains visible.
(You can't turn off all channels in an image; at least one must remain visible.)

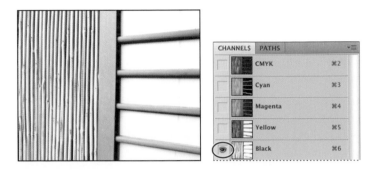

Individual channels appear in grayscale. In grayscale, you can evaluate the tonal values of the color components of the color channels, and decide which channel is the best candidate for corrections.

5   In the Channels panel, click the Yellow channel name to turn off the Black channel and turn on the Yellow channel, and then examine the contrast in the image. Repeat this step for the Magenta and Cyan channels. You're looking for the channel that offers the easiest selection for the blue background.

Notice that in all channels but Cyan, the panels have a vertical dark streak. The Cyan channel shows the panel background as solid black. The solid black offers the most contrast, making the Cyan channel the easiest to select.

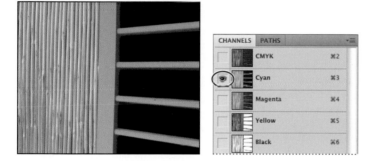

You'll apply a levels adjustment to the channel, to make it easier to select.

Adjusting individual channels

Now that you've identified the Cyan channel as the channel with the most contrast, you'll copy it and make adjustments to the copy.

1   Make sure that only the Cyan channel is visible in the Channels panel. Drag the Cyan channel to the New Channel button (⊡) at the bottom of the Channels panel. A channel named Cyan copy appears in the Channels panel.

2 Double-click the Cyan copy name and rename it **Panel Mask**.

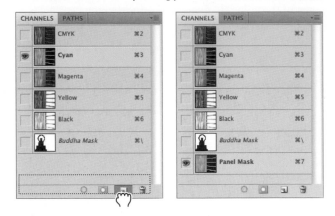

You'll isolate the black panels with a levels adjustment.

3 Choose Image > Adjustments > Levels to open the Levels dialog box. Notice the nearly flat part of the histogram: you'll isolate these values.

4 Drag the black (shadows) slider to the right to the point where the black begins to flatten out on the left side of the histogram; drag the white (highlights) slider to the left to where the black values start to climb again. (We used values of 23, 1.00, and 45.) The preview shows the image as black and white. Click OK.

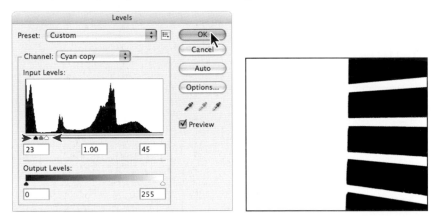

5 Choose File > Save to save your work so far.

Loading a mask as a selection

You will load the channel mask you just created as a selection, which you can then convert to a layer mask.

1 In the Layers panel, make the Garden layer visible, and then select it.

2 Double-click the Hand tool to change the view to 100%.

3 Choose Select > Load Selection. Choose Panel Mask from the Channel menu, and then select Invert to reverse the selection so that the panels—not the background—will be selected. Click OK.

A selection marquee appears on the image.

4 With the selection active, click the Add Layer Mask button (▣) at the bottom of the Layers panel to mask the selection.

Notice that a new channel, named Garden Mask, appears in the Channels panel. As long as the Garden layer is selected, the Channels panel displays its mask.

5 In the Layers panel, click the Link icon (🔗) between the image thumbnail and mask thumbnail on the Garden layer to unlink the two.

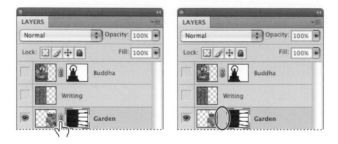

6 On the Garden layer, click the image thumbnail to make it active.

You want to reposition the temple within the mask.

7 Select the Move tool (▶⊕) in the Tools panel. With the selection still active, drag to reposition the image within the mask, so that the peak of the temple is visible in the top panel.

8 When you are satisfied with how the image looks within the mask, relink the image and the layer mask in the Garden layer. (To relink them, click the area between the image thumbnail and the layer mask thumbnail.)

9 Save your work so far.

Loading a selection into an image using shortcuts

You can reuse a previously saved selection by loading it into an image.

To load a saved selection using shortcuts, do one of the following in the Channels panel:

- Select the alpha channel, click the Load Channel As Selection button at the bottom of the panel, and then click the composite color channel near the top of the panel.

- Drag the channel that contains the selection you want to load onto the Load Channel As Selection button.

- Control-click (Windows) or Command-click (Mac OS) the channel containing the selection you want to load.

You can choose how the mask interacts with an existing selection:

- To add the mask to an existing selection, press Ctrl+Shift (Windows) or Command+Shift (Mac OS), and click the channel.

- To subtract the mask from an existing selection, press Ctrl+Alt (Windows) or Command+Option (Mac OS), and click the channel.

- To load the intersection of the saved selection and an existing selection, press Ctrl+Alt+Shift (Windows) or Command+Option+Shift (Mac OS), and select the channel.

Applying filters to a mask

You worked in CMYK mode to isolate the Cyan channel. Now you'll convert the image to RGB mode to apply an RGB filter from the Filter Gallery. A limited number of filters are available in CMYK mode; Filter Gallery filters work only on RGB images. You will refine the selection of panels so that they appear to be glass.

1 In the Channels panel, make sure that the CMYK composite channel is visible.

2 Choose Image > Mode > RGB Color. In the alert dialog box, click Don't Flatten. The image is converted to RGB. If a compatibility alert appears, click OK.

3 Choose Filter > Filter Gallery to display the Filter Gallery dialog box.

4 In the Filter Gallery, expand the Distort folder. Then select Glass. On the right side of the dialog box, set the Distortion value to **2** and Smoothness to **4** to make it look like glass on a rainy day. Click OK.

Applying effects using a gradient mask

In addition to using black to indicate what's hidden and white to indicate what's selected, you can paint with shades of gray to indicate partial transparency. For example, if you paint in a mask with a shade of gray that is at least halfway between white and black, the underlying image becomes partially (50% or more) visible.

You'll create a gradient mask and use it to apply a filter that fades into the image.

1 In the Layers panel, make the Writing layer visible, and then select it. The layer contains an image of bronze lettering.

2 At the bottom of the Layers panel, click the Add Layer Mask button (⬛) to add a layer mask to the Writing layer.

3 Click the Writing layer mask thumbnail (currently a white box) to select it. A black border appears around the layer mask, indicating that it, not the image, is selected. You will apply an effect to the mask, not the image.

4 Click the Gradient tool (⬛) in the Tools panel to select it. In the options bar, make sure that the default Linear Gradient button is selected.

You want the gradient to move from white to black, so the foreground color should be white and the background color should be black.

5 If the foreground color is black and the background color is white, click the double-arrow icon in the Tools panel to switch the foreground and background colors.

6 In the image window, hold down the Shift key as you drag the Gradient tool from the center-left side of the image straight across to the right, where the wall meets the window. The layer mask thumbnail in the Layers panel displays the gradient.

Where the gradient is white, it will reveal the filter you're about to add to the layer mask. As it moves from white to black, it will gradually hide the effect. Gradient pixel values that decrease from 255 (black) to 0 (white) gradually reveal more of what's under the mask.

7 Make sure that the black border still appears around the layer mask thumbnail, indicating that it, not the image thumbnail, is selected.

8 Choose Filter > Texture > Mosaic Tiles. Photoshop opens the Filter Gallery.

9 Adjust the Mosaic Tiles settings. For Tile Size, enter **18**; for Grout Width, enter **4**; and for Lighten Grout, enter **1**. Then, click OK.

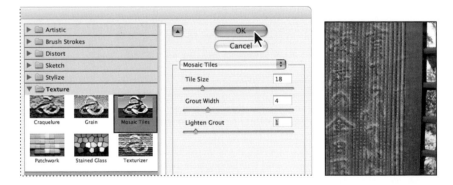

10 Choose File > Save to save your work.

Resizing the canvas

Next, you'll add canvas area to the image so that you can create a background for the cover title and byline.

1   In the Tools panel, set the background color to white. (To set it quickly, click the Default Colors button in the Tools panel, and then click the double-arrow icon to switch the foreground and background colors.)

2   Choose Image > Canvas Size. In the Canvas Size dialog box, select Relative to add to the existing image size. Enter **2** inches for the Height. In the Anchor area, click the lower center square to add canvas to the top of the image. Click OK.

● **Note:** Ordinarily, the default background color is white and the default foreground color is black. When you have a mask selected, however, the defaults are reversed.

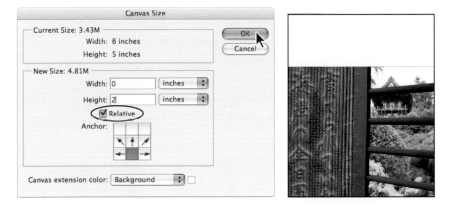

You'll perform the same action again to add canvas to the bottom of the image.

3   Choose Image > Canvas Size. In the Canvas Size dialog box, make sure that Relative is still selected, change the Height to **1** inch, and in the Anchor area, click the upper center square. Click OK.

4   Double-click the Hand tool to see the entire image, and then save your work.

Removing the background from an image

You'll add a torn-paper background to the canvas you just created. The paper was scanned against a white background. To use the paper without the background, you'll need to select it and copy it to its own layer. One way to select a delicate edge is to team up the Color Range selection feature with the Quick Selection tool and the Refine Edge option. Using this method, even objects with wispy, intricate, or undefinable edges can be clipped from their backgrounds with a minimum of effort.

▶ **Tip:** For best results, combine files that have the same image resolution. For information on image resolution, see "Pixel dimensions and image resolution" in Photoshop Help.

1   Click the Launch Bridge button (▣) in the application bar to jump to Adobe Bridge. Then double-click the 05Paper.psd thumbnail (in the Lesson05 folder) to open the file in Photoshop.

2   Choose Select > Color Range. In the Color Range dialog box, enter **200** for Fuzziness. Click the pointer, which looks like an eyedropper, on the paper. The preview window shows you the selection. Click OK.

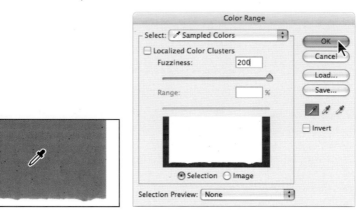

Most of the paper is selected, but some of the darker colors aren't included. You'll use the Quick Selection tool to add them.

3   Select the Quick Selection(🖌) tool in the Tools panel. Drag it across the paper until it finds and selects the paper's edges, selecting the entire paper image.

4   In the options bar, click Refine Edge. Specify **5.0** for the Radius, **50%** for Contrast, **3** for Smooth, **0** for Feather, and **-55** for Contract/Expand to smooth the edges. Then, click OK.

5   Choose Layer > New > Layer Via Copy. A new layer appears in the Layers panel, named Layer 1. Hide the Background layer to see it clearly. Only the paper is on the layer, not the white background.

Moving layers between documents

Often, you may need to add layers from one Photoshop document to another. It's very easy to do. Here, you'll move the paper texture you just copied to the book cover composition to add a background texture.

1   Click the Arrange Documents button (▦) in the application bar, and select a 2 Up layout. Make sure the Writing layer is active in the 05Working.psd Layers panel, and then select the 05Paper.psd document to make it active.

2 Drag Layer 1 from the 05Paper.psd file's Layers panel into the center of the 05Working.psd image. The layer is added as Layer 1, just below the top layer, Buddha.

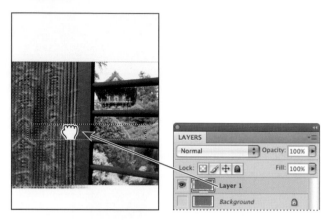

3 In the Layers panel, double-click the layer name and rename it **Paper**.

4 Close the 05Paper.psd file without saving changes.

5 Choose View > Rulers. Drag a ruler guide down from the top of the document to 2¼ inches.

6 Select the Move tool (◄⊕) in the Tools panel. Move the paper up so that its bottom edge aligns with the ruler guide. The top portion of the paper will be out of the image area.

Colorizing with an adjustment layer

Now you'll create an adjustment layer to colorize the paper.

1 In the Layers panel, make sure that the Paper layer is selected.

2 Click the Adjustments tab to display the Adjustments panel. Click the Hue/Saturation button in the Adjustments layer.

3 Enter these values to give the paper a violet cast: Hue: **-125**, Saturation **-56**, Lightness **-18**.

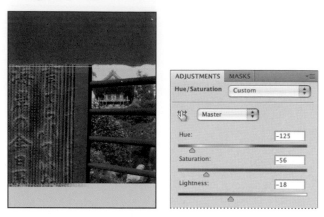

Because adjustment layers affect all the layers beneath them, the entire image is purple. You'll confine the effect to just the paper by creating a clipping layer.

4 In the Layers panel, hold down Alt (Windows) or Option (Mac OS), and position the pointer between the Hue/Saturation adjustment layer and the Paper layer until the pointer becomes a double-circle icon (⟲). Then, click to create a clipping layer.

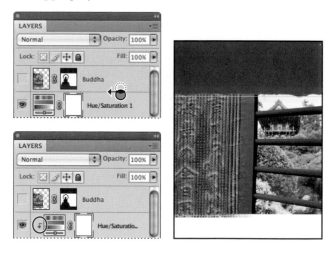

In the Layers panel, the Hue/Saturation layer indents, and an arrow points to the layer beneath it, Paper, which is now underlined. The Paper layer is clipped to the adjustment layer, meaning that the effect applies only to that layer.

5 Choose File > Save to save your work so far.

Grouping and clipping layers

You'll complete the composition by rearranging some layers and adding text.

1   In the Layers panel, make the Buddha layer visible. It should be the top layer in the Layers panel.

2   In the Layers panel, select the Paper layer and the Hue/Saturation adjustment layer. (Press the Shift key to select both layers.) From the Layers panel menu, choose New Group From Layers. Name this group **Top Paper.** Click OK.

Now you'll duplicate this layer group for the bottom part of the book cover.

3   Choose Duplicate Group from the Layers panel menu.

4   In the Duplicate Group dialog box, name the duplicate group **Bottom Paper**. Click OK.

5   In the Layers panel, click the triangles next to the Bottom Paper and Top Paper layer groups to expand them. As you can see, the Bottom Paper layer now has the same contents as the Top Paper layer, duplicated in the same location in the image. Click the triangles again to collapse the groups.

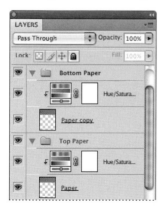

6 In the Layers panel, hide the Top Paper layer group.

7 With the Bottom Paper layer selected in the Layers panel, choose Edit > Transform > Rotate 180°.

8 Use the Move tool (⯈⊕) to drag the rotated paper to the bottom of the composition, so that the top of the lower edge is at about 6½ inches on the ruler. You can drag a ruler guide from the top ruler if it helps you.

9 In the Layers panel, make the Top Paper layer group visible again.

10 Choose View > Rulers to hide the rulers, and then choose View > Clear Guides to hide any ruler guides.

Inverting a mask

Remember the beautiful mask that you created at the start of this lesson? Now it's time to retrieve it to mask out the background.

1 Select the Buddha layer at the top of the Layers panel.

2 Select the layer mask thumbnail in the Buddha layer.

3 Click the Masks tab to open the Masks panel, and then click Invert in the Masks panel. The statue appears, and its background is gone.

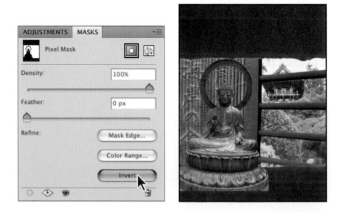

Notice that the Buddha Mask channel is selected in the Channels panel.

You can see how helpful it is to have the flexibility to apply saved alpha channels at various stages of your workflow.

Remember that you can adjust the image within the mask: In this case, you'll move the mask and the masked image together.

4   Use the Move tool to adjust the masked image so that both the top halo and base of the statute extend about half an inch into the paper.

Now you'll adjust how the statue appears on the paper.

5   In the Layers panel, drag the Bottom Paper layer group above the Buddha layer so the paper covers the base of the Buddha statue.

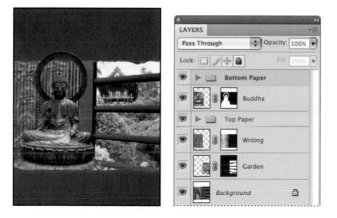

6   Choose File > Save to save your work.

Using type as a mask

Just as you can use selections to mask areas of an image, you can use type as a mask. You'll reveal the original paper texture, using type to mask the colorized paper.

1   Select the Type tool (T) in the Tools panel. In the options bar, set the font to Minion Pro Regular, Center alignment, and **75** points. Set black as the text color.

2   Click with the Type tool in the center of the top paper background, and type **Zen Garden**.

To add the paper texture, first you will copy it.

3   In the Layers panel, expand the Top Paper layer group.

4   Press the Alt (Windows) or Option (Mac OS) key, and drag the Paper layer to just above the Zen Garden type layer. This makes a copy of the Paper layer on top of the type layer.

You copied the layer out of its layer group to create a clipping group in the next step. You can clip two layers together, but you cannot clip a layer group with a layer.

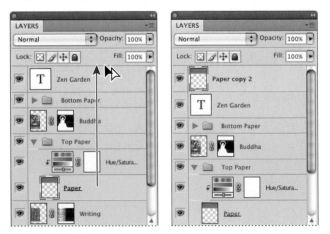

5 Position the pointer between the Paper copy 2 layer and the Zen Garden type layer, and hold down Alt (Windows) or Option (Mac OS) until the pointer becomes a double-circle clipping layer icon (⇥). Click when this icon appears.

The original gold paper texture shows through the type. Now you'll make the type pop a bit more with a drop shadow.

6 To add a drop shadow, select the Zen Garden type layer. Click the Add A Layer Style button (*fx*) at the bottom of the Layers panel, and choose Drop Shadow. In the Layer Style dialog box, choose Multiply from the Blend Mode menu; set the Distance to **12**, Spread to **5**, and Size to **29**. Click OK.

● **Note:** If you make a mistake and inadvertently add the Drop Shadow effect to the Paper copy 2 layer, simply drag the effect to the Zen Garden type layer to apply it there.

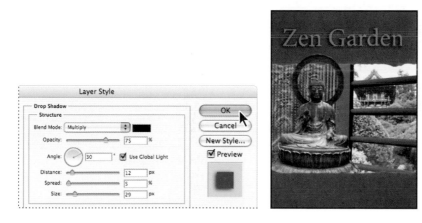

To complete the composition and this lesson, you'll add your name as the author to the bottom paper texture.

7 In the Layers panel, select the Paper copy 2 layer, so that the new type layer will be added above it.

8 To color the type, select the Eyedropper tool (✐) in the Tools panel. Click a light green color from the shrubbery in the panel area to sample the color.

9 Select the Type tool (T) in the Tools panel. In the options bar, choose Minion Pro Regular for the font, and **15** pt for the size.

10 Position the Type tool over the center of the bottom paper texture. Type the author name [**your name here**].

11 Press Control (Windows) or Command (Mac OS) to switch to the Move tool, and drag to position the type in the center of the bottom paper.

Your book cover is complete.

12 Choose File > Save.

You have completed this lesson. Although it takes some practice to become comfortable using channels, you've learned all the fundamental concepts and skills you need to get started using masks and channels.

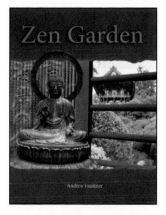

About masks and masking

Alpha channels, channel masks, clipping masks, layer masks, vector masks—what's the difference? In some cases, they're interchangeable: a channel mask can be converted to a layer mask, a layer mask can be converted to a vector mask, and vice versa.

Here's a brief description to help you keep them all straight. What they have in common is that they all store selections, and they all let you edit an image nondestructively so that you can return at any time to your original.

- An **alpha channel**—also called a *mask* or *selection*—is an extra channel added to an image that stores selections as grayscale images. You can add alpha channels to create and store masks.

- A **layer mask** is like an alpha channel, but it's attached to a specific layer. A layer mask controls which part of a layer is revealed or hidden. A layer mask appears as a blank thumbnail next to the layer thumbnail in the Layers panel until you add content to it; a black outline indicates that it's selected.

- A **vector mask** is essentially a layer mask made up of vectors, not pixels. Resolution-independent, vector masks have crisp edges and are created with the pen or shape tools. They do not support transparency, so their edges cannot be feathered. Their thumbnails appear the same as layer mask thumbnails.

- A **clipping mask** applies to a layer. It confines the influence of an effect to specific layers, rather than to everything below the layer in the layer stack. Using a clipping mask clips layers to a base layer; only that base layer is affected. Thumbnails of a clipped layer are indented with a right-angle arrow pointing to the layer below. The clipped base layer is underlined.

- A **channel mask** restricts editing to a specific channel (for example, a Cyan channel in a CMYK image). Channel masks are useful for making intricate, fringed, or wispy-edged selections. You can create a channel mask based on a dominant color in an image or pronounced contrast in an isolated channel, for example, between the subject and the background.

Review questions

1 What is the benefit of using a quick mask?

2 What happens to a quick mask when you deselect it?

3 When you save a selection as a mask, where is the mask stored?

4 How can you edit a mask in a channel once you've saved it?

5 How do channels differ from layers?

Review answers

1 Quick masks are helpful for creating quick, one-time selections. In addition, using a quick mask is an easy way to edit a selection using the painting tools.

2 The quick mask disappears when you deselect it.

3 Masks are saved in channels, which can be thought of as storage areas for color and selection information in an image.

4 You can paint on a mask in a channel using black, white, and shades of gray.

5 Channels are used as storage areas for saved selections. Unless you explicitly display a channel, it does not appear in the image or print. Layers can be used to isolate various parts of an image so that they can be edited as discrete objects with the painting or editing tools or other effects.

6 CORRECTING AND ENHANCING DIGITAL PHOTOGRAPHS

Lesson overview

In this lesson, you'll learn how to do the following:

- Process a proprietary camera raw image and save your adjustments.

- Make typical corrections to a digital photograph, including removing red eye and noise and bringing out shadow and highlights detail.

- Adjust the visual perspective of objects in an image using the Vanishing Point filter.

- Apply optical lens correction to an image.

- Align and blend two images to extend the depth of field.

- Prepare a PDF image gallery of your corrected images.

- Adopt best practices for organizing, managing, and saving your images.

 This lesson will take 1½ to 2 hours to complete. Copy the Lesson06 folder onto your hard drive if you haven't already done so. As you work on this lesson, you'll preserve the start files. If you need to restore the start files, copy them again from the *Adobe Photoshop CS4 Classroom in a Book CD.*

Whether you have a collection of digital images amassed for clients or projects, or a personal collection that you want to refine, archive, and preserve for posterity, Photoshop has an array of tools for importing, editing, and archiving digital photographs.

Getting started

In this lesson, you'll edit several digital images using Photoshop and Adobe Camera Raw, which comes with Photoshop. You will save each edited image in a Gallery folder, and then prepare a PDF slide show of the final images. Start by viewing the before and after images in Adobe Bridge.

1 Start Photoshop and then immediately hold down Ctrl+Alt+Shift (Windows) or Command+Option+Shift (Mac OS) to restore the default preferences. (See "Restoring default preferences" on page 4.)

2 When prompted, click Yes to confirm that you want to reset preferences.

3 Click the Launch Bridge button (Br) in the application bar to open Adobe Bridge.

4 In the Favorites panel in Bridge, click the Lessons folder. Then, in the Content panel, double-click the Lesson06 folder to open it.

5 Adjust the thumbnail slider, if necessary, so that you can see the thumbnail previews clearly. Then, look at the 06A_Start.crw and 06A_End.psd files.

06A_Start.crw   06A_End.psd

The original photograph of a Spanish-style church is a camera raw file, so it doesn't have the usual .psd file extension you've worked with so far in this book. It was shot with a Canon Digital Rebel camera and has the Canon proprietary .crw raw file extension instead. You will process this proprietary camera raw image to make it brighter, sharper, and clearer, and then save it as an industry-standard Digital Negative (DNG) file.

6 Look at the 06B_Start.psd and 06B_End.psd thumbnail previews.

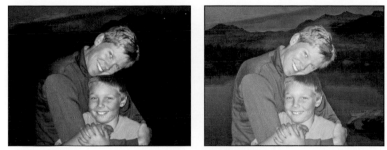

06B_Start.psd   06B_End.psd

You'll make several corrections to this portrait of mother and son, including bringing out shadow and highlight detail, removing red eye, and sharpening the image.

7 Look at the 06C_Start.psd and 06C_End.psd thumbnail previews.

06C_Start.psd   06C_End.psd

You'll add a window to the red clapboard farmhouse in this image, and you'll
remove the seasonal wreath, preserving the vanishing-point perspective as you make
corrections.

8 Look at the 06D_Start.psd and 06D_End.psd thumbnail previews.

06D_Start.psd   06D_End.psd

The original image is distorted, with the columns appearing to be bowed. You'll correct the lens barrel distortion.

9 Look at the 06E_Start.psd and 06E_End.psd thumbnail previews.

06E_Start.psd   06E_End.psd

In the first image, either the glass in the foreground or the beach in the background is in focus. You'll extend the depth of field to make both clear.

About camera raw

A *camera raw* file contains unprocessed picture data from a digital camera's image sensor. Many digital cameras can save images as camera raw format files. The advantage of camera raw files is that they let the photographer—rather than the camera—interpret the image data and make adjustments and conversions. (In contrast, shooting JPEG images with your camera locks you into your camera's processing.) Because the camera doesn't do any image processing when you shoot a camera raw photo, you can use Adobe Camera Raw to set the white balance, tonal range, contrast, color saturation, and sharpening. Think of camera raw files as photo negatives. You can go back and reprocess the file anytime you like to achieve the results you want.

To create camera raw files, set your digital camera to save files in its own, possibly proprietary, raw file format. When you download the file from your camera, it will have a file extension such as .nef (from Nikon) or .crw (from Canon). In Bridge or Photoshop, you can process camera raw files from a myriad of supported digital cameras from Canon, Kodak, Leica, Nikon, and other makers—and even process multiple images simultaneously. You can then export the proprietary camera raw files to the Digital Negative (DNG) file format, the nonproprietary Adobe format for standardizing camera raw files; or to such other formats as JPEG, TIFF, and PSD.

Note: The Photoshop Raw format (.raw extension) is a file format for transferring images between applications and computer platforms. Don't confuse Photoshop Raw with camera raw file formats.

You can process camera raw files obtained from supported cameras, but you can also open TIFF and JPEG images in Camera Raw, which includes some editing features that aren't in Photoshop. However, you won't have the same flexibility with white balance and other settings if you're using a TIFF or JPEG image. Although Camera Raw can open and edit a camera raw image file, it cannot save an image in camera raw format.

Processing files in Camera Raw

When you make adjustments to an image in Camera Raw, such as straightening or cropping the image, Photoshop and Bridge preserve the original file data. This way, you can edit the image as you desire, export the edited image, and keep the original intact for future use or other adjustments.

Opening images in Camera Raw

You can open Camera Raw from either Bridge or Photoshop, and you can apply the same edits to multiple files simultaneously. This is especially useful if you are working with images that were all shot in the same environment, and which therefore need the same lighting and other adjustments.

Camera Raw provides extensive controls for adjusting white balance, exposure, contrast, sharpness, tone curves, and much more. In this exercise, you'll edit one image and then apply the settings to similar images.

1   In Bridge, open the Lessons/Lesson06/Mission folder, which contains three shots of the Spanish church you previewed in the previous exercise.

2   Shift-click to select all of the images—Mission01.crw, Mission02.crw, and Mission03.crw, and then choose File > Open In Camera Raw.

A. Filmstrip
B. Toggle Filmstrip
C. Toggle Full-Screen Mode
D. RGB values
E. Image adjustment tabs
F. Histogram
G. Camera Raw Settings menu
H. Zoom levels
I. Click to display workflow options
J. Multi-image navigation controls
K. Adjustment sliders

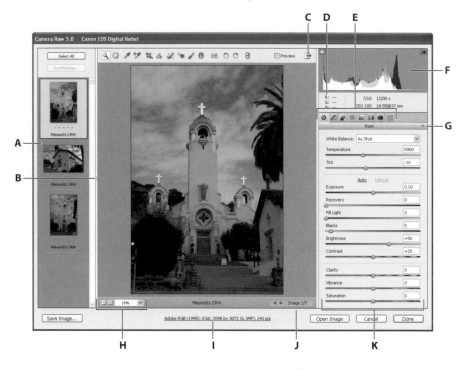

The Camera Raw dialog box displays a large preview of the first image, and a filmstrip down the left side displays all open images. The histogram in the upper-right corner shows the tonal range of the selected image; the workflow options at the bottom center of the dialog box displays the selected image's color space, bit depth, size, and resolution. Tools along the top of the dialog box let you zoom, pan, straighten, and make other adjustments to the image. Tabbed panels on the right side of the dialog box give you more nuanced options for adjusting the image: you can correct the white balance, adjust the tone, sharpen the image, remove noise, adjust color, and make other changes. You can also save settings as a preset, and then apply them later.

For the best results using Camera Raw, plan your workflow to move from left to right and top to bottom. That is, you'll often want to use the tools across the top first, and then move through the panels in order, making changes as necessary.

You will explore these controls now as you edit the first image file.

3 Click each thumbnail in the filmstrip to preview each image before you begin. Or, you can click the forward button under the main preview window to cycle through the images. When you've seen all three images, select the Mission01.crw image again.

4 Make sure that Preview is selected at the top of the dialog box so that you can see the effect of the adjustments you're about to make.

Adjusting white balance

An image's white balance reflects the lighting conditions under which it was captured. A digital camera records the white balance at the time of exposure; this is the value that initially appears in the Camera Raw dialog box image preview.

White balance comprises two components. The first is *temperature*, which is measured in kelvins and determines the level of "coolness" or "warmness" of the image—that is, its cool blue-green tones or warm yellow-red tones. The second component is *tint*, which compensates for magenta or green color casts in the image.

Depending on the settings you're using on your camera and the environment in which you're shooting (for example, if there's glare or uneven lighting), you may want to adjust the white balance for the image. If you plan to modify the white balance, make that the first thing you do, as it will affect all other changes in the image.

1 If the Basic panel isn't already displayed on the right side of the dialog box, click the Basic button (◉) to open it.

By default, As Shot is selected in the White Balance menu. Camera Raw is applying the white balance settings in your camera at the time of exposure. You'll use the White Balance tool to change the temperature of the image.

2 Select the White Balance tool (🖋) at the top of the Camera Raw dialog box.

To set an accurate white balance, select an object that should be white or gray. Camera Raw uses that information to determine the color of the light in which the scene was shot and then adjusts for scene lighting automatically.

3 Click the white clouds in the image. The lighting of the image changes.

4 Click a different area of the clouds. The lighting shifts.

You can use the White Balance tool to find the best lighting for the scene quickly and easily. Clicking different areas changes the lighting without making any permanent changes to the file, so you can experiment freely.

Camera Raw also includes several White Balance presets, which you can use as a starting point to see different lighting effects.

5 In the Basics panel, choose different options from the White Balance menu, and observe how the lighting changes the image.

6 Choose Cloudy from the White Balance menu.

▶ **Tip:** To undo the settings, press Ctrl+Z (Windows) or Command+Z (Mac OS). To compare the changes you've made in the current panel with the original image, deselect Preview. Select Preview again to see the modified image.

The Cloudy preset suits this image, which was taken on a cloudy day.

Making tonal adjustments in Camera Raw

Other sliders in the Basic panel affect exposure, brightness, contrast, and saturation in the image. Exposure essentially defines the *white point*, or the lightest point of the image, so that Camera Raw adjusts everything else accordingly. Conversely, the Blacks slider sets the *black point*, or the darkest point in the image. The Fill Light slider adjusts the midtones.

The Brightness slider determines how bright the image is, and the Contrast slider adjusts the contrast. For more nuanced contrast adjustments, you can use the Clarity slider, which adds depth to an image by increasing local contrast, especially on the midtones.

The Saturation slider adjusts the saturation of all colors in the image equally. The Vibrance slider, on the other hand, has a greater effect on undersaturated colors, so you can bring life to a background without oversaturating skin tones, for example.

You can use the Auto option to let Camera Raw attempt to correct the image tone, or you can select your own settings.

1 Click Auto in the Basic panel.

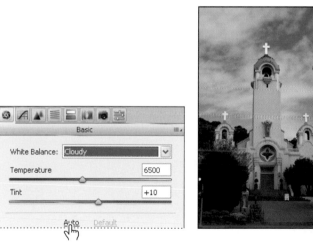

▶ **Tip:** For the best effect, increase the Clarity slider until you see halos near the edge details, and then reduce the setting slightly.

Camera Raw increases the saturation and decreases the blacks and the contrast. You could use this as a starting point. However, in this exercise, you'll return to the default settings and adjust them yourself.

2 Click Default in the Basic panel.

3 Change the sliders as follows:

- Increase Exposure to **+1.20**.

- Leave Brightness at **50**.

- Increase Contrast to **+29**.

- Decrease Clarity to **-75**.

- Decrease Saturation to **-5**.

These settings help pump up the midtones of the image, so that it looks bolder and more dimensional without being oversaturated. However, it's quite soft. You'll adjust the Clarity setting to sharpen it up a little bit.

4 Increase Clarity to **+25**.

About the Camera Raw histogram

The histogram in the upper-right corner of the Camera Raw dialog box simultaneously shows the red, green, and blue channels of the selected image, and it updates interactively as you adjust any settings. Also, as you move any tool over the preview image, the RGB values for the area under the cursor appear below the histogram

Applying sharpening

Photoshop offers several sharpening filters, but when you need to sharpen an entire image, Camera Raw provides the best control. The sharpening controls are in the Detail panel. To see the effect of sharpening in the preview panel, you must view the image at 100% or greater.

1   Double-click the Zoom tool (🔍) on the left side of the toolbar to zoom in to 100%. Then select the Hand tool (✋), and pan the image to see the cross at the top of the mission tower.

2   Click the Detail button to open the Detail panel (▲).

The Amount slider determines how much sharpening Camera Raw applies. Typically, you'll want to exaggerate the amount of sharpening first, and then adjust it after you've set the other sliders.

3   Move the Amount slider to **100**.

The Radius slider determines the pixel area Camera Raw analyzes as it sharpens the image. For most images, you'll get the best results if you keep the radius low, even below 1 pixel, as a larger radius can begin to cause an unnatural look, almost like a watercolor.

4   Move the Radius slider to **0.9**.

The Detail slider determines how much detail you'll see. Even when this slider is set to 0, Camera Raw performs some sharpening. Typically, you'll want to keep the Detail setting relatively low.

5   Move the Detail slider to **25**, if it isn't already there.

The Masking slider determines which parts of the image Camera Raw sharpens. When the Masking value is high, Camera Raw sharpens only those parts of the image that have strong edges.

▶ **Tip:** Press Alt (Windows) or Option (Mac OS) as you move the Masking slider to see what Camera Raw will sharpen.

6 Move the Masking slider to **61**.

After you've adjusted the Radius, Detail, and Masking sliders, you can lower the Amount slider to finalize the sharpening.

7 Decrease the Amount slider to **50**.

● **Note:** If you zoom out, the image won't appear to be sharpened. You can preview sharpening effects only at zoom levels of 100% or greater.

Sharpening the image gives stronger definition to the details and edges. The Masking slider lets you target the sharpening effect to the lines in the image, so that artifacts don't appear in unfocused or background areas.

When you make adjustments in Camera Raw, the original file data is preserved. Your adjustment settings for the image are stored either in the Camera Raw database file or in "sidecar" XMP files that accompany the original image file in the same folder. These XMP files retain the adjustments you made in Camera Raw when you move the image file to a storage medium or another computer.

Synchronizing settings across images

All three of the mission images were shot at the same time under the same lighting conditions. Now that you've made the first look stunning, you can automatically apply the same settings to the other two images. You do this using the Synchronize command.

1 In the upper-left corner of the Camera Raw dialog box, click Select All to select all of the images in the filmstrip.

2 Click the Synchronize button.

The Synchronize dialog box appears. This dialog box lists all the settings you can apply to the images. By default, all options except Crop and Spot Removal are selected. You can accept the default for this project, even though you didn't change all the settings.

3 Click OK in the Synchronize dialog box.

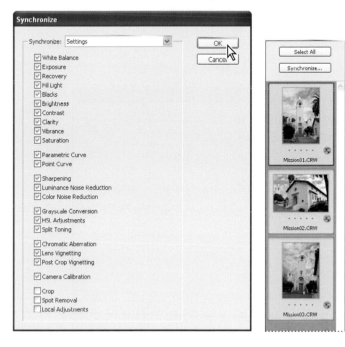

When you synchronize the settings across all of the selected images, the thumbnails update to reflect the changes you made. To preview the images, click each thumbnail in the filmstrip.

Saving Camera Raw changes

First, you'll save the images with adjustments as low-resolution JPEG files that you can share on the web. Then, you'll save one image, Mission01, as a Photoshop file that you can add to a PDF image gallery later in this lesson. You'll open the Mission01 image as a Smart Object in Photoshop so that you can return to Camera Raw at any time to make further adjustments.

1 Click Select All in the Camera Raw dialog box to select all three images.

2 Click Save Images in the lower-left corner.

3 In the Save Options dialog box, do the following:

- Select Save In Same Location from the Destination menu.

- In the File Naming area, leave *Document Name* in the first box.

- Choose JPEG from the Format menu.

These settings will save your corrected images as smaller, downsampled JPEG files, which you can share with colleagues on the web. Your files will be named Mission01.jpg, Mission02.jpg, and Mission03.jpg.

4 Click Save.

● **Note:** Before sharing these images on the web, you would probably want to open them in Photoshop and resize them to 640 x 480 pixels. They are currently much larger, and most viewers would need to scroll to see the full-size images.

Bridge returns you to the Camera Raw dialog box and indicates how many images have been processed until all the images have been saved. The CRW thumbnails still appear in the Camera Raw dialog box. In Bridge, however, you now also have JPEG versions as well as the original, unedited CRW image files, which you can continue to edit or leave for another time.

Now, you will save a copy of the Mission01 image to the Gallery folder, where you'll save all the images for the gallery.

5 Select the Mission01.crw image thumbnail in the filmstrip in the Camera Raw dialog box. Then, press the Shift key, and click Open Object at the bottom of the dialog box.

The Open Object button opens the image as a Smart Object in Photoshop, and you can return to Camera Raw to continue making adjustments at any time. If you click Open Image, the image opens as a standard Photoshop image. Pressing the Shift key changes the Open Image button to the Open Object button.

6 In Photoshop, choose File > Save As. In the Save As dialog box, choose Photoshop for the Format, rename the file **Mission_Final.psd**, navigate to the Lesson06/Gallery folder, and click Save. Click OK if a compatibility dialog box appears. Then close the file.

▶ **Tip:** To make the Open Object button the default, click the workflow options link (in blue) below the preview window, select Open In Photoshop As Smart Objects, and click OK.

About saving files in Camera Raw

Every camera model saves raw images in a unique format, but Adobe Camera Raw can process many raw file formats. Camera Raw processes the raw files with default image settings based on built-in camera profiles for supported cameras and the EXIF data.

You can save the proprietary files in DNG format (the format saved by Adobe Camera Raw), JPEG, TIFF, and PSD. All of these formats can be used to save RGB and CMYK continuous-tone, bitmapped images, and all of them except DNG are also available in the Photoshop Save and Save As dialog boxes.

- The *Adobe Digital Negative (DNG)* format contains raw image data from a digital camera and metadata that defines what the image data means. DNG is meant to be an industry-wide standard format for raw image data, helping photographers manage the variety of proprietary raw formats and providing a compatible archival format. (You can save this format only from the Camera Raw dialog box.)

- The *JPEG (Joint Photographic Experts Group)* file format is commonly used to display photographs and other continuous-tone RGB images on the web. Higher-resolution JPEG files may be used for other purposes, including high-quality printing. JPEG format retains all color information in an image but compresses file size by selectively discarding data. The greater the compression, the lower the image quality.

- *TIFF (Tagged Image File Format)* is used to exchange files between applications and computer platforms. TIFF is a flexible format supported by virtually all paint, image-editing, and page-layout applications. Also, virtually all desktop scanners can produce TIFF images.

- The *PSD format* is the Photoshop native file format. Because of the tight integration between Adobe products, other Adobe applications such as Adobe Illustrator, Adobe InDesign, and Adobe GoLive can directly import PSD files and preserve many Photoshop features.

Once you open a file in Photoshop, you can save it in many different formats, including Large Document Format (PSB), Cineon, Photoshop Raw, or PNG. Not to be confused with camera raw file formats, the Photoshop Raw format (RAW) is a file format for transferring images between applications and computer platforms.

For more information about file formats in Camera Raw and Photoshop, see Photoshop Help.

Correcting digital photographs in Photoshop

Photoshop provides many features to help you easily improve the quality of digital photographs. These include the ability to bring out details in the shadow and highlight areas of an image, gracefully remove red eye, reduce unwanted noise, and sharpen targeted areas of an image. To explore these capabilities, you will edit a different digital image now: a portrait of a mother and a child.

Adjusting shadows and highlights

To bring out the detail in dark or light areas of an image, you can use the Shadows/Highlights command. Shadows/Highlights adjustments work best when the subject of the image is silhouetted against strong backlighting or is washed out because the camera flash was too close. You can also use the adjustments to pull details from the shadows in an image that is otherwise well-lit.

1 Click the Launch Bridge button (![Br]).
In the Favorites panel in Bridge, click the Lessons folder. In the Content panel, double-click the Lesson06 folder. Double-click the 06B_Start.psd image to open it in Photoshop.

2 Choose File > Save As. Name the file **06B_Working.psd**.

3 Choose Image > Adjustments > Shadows/Highlights. Photoshop automatically applies default settings to the image, lightening the background. You'll customize the settings to bring out more detail in both the shadows and the highlights, and to enhance the red sunset in the sky.

4 In the Shadows/Highlights dialog box, select Show More Options to expand the dialog box. Then, do the following:

- In the Shadows area, set Amount to **80**% and Tonal Width to **65**%.

- In the Highlights area, set Amount to **5**%.

- In the Adjustments area, drag the Color Correction slider to **+45**.

5 Click OK to accept your changes.

6 Choose File > Save to save your work so far.

Correcting red eye

Red eye occurs when the retina of a subject's eye is reflected by the camera flash. It commonly occurs in photographs of a subject in a darkened room, because the subject's irises are wide open. Red eye is easy to fix in Photoshop. In this exercise, you will remove the red eye from the boy's eyes in the portrait.

1 Select the Zoom tool (🔍), and then drag a marquee around the boy's eyes to zoom into them.

2 Select the Red Eye tool (👁), hidden under the Spot Healing Brush tool (🖌).

3 In the options bar, leave Pupil Size set to 50%, but change Darken Amount to **10%**. The Darken Amount specifies how dark the pupil should be. Because this child's eyes are blue, the Darken Amount setting should be lighter than the default.

4 Click on the red area in the boy's left eye. The red reflection disappears.

5 Click on the red area in the boy's right eye to remove that reflection, as well.

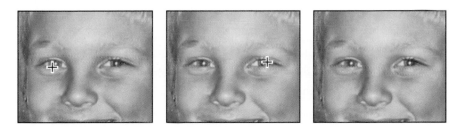

6 Double-click the Zoom tool to zoom out to 100%.

7 Choose File > Save to save your work so far.

Reducing noise

Random, extraneous pixels that aren't part of the image detail are called *noise*. Noise can result from using a high ISO setting on a digital camera, from underexposure, or from shooting in darkness with a long shutter speed. Scanned images may contain noise that results from the scanning sensor, or from a grain pattern from the scanned film.

There are two types of image noise: *luminance noise*, which is grayscale data that makes an image look grainy or patchy; and *color noise*, which appears as colored artifacts in the image. The Reduce Noise filter can address both types of noise in individual color channels while preserving edge detail, as well as correct JPEG compression artifacts.

First, zoom in to the sky to get a good look at the noise in this image.

1 Using the Zoom tool (🔍), click in the center of the sky above the woman's head and zoom in to about 300%.

The noise in this image is speckled and rough, with uneven graininess in the sky. Using the Reduce Noise filter, you can smooth out this area and give the sky more depth.

2 Choose Filter > Noise > Reduce Noise.

3 In the Reduce Noise dialog box, do the following:

- Increase Strength to **8**. (Strength controls the amount of luminance noise.)

- Decrease Preserve Details to **45**%.

- Increase Reduce Color Noise to **50**%.

- Move Sharpen Details to **35**%.

● **Note:** To correct noise in individual channels of the image, select Advanced and click the Per Channel tab to adjust the settings in each channel.

You don't need to select Remove JPEG Artifact, because this image is not a JPEG and has no JPEG artifacts.

4 Click the plus button at the bottom of the dialog box twice to zoom in to about 300%, and then drag to position the sky in the preview area. Click and hold the mouse button down in the preview area to see the "before" image, and release the mouse button to see the corrected result.

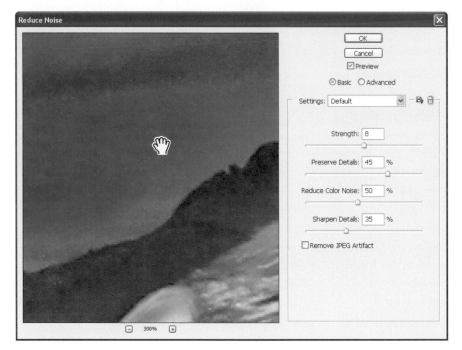

5 Click OK to apply your changes and to close the Reduce Noise dialog box, and then double-click the Zoom tool to return to 100%.

6 Choose File > Save to save your work so far.

Sharpening edges

Reducing noise can soften an image, so, as a final correction to this photograph, you will sharpen it to improve its clarity.

Photoshop includes several filters that sharpen areas of an image, including Sharpen, Unsharp Mask, Sharpen Edges, and Smart Sharpen. All of them focus blurry images by increasing the contrast of adjacent pixels, but some are better for individual images than others, depending on whether all or part of an image needs to be sharpened. Smart Sharpen sharpens an image while also reducing noise and lets you specify whether the filter is applied to the overall image, to its shadows, or to its highlights.

For more on the other filters in the Sharpen submenu, see Photoshop Help.

1   Choose Filter > Sharpen > Smart Sharpen.

2   In the Smart Sharpen dialog box, do the following:

 • Reduce the Amount to **40**%.

 • Set the Radius to **5** pixels.

 • Choose Lens Blur from the Remove menu.

 • At the bottom of the dialog box, select More Accurate.

The Remove option determines which algorithm is used to sharpen the image. Gaussian Blur uses the same method as the Unsharp Mask filter. Lens Blur detects the edges and detail in an image and sharpens finer detail with fewer sharpening halos. Motion Blur reduces blurring due to camera or subject movement, and includes an Angle control.

A photographer for more than 22 years, Jay Graham began his career designing and building custom homes. Today, Graham has clients in the advertising, architectural, editorial, and travel industries.

See Jay Graham's portfolio on the web at jaygraham.com.

Pro Photo Workflow

Good habits make all of the difference

A sensible workflow and good work habits will keep you enthused about digital photography, help your images shine—and save you from the night terrors of losing work you never backed up. Here's an outline of the basic workflow for digital images from a professional photographer with more than 22 years' experience. To help you get the most from the images you shoot, Jay Graham offers guidelines for setting up your camera, creating a basic color workflow, selecting file formats, organizing images, and showing off your work.

Graham uses Adobe Bridge to organize thousands of images.

"The biggest complaint from people is they've lost their image. Where is it? What does it look like?" says Graham. "So naming is important."

Start out right by setting up your camera preferences

If your camera has the option, photograph only in its camera raw file format, which captures all the image information you need. With one camera raw photo, says Graham, "You can go from daylight, to an indoor tungsten image without degradation" when it's reproduced.

Start with the best material

Get all the data when you capture—at fine compression and high resolution. You can't go back later.

Transfer images to your computer

Use a card reader rather than plugging your camera into the computer to download images. Card readers don't require that the camera be on; use multiple cards as needed to store your images.

Organize your files

Name and catalog your images as soon after downloading them as possible. "If the camera names files, eventually it resets and produces multiple files with the same name," says Graham. Use Adobe Bridge to rename, rank, and add metadata to the photos you plan to keep; cull those you don't.

Graham names his files by date (and possibly subject). He would store a series of photos taken Dec. 12, 2006, at Stinson Beach in a folder named "20061212_Stinson"; within the folder, he names each image incrementally—"2006_1212_01" or "001" and so on. "That way, it lines up on the hard drive real easily," he says. Follow Windows naming conventions to keep filenames usable on non-Macintosh platforms (32 characters maximum; only numbers, letters, underscores and hyphens).

Convert raw images to Adobe Camera Raw

Save edited camera raw images in the DNG format. This open-source format can be read by any device, unlike many cameras' proprietary raw formats.

Keep a master image

Save your master in PSD, TIFF, or DNG format, not in JPEG. Each time a JPEG is reedited and saved, compression is reapplied and the image quality degrades.

Show off to clients and friends

Pick the best color profile for converting your work for screen or print, and set the final image resolution for quality and file size. For a comp, online display, or web photo service, use sRGB at 72 dpi resolution. For inkjet printing, use Adobe 1998 to reproduce images at 180 dpi and higher resolutions.

Back up your images

You've devoted a lot of time and effort to your images: don't lose them. Use a CD or DVD for backup. Even better: use an external hard drive set to back up automatically. "The question is not if your [internal] hard drive is going to crash," says Graham, reciting a common adage. "It's when."

Selecting More Accurate yields more accurate sharpening, but takes longer to process.

3 To examine the results of Smart Sharpen, click and hold the mouse button in the preview area, then release.

4 Click OK to apply your changes.

5 Choose File > Save As. Name the file **Portrait_Final.psd**, and save it in the Lesson06/Gallery folder. Then, close the file.

You made several typical corrections to the portrait. Next, you will do something a little more unusual: editing an image while preserving its perspective.

Editing images with a vanishing-point perspective

Using the Vanishing Point filter, you can define the planes in an image and then paint, clone, and transform the image according to that perspective. You can create multiple planes that are related to each other. Photoshop automatically scales and orients your edits in the proper perspective throughout the image.

The Vanishing Point filter works with 8-bit-per-channel images, but not with vector data. To use it, you first create a grid that defines your perspective, and then you edit your image normally. Vanishing Point adjusts your editing to the defined perspective.

Defining a grid

In this exercise, you'll work with an image of a snow-covered house. You will use the Vanishing Point filter to add a window to the wall and to remove the seasonal holiday wreath, all while maintaining perspective.

1 Click the Launch Bridge button (![Br]). Navigate to the Lesson06 folder. Double-click the 06C_Start.psd image to open it in Photoshop.

First, you'll define the perspective grid. Then you'll add a fourth window and remove the wreath.

2 Choose Filter > Vanishing Point.

The Vanishing Point dialog box contains a preview of the image, as well as a variety of tools and options for working with perspective. The Create Plane tool (⊞) is selected to get you started.

3 Using the Create Plane tool (⊞), click each of the four corner points of the main wall of the house: Click just under the white trim where the red siding meets it, and over the plant in the lower right corner, to define the size and shape of the perspective plane. As you click, a blue outline appears. When you finish, Photoshop displays a blue grid over the plane that you just defined.

● **Note:** The grid appears only when a plane has parallel edges. If you see a red border instead of the grid, drag the handles to adjust the plane.

4 If necessary, drag a corner or a side handle to adjust the grid.

Editing objects in the image

Now that the perspective grid is created, you can select and move the window.

1 Select the Marquee tool (⬚) from the Tools panel in the Vanishing Point dialog box. The detailed grid disappears and the plane is outlined in blue.

2 To slightly blur the edge of the selection you're about to make, at the top of the dialog box, set the Feather option to **3**. Leave the other options unchanged.

● **Note:** The Heal option determines how the selection, cloning, or paint stroke blends with the color, lighting, and shading of the surrounding pixels. For more on Vanishing Point options, see Photoshop Help.

3 Drag a selection marquee a little larger than the center window. Then, press Alt (Windows) or Option (Mac OS) to copy the selection, press Shift to keep the plane aligned, and drag the copy to the right. Release the mouse when the new window is positioned between the right window and the far end of the wall. As you drag, Photoshop scales the selection according to the perspective of the wall.

4 Select the Zoom tool (🔍), and drag it over the three original windows to get a closer view of them.

5 Select the Marquee tool (⬚), and drag to select the empty wall between the first two windows.

6 Press Alt+Shift (Windows) or Option+Shift (Mac OS) as you drag the selection between the second and third windows, over the wreath.

Although the copied selection keeps perspective in its new location, it doesn't cover the whole wreath. Some of the wreath still shows in the image. You will fix this next.

7 Select the Transform tool (⬚). Handles appear on the selection.

8 Drag the transform handles to expand the selection and cover the wreath. If necessary, use the Up, Down, Right, and Left Arrow keys to nudge the selection and align the cloned clapboards.

9 Select the Marquee tool, and then click outside the selection to deselect it. Zoom back out to see the results of your work. Then, click OK to apply the Vanishing Point filter.

10 Choose File > Save As. In the Save As dialog box, name the file **Farmhouse_Final.psd** and save it in the Lesson06/Gallery folder. Then, close the image window.

● **Note:** To preserve the perspective plane information in the image, you must save the image in PSD, TIFF, or JPEG format.

Correcting image distortion

The Lens Correction filter fixes common camera lens flaws, such as barrel and pincushion distortion, chromatic aberration, and vignetting. *Barrel distortion* is a lens defect that causes straight lines to bow out toward the edges of the image. *Pincushion distortion* is the opposite effect, causing straight lines to bend inward. *Chromatic aberration* appears as a color fringe along the edges of image objects. *Vignetting* occurs when the edges of an image, especially the corners, are darker than the center.

Some lenses exhibit these defects depending on the focal length or the f-stop used. The Lens Correction filter can apply settings based on the camera, lens, and focal length used to make the image. The filter can also rotate an image or fix image perspective caused by tilting a camera vertically or horizontally. The filter's image grid makes it easier and more accurate to make these adjustments than using the Transform command.

In this exercise, you will adjust the lens distortion in an image of a Greek temple.

1 Click the Launch Bridge button (). In Bridge, navigate to the Lesson06 folder. Double-click the 06D_Start.psd image to open it in Photoshop.

The columns in this image bend toward the camera and appear to be warped. This photo was shot at a range that was too close with a wide-angle lens.

2 Choose Filter > Distort > Lens Correction. The Lens Correction dialog box opens. An alignment grid overlays the image, next to options for removing distortion, correcting chromatic aberration, removing vignettes, and transforming perspective.

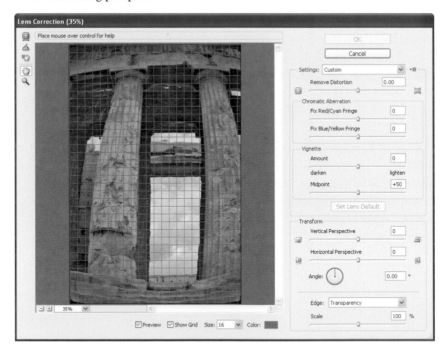

3 In the Lens Correction dialog box, do the following:

- Drag the Remove Distortion slider to about **+52.00** to remove the barrel distortion in the image. Alternatively, you could select the Remove Distortion tool (▣) and drag in the image preview area until the columns are straight.

The adjustment causes the image borders to bow inward; you'll scale the image to correct this.

- At the bottom of the dialog box, choose Transparency from the Edge menu.

- Drag the Scale slider to **146**%.

4 Click OK to apply your changes and close the Lens Correction dialog box.

► **Tip:** Watch the alignment grid as you make these changes so that you can see when the vertical columns are straightened in the image.

The curving distortion caused by the wide-angle lens and low shooting angle are eliminated.

5 (Optional) To see the effect of your change in the main image window, press Ctrl+Z (Windows) or Command+Z (Mac OS) twice to undo and redo the filter.

6 Choose File > Save As. In the Save As dialog box, name the file **Columns_Final.psd** and save it in the Lesson06/Gallery folder. Click OK if a compatibility warning appears. Then, close the image.

Adding depth of field

When you're shooting a photo, you often have to choose to focus either the background or the foreground. If you want the entire image to be in focus, take two photos—one with the background in focus and one with the foreground in focus—and then merge the two in Photoshop.

Because you'll need to align the images exactly, it's helpful to use a tripod to keep the camera steady. Even with a handheld camera, though, you can get some amazing results. You'll use this technique on an image of a wine glass on a beach.

1 In Photoshop, choose File > Open. Navigate to the Lessons/Lesson06 folder, and double-click the 06E_Start file to open it.

2 In the Layers panel, hide the Beach layer, so that only the Glass layer is visible. The glass is in focus, but the background is blurred. Then, show the Beach layer and hide the Glass layer. Now the beach is in focus, but the glass is blurred.

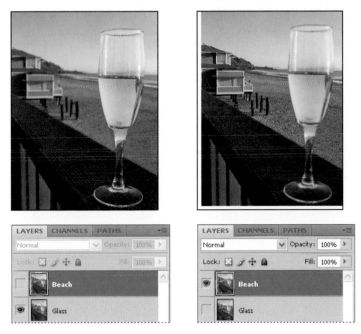

You'll merge the layers, using the part of each layer that is in focus. First, you need to align the layers.

3 Show both layers again, and then Shift-click to select both of them.

4 Choose Edit > Auto-Align Layers.

Auto is selected by default in the Projection area of the Auto-Align Layers dialog box. Because these images were shot from the same angle, Auto will work just fine.

5 Click OK to align the layers.

Now that the layers are perfectly aligned, you're ready to blend them.

6 Make sure both layers are still selected in the Layers panel. Then, choose Edit > Auto-Blend Layers.

7 Select Stack Images, and make sure Seamless Tones And Colors is selected. Then, click OK.

Both the wine glass and the beach behind it are in focus. Now, you'll add a Vibrance adjustment layer to give the image a little extra punch.

8 Click the Vibrance button in the Adjustments panel.

9 Move the Vibrance slider to **+33**, and then move the Saturation slider to **-5**.

The Vibrance adjustment layer affects all the layers beneath it.

10 Choose File > Save As. Name the file **Glass_Final.psd**, and save it in the Lesson06/Gallery folder. Click OK if a compatibility warning appears. Then, close the file.

About Adobe Photoshop Lightroom®

Modular and task-based, Adobe Photoshop Lightroom offers a streamlined environment from digital capture to print.

Incorporating raw conversion into a single workflow, Adobe Photoshop Lightroom speeds up the professional photographer's work. Think of Lightroom as a digital lightbox—on steroids. Click to make control panels and tools fade into the background in Lights-Out mode and place the image center stage. Use the Identity Plate feature to personally brand the application and its output, and showcase your work. Rapidly scroll through hundreds of images or instantly magnify finer points within an image.

Lightroom leverages Adobe Camera Raw technology to support more than 190 native raw file formats—including those from the latest camera models.

Just some of the features in Lightroom:

- Intuitive image-correction features, including tone curve adjustments for midtones, shadows, and highlights. Split-toning controls create richer black-and-white images—with greater control to make adjustments and address precise image areas on the histogram.

- Time-saving ability to convert and rename imported files to Digital Negative format (DNG) or rename and segment them by folder or date.

- Quick retrieval of images with search filters and presets, and organizing options.

- Features for showcasing images via slide shows with drop shadows, borders, Identity Plates, and different colored backgrounds. You can deliver the images in Adobe Flash, Adobe PDF or HTML formats.

- Contact sheet templates can be customized to add identity plates or produce a fine art print.

For a showcase of work by a Lightroom online community that Adobe hosts, see the Lightroom slide show at www.adobe.com/products/photoshoplightroom/.

Creating a PDF image gallery

You can create an Adobe PDF slide show or a multiple-page PDF document from a set of Photoshop files using the PDF Presentation command in Photoshop or Bridge. You can select which files within a folder you want to include, or select a folder to include all the files stored inside it. You can easily turn the files you saved in the Gallery folder into a PDF gallery to share with clients and colleagues.

1 Click the Launch Bridge button (![Br]). In Bridge, navigate to the Lesson06/Gallery folder. The Gallery folder should contain 11 images that we provided for you plus the following image files you saved: Mission_Final.psd, Portrait_Final.psd, Farmhouse_Final.psd, Columns_Final.psd, and Glass_Final.psd.

2 Choose Window > Workspace > Output to change the workspace.

3 Select the Buddha.psd image, then scroll through the files in the Content panel, and press Shift as you select the Zoo_2.psd image. All the images in the folder should be selected.

4 Click the PDF button in the Output panel.

5 From the Template menu, select 4*5 Contact Sheet, and then click Refresh Preview. The images appear on a single page, four images across.

6 From the Template menu, select 2*2 Cells, and click Refresh Preview again. The preview changes. Now there are four images on each page. It's easier to see the images in the 2 x 2 layout, so leave that option selected.

7 If the Document section isn't visible, click the triangle next to Document to expand it.

8 Choose U.S. Paper from the Page Preset menu. Click the triangle next to Document to collapse the section.

9 Expand the Playback section, and then choose Dissolve from the Transition menu. Then, collapse the Playback section.

10 Expand the Watermark section. Type **not for reproduction** in the Watermark Text box. Select a type size of **29**; choose Black for the Color; and specify **20**% for Opacity.

11 At the very bottom of the Output panel, select View PDF After Save, and then click Save.

12 Name the file **PDF_Presentation**, and save it in the Lesson06 folder.

The PDF image gallery opens in Adobe Acrobat, if it is installed on your system, or in Adobe Reader. It appears in Full Screen mode and transitions from one page to another.

13 Close the PDF presentation when you're done viewing it, and return to Bridge.

14 In Bridge, choose Window > Workspace > Essentials to return to the default workspace.

Review questions

1 What happens to camera raw images when you edit them in Camera Raw?

2 What is the advantage of the Adobe Digital Negative (DNG) file format?

3 How do you correct red eye in Photoshop?

4 Describe how to fix common camera lens flaws in Photoshop. What causes these defects?

Review answers

1 A camera raw file contains unprocessed picture data from a digital camera's image sensor. Camera raw files give photographers control over interpreting the image data, rather than letting the camera make the adjustments and conversions. When you edit the image in Camera Raw, it preserves the original raw file data. This way, you can edit the image as you desire, export it, and keep the original intact for future use or other adjustments.

2 The Adobe Digital Negative (DNG) file format contains the raw image data from a digital camera as well as metadata that defines what the image data means. DNG is an industry-wide standard for camera raw image data that helps photographers manage proprietary camera raw file formats and provides a compatible archival format.

3 Red eye occurs when the retinas of a subject's eyes are reflected by the camera flash. To correct red eye in Adobe Photoshop, zoom in to the subject's eyes, select the Red Eye tool, and then click the red eyes. The red reflection disappears.

4 The Lens Correction filter fixes common camera lens flaws, such as barrel and pincushion distortion, in which straight lines bow out towards the edges of the image (barrel) or bend inward (pincushion); chromatic aberration, where a color fringe appears along the edges of image objects; and vignetting at the edges of an image, especially corners, that are darker than the center. Defects can occur from incorrectly setting the lens's focal length or f-stop, or by tilting the camera vertically or horizontally.

7 TYPOGRAPHIC DESIGN

Lesson overview

In this lesson, you'll learn how to do the following:

- Use guides to position text in a composition.

- Make a clipping mask from type.

- Merge type with other layers.

- Use layer styles with text.

- Preview typefaces interactively to choose them for a composition.

- Control type and positioning using advanced type panel features.

- Warp a layer around a 3D object.

 This lesson will take about an hour to complete. Copy the Lesson07 folder onto your hard drive if you haven't already done so. As you work on this lesson, you'll preserve the start files. If you need to restore the start files, copy them from the *Adobe Photoshop CS4 Classroom in a Book* CD.

Photoshop has powerful, flexible text tools so you can add type to your images with great control and creativity.

About type

Type in Photoshop consists of mathematically defined shapes that describe the letters, numbers, and symbols of a typeface. Many typefaces are available in more than one format, the most common formats being Type 1 or PostScript fonts, TrueType, and OpenType (see "OpenType in Photoshop" later in this lesson).

When you add type to an image in Photoshop, the characters are composed of pixels and have the same resolution as the image file—zooming in on characters shows jagged edges. However, Photoshop preserves the vector-based type outlines and uses them when you scale or resize type, save a PDF or EPS file, or print the image to a PostScript printer. As a result, you can produce type with crisp, resolution-independent edges, apply effects and styles to type, and transform its shape and size.

Getting started

In this lesson, you'll work on the layout for the label of a bottle of olive oil. You will start from an illustration of a bottle, created in Adobe Illustrator, and then add and stylize type in Photoshop, including warping the text to conform to the 3D shape. The start file has a blank label on a layer above the bottle background.

You'll start the lesson by viewing an image of the final composition.

1   Start Photoshop and then immediately hold down Ctrl+Alt+Shift (Windows) or Command+Option+Shift (Mac OS) to restore the default preferences. (See "Restoring default preferences" on page 4.)

2   When prompted, click Yes to confirm that you want to reset preferences.

3   Click the Launch Bridge button (![Br]) in the application bar to open Adobe Bridge.

4   In the Favorites panel on the left side of Bridge, click the Lessons folder, and then double-click the Lesson07 folder in the Content panel.

5   Select the 07End.psd file. Increase the thumbnail size to see the bottle clearly by dragging the thumbnail slider to the right.

This layered composite represents a comp of packaging for a new brand of olive oil. For this lesson, you are a designer creating the comp for the product. The bottle shape was created by another designer in Adobe Illustrator. Your job is to apply the type treatment in Photoshop to prepare for a client review. All of the type controls you need are available in Photoshop, so you don't have to switch to another application to complete the project.

6 Double-click the 07Start.psd file to open it in Photoshop.

7 Choose File > Save As, rename the file **07Working.psd**, and click Save.

8 Click OK if the Photoshop Format Options dialog box appears.

Creating a clipping mask from type

A *clipping mask* is an object or a group of objects whose shape masks other artwork so that only areas that lie within the clipping mask are visible. In effect, you are clipping the artwork to conform to the shape of the object (or mask). In Photoshop, you can create a clipping mask from shapes or letters. In this exercise, you will use letters as a clipping mask to allow an image in another layer to show through the letters.

Adding guides to position type

The 07Working.psd file includes a background layer, which contains the bottle, and a Blank Label layer, which will be the foundation for your typography. The Blank Label layer is the active layer on which you will begin your work. You'll start by zooming in on the work area and using ruler guides to help position the type.

1 Select the Zoom tool ($\mathcal{Q}$) and drag over the black-and-white portion of the blank label to zoom in to the area and center it in the image window.

2 Choose View > Rulers to display rulers along the left and top borders of the image window. Then, drag a vertical guide from the left ruler to the center of the label (3½ inches) and release.

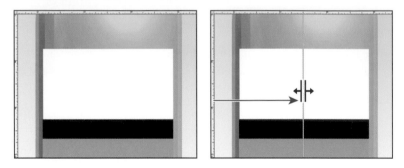

Adding point type

Now you're ready to actually add type to the composition. Photoshop lets you create horizontal or vertical type anywhere in an image. You can enter *point type* (a single letter, word, or line) or *paragraph type*. You will do both in this lesson. First, you'll create point type.

1 Make sure that the Blank Label layer is selected in the Layers panel. Then, select the Horizontal Type tool (T), and in the options bar, do the following:

- Choose a sans serif typeface, such as Myriad Pro, from the Font Family pop-up menu, and choose Bold from the Font Style pop-up menu.

- Type **79 pt** for the Size and press Enter or Return.

- Click the Center Text button.

2 Click on the center guide in the white area of the label to set an insertion point, and type **OLIO** in all caps. Then click the Commit Any Current Edits button (✔) in the options bar.

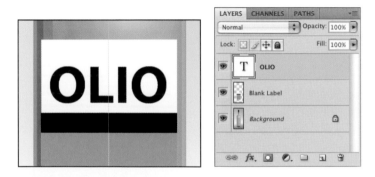

The word "Olio" is added to the label, and it appears in the Layers panel as a new type layer, OLIO. You can edit and manage the type layer as you would any other layer. You can add or change the text, change the orientation of the type, apply anti-aliasing, apply layer styles and transformations, and create masks. You can move, restack, and copy a type layer, or edit its layer options, just as you would for any other layer.

3 Press Ctrl (Windows) or Command (Mac OS), and drag the OLIO type to visually center it vertically in the white box.

4 Choose File > Save to save your work so far.

Making a clipping mask and applying a drop shadow

You added the letters in black, the default text color. However, you want the letters to appear to be filled with an image of olives, so you'll use the letters to make a clipping mask that will allow another image layer to show through.

1 Open the Olives.psd file, which is in the Lesson07 folder. You can open it using Bridge or by choosing File > Open.

2 In Photoshop, click the Arrange Documents button (▦) in the application bar, and then select a 2 Up layout option. The Olives.psd and 07Working.psd files appear onscreen together. Click the Olives.psd file to ensure that it's the active window.

3 Hold down the Shift key as you drag the Background layer from the Layers panel in the Olive.psd file onto the center of the 07Working.psd file. Pressing Shift as you drag centers the Olives.psd image in the composition.

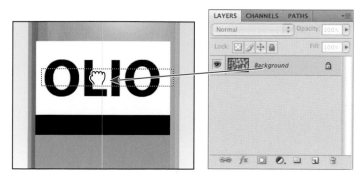

A new layer appears in the Layers panel for the 07Working.psd file: Layer 1. This new layer contains the image of olives, which will show through the type. But before you make the clipping mask, you'll resize the olives image, as it is too large for the composition.

4   Close the Olives.psd file without saving any changes to it.

5   In the 07Working.psd file, select Layer 1, and then choose Edit > Transform > Scale.

6   Grab a corner handle on the bounding box for the olives. Press Shift as you resize it to approximately the same width as the white area of the label. Pressing Shift retains the image proportions. You may need to reposition the olives so that the image remains centered on the label.

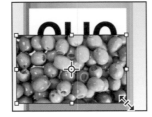  

7   Press Enter or Return to apply the transformation.

8   Double-click the Layer 1 name and change it to **Olives**. Then, press Enter or Return, or click away from the name in the Layers panel, to apply the change.

9 Select the Olives layer, if it isn't already selected, and choose Create Clipping Mask from the Layers panel menu.

▶ **Tip:** You can also make a clipping mask by holding down the Alt (Windows) or Option (Mac OS) key and clicking between the Olives and OLIO type layers.

The olives now show through the OLIO letters. A small arrow in the Olives layer and the underlined Type layer name indicate the clipping mask is applied. Next, you'll add a drop shadow to give the letters depth.

10 Select the OLIO layer to make it active, and then click the Add A Layer Style button (*fx*) at the bottom of the Layers panel, and choose Drop Shadow from the pop-up menu.

11 In the Layer Style dialog box, change the Opacity to **35%**, accept all other default settings, and click OK.

12 Choose File > Save to save your work so far.

Creating a design element from type

Next, you'll use a type trick to add vertical lines at the top of the label. These vertical lines need to be perfectly aligned, so you will use the capital "I" of a sans serif font instead of creating, copying, and moving individual lines. You will also easily adjust the size and spacing of the "lines" using the Character panel.

1 Click a blank area in the Layers panel to deselect all layers. Expand the panel if no blank area is visible.

2 Select the Horizontal Type tool (T). In the options bar, do the following:

- Choose a sans serif typeface, such as Myriad Pro.

- Choose Condensed for the font style, if it is available.

- Set the size to **36 pt**, and press Enter or Return.

- Leave the Anti-aliasing pop-up menu set to Sharp.

- Select the Left Align Text button.

- Click the color swatch to open the Color Picker. Move the cursor, which looks like an eyedropper, over the olives showing through the OLIO letters. Select a dark green color from the image, and click OK.

3   Click in the upper-left corner of the white box and hold down the Shift key as you type **I** 12 times.

This creates a new type layer in the Layers panel.

4   Select the Move tool (⯈⊕), position it inside the box, and drag the letters so that their tops touch the top edge of the white box.

● **Note:** After you type, you must commit your editing in the layer by clicking the Commit Any Current Edits button or switching to another tool or layer. You cannot commit to current edits by pressing Enter or Return; this action merely creates a new line for typing.

Julieanne Kost is an official Adobe Photoshop evangelist.

Tool tips from the Photoshop evangelist

Type tool tricks

- Shift-click in the image window with the Type tool (T) to create a new type layer—in case you're close to another block of type and Photoshop tries to autoselect it.

- Double-click the thumbnail icon on any type layer in the Layers panel to select all of the type on that layer.

- With any text selected, right-click (Windows) or Control-click (Mac OS) on the text to access the context menu. Choose Check Spelling to run a spell check.

Now, you will adjust the tracking to space the "lines" a bit wider apart.

5 Choose Window > Character to open the Character panel.

6 Type **40** in the Tracking box, and press Enter or Return. Or, scrub the Tracking label to set the value.

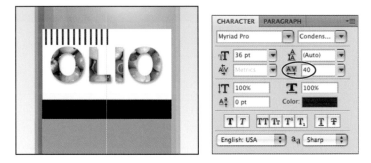

Now you'll adjust the position of the OLIO letters so that they're not too close to the vertical lines. To do that, you need to link the OLIO type layer and the olive image mask layer and move them as a unit.

7 Select the Olives layer, and then Shift-click the OLIO type layer to also select it. Then choose Link Layers from the Layers panel pop-up menu. A link icon appears next to the names of both layers.

8 Select the Move tool (⤧) and drag the type lower in the white box.

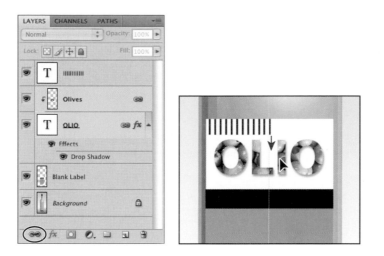

9 Choose File > Save to save your work so far.

Using interactive formatting controls

The Character panel in Photoshop contains many options to help you set beautiful type, but not all of the choices and controls are obvious—as in the trick of scrubbing the Tracking icon to choose a tracking value. In this exercise, you will make a type selection using another advanced trick for previewing type in the Character panel.

1 Click in a blank area of the Layers panel to deselect all layers.

2 Select the Horizontal Type tool (T). In the options bar, do the following:

- Click the Center Text button.

- Click the color box and select a bright red color. Click OK to close the Color Picker.

| 'T' ▾ | ⬆T | Myriad Pro ▾ | Condens... ▾ | ᵀT 36 pt ▾ | aₐ Sharp ▾ | ☰ ☰ ☰ | ■ |

For the moment, don't worry about which typeface or size you're using.

3 Click the center guide in the black stripe in the label. To be sure that you don't accidentally start editing the OLIO text, make sure that the pointer has a thin dotted line around it (Ⅱ) when you click. This means you'll create a new type layer when you type.

4 Type **EXTRA VIRGIN** in all caps.

Photoshop adds the text in whatever typeface and size were previously specified. But what if you want to use a different typeface? What if you're not sure which typeface you want to use?

5   Select the EXTRA VIRGIN text in the image window, and then, in the Character panel, click on the name in the Font Family pop-up menu. The name becomes highlighted.

6   Press the Up or Down Arrow key to cycle through the available fonts, and watch as Photoshop interactively previews each font in the highlighted EXTRA VIRGIN letters onscreen.

7   After experimenting, choose the sans serif typeface that you used for the OLIO letters—Myriad Pro, in our example—and then use the Tab key to jump to the Font Style box.

8   Again, use the Up and Down Arrow keys to cycle through available styles (if available) to choose one (we chose Bold), and watch as the styles preview interactively in the image window.

▶ **Tip:** Press Shift as you use the Up and Down Arrow keys to change the Size increment by 10 points.

9   Tab to the Size box, and use the Up or Down Arrow keys to set the type at **11** points.

10 Tab to the Tracking field, and set the Tracking to **280**: Type the value, use the Up Arrow key (press Shift as you press the key to increase the increment by 100), or scrub to set it.

11 Select the Move tool (⬥) and drag the EXTRA VIRGIN text so that it is centered in the black bar of the label.

12 Choose File > Save to save your work so far.

Warping point type

Now you will add the words "Olive Oil" to the label, and then warp them to make them more playful. *Warping* lets you distort type to conform to a variety of shapes, such as an arc or a wave. The warp style you select is an attribute of the type layer—you can change a layer's warp style at any time to change the overall shape of the warp. Warping options give you precise control over the orientation and perspective of the warp effect.

1   Scroll or use the Hand tool (🖐) to move the visible area of the image window so that the orange part of the label, below the black bar, is in the center of the screen.

2   Click in a blank area of the Layers panel to deselect all layers.

3   Select the Horizontal Type tool (T), and in the Character panel, do the following:

   • Choose a traditional serif typeface, such as Garamond.

   • Select Regular for the font style.

   • Set the size to **40 points**.

   • Set the tracking to **0**.

   • Make the color white.

4   Click and drag a text box in the upper area of the orange box, and then type **Olive Oil**. Then click the Commit Any Current Edits button (✔) in the options bar.

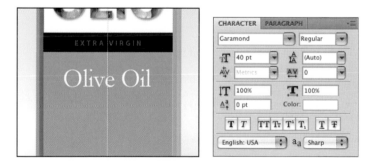

The words appear on the label, and a new layer, Olive Oil, appears in the Layers panel.

5   Right-click (Windows) or Control-click (Mac OS) the Olive Oil layer in the
    Layers panel, and choose Warp Text from the context menu.

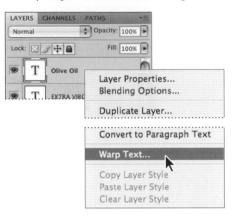

6   In the Warp Text dialog box, choose Wave from the Style menu, and click
    the Horizontal option. Specify the following values: Bend, +77%; Horizontal
    Distortion, -7%; and Vertical Distortion, -24%. Then click OK.

The words "Olive Oil" appear to float like a wave on the label.

Designing a paragraph of type

All of the text you've written on this label so far has been a few discrete words or
lines—point type. However, many designs call for full paragraphs of text. You can
design complete paragraphs of type in Photoshop; you don't have to switch to a
dedicated page-layout program for sophisticated paragraph type controls.

Using guides for positioning

Next, you will add a paragraph of descriptive content to the label in Photoshop. First, you'll add some guides to the work area to help you position the paragraph.

1   Drag two guides from the left vertical ruler, placing the first one at 2½ inches and the second at 4½ inches.

2   Drag two guides down from the top horizontal ruler, placing the first one at 10¾ inches and the second at 13 inches.

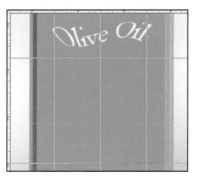

Adding paragraph type from a sticky note

You're ready to add the text. In a real design environment, the text might be provided to you in the form of a word processing document, or perhaps in the body of an email message, which you could copy and paste into Photoshop. Or you might have to type it in. Another easy way to add a bit of text is for the copywriter to attach it to the image file in a sticky note.

1   Double-click the yellow sticky note in the lower-right corner of the image window to open the Notes panel. Expand the Notes panel, if necessary, to see all the text.

● **Note:** You may need to change the view or scroll to see the open note onscreen.

2   Select all of the text in the note, and then press Ctrl+C (Windows) or Command+C (Mac OS) to copy it to the clipboard. Close the Notes panel.

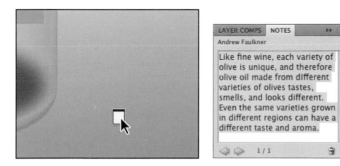

Before you paste the text, specify your type options.

3   Choose Select > Deselect Layers to ensure no layers are selected.

4 Select the Horizontal Type tool (T), and in the Character panel, do the following:

- Choose a sans serif typeface, such as Myriad Pro.

- Choose Regular for the font style, if it's available.

- Set the size to **10 pt**.

- Set the leading to **24 pt**.

- Set the tracking to **5**.

- Make the color black.

5 Click the Paragraph tab to open the Paragraph panel, and click the Justify All button (▤).

6 Drag the Type tool to create a text box that matches the guides you positioned in the previous exercise, and then press Ctrl+V (Windows) or Command+V (Mac OS) to paste the text from the clipboard into the text box.

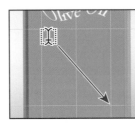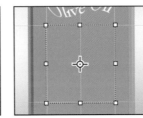

▶ **Tip:** If you resize the bounding box, the type will reflow within the adjusted rectangle.

The text appears in the image window with the styles you specified, and it wraps to the dimensions of the bounding box. The second-to-last line has some unsightly gaps, so as a fine-tuning measure, you'll fix that now.

7 Position the Horizontal Type tool (T) over the second-to-last line of the paragraph, and triple-click to select the line.

8 Click the Character tab to open the Character panel, and set tracking to **60**.

9 Click the Commit Any Current Edits button (✔) in the options bar. The paragraph text now appears as the layer named, "Like fine wine. . . ."

10 Choose File > Save to save your work so far.

OpenType in Photoshop

OpenType is a cross-platform font file format developed jointly by Adobe and Microsoft. The format uses a single font file for both Mac OS and Windows, so you can move files from one platform to another without font substitution or reflowed text. Supported in Photoshop CS4, OpenType offers widely expanded character sets and layout features, such as swashes and discretionary ligatures, that aren't available in traditional PostScript and TrueType fonts. This, in turn, provides richer linguistic support and advanced typography control. Here are some highlights of OpenType.

The OpenType menu The Character panel menu includes an OpenType submenu that displays all available features for a selected OpenType font, including ligatures, alternates, and fractions. Dimmed features are unavailable for that typeface; a check mark appears next to features that have been applied.

Discretionary ligatures To add a discretionary ligature to two OpenType letters, such as to a "th" in the Bickham Script Standard typeface, select them in the image, and choose OpenType > Discretionary Ligatures from the Character panel menu.

Swashes Adding swashes or alternate characters works the same way: Select the letter, such as a capital "T" in Bickham Script, and choose OpenType > Swash to change the ordinary capital into a dramatically ornate swash T.

Creating true fractions Type fractions as usual—for example, 1/2—and then select the characters, and from the Character panel menu, choose OpenType > Fractions. Photoshop applies the true fraction (½).

▶ **Tip:** Use the Adobe Illustrator CS4 Glyphs panel to preview OpenType options: Copy your text in Photoshop and paste it into an Illustrator document. Then, choose Window > Type > Glyphs. Select the text you want to change, and choose Show > Alternates For Current Selection. Double-click a glyph to apply it, and when you've finished, copy and paste the new type into your Photoshop file.

Adding the last two lines

You've almost finished adding text to the label. You need to add just two more lines.

1 With the Like fine wine. . . layer selected, click inside the paragraph of text, and then drag the handle in the middle of the lower edge of the text box down to the bottom of the edge of the label.

2 Click an insertion point at the end of the paragraph of text and press Enter or Return.

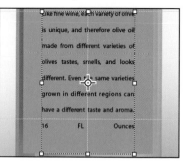

3   Type **16 FL Ounces**.

4   Triple-click to select "16 FL Ounces." In the Character panel, set the font size
    to **13 pt** and set the Baseline Shift to **-10**. The baseline shift option moves
    characters up or down relative to the baseline of the surrounding text.

5   In the Tools panel, click the Switch Colors button so that white is the foreground
    color.

6   In the Paragraph panel, click the Center Text button (≣). Then, click the
    Commit Any Current Edits button (✔) in the options bar.

Adding vertical type

The last line will be vertical.

1   Choose Select > Deselect Layers. Then, select the Vertical Type tool (↓T), which
    is hidden under the Horizontal Type tool.

2   Drag in the orange area of the label to the right of the descriptive text to create
    a long, narrow text box. Start from the lower or upper right corner so that you
    don't accidentally select the paragraph text.

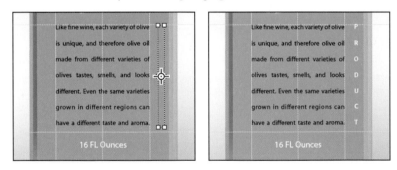

3 Type **PRODUCT OF ITALY**, all caps.

4 Select the letters either by dragging or triple-clicking them, and then, in the Character panel, do the following:

- Choose a serif typeface, such as Adobe Garamond.

- Set the size to **8 pt**.

- Set the tracking to **300**.

- Make the color red.

5 Click the Commit Any Current Edits button (✔) in the options bar. Your vertical text now appears as the layer named PRODUCT OF ITALY. Use the Move tool (▶⊕) and drag to center it if necessary.

Now, you'll clean up a bit.

6 Click the note to select it. Then right-click (Windows) or Control-click (Mac OS) and choose Delete Note from the context menu; click Yes to confirm that you want to delete the note.

7 Hide the guides: choose the Hand tool (✋) and then press Ctrl+; (Windows) or Command+; (Mac OS). Then, zoom out to get a nice look at your work.

8 Choose File > Save to save your work so far.

Warping a layer

All of the text is now on the label, but there's one problem: the bottle looks three-dimensional, while the label looks unrealistically flat on its surface. So your final effect will be to warp the label and its contents to look like they conform to the bottle shape.

Earlier in this lesson, you warped the words "Olive Oil" so that the letters appeared wavy. For this exercise, however, you'll apply the warp transformation to a layer, rather than to individual letters. To do this, you'll convert the label and type layers into a Smart Object, and then transform the new Smart Object. Using a Smart Object allows you to continue to edit both the contents of the layer (the type) and the warp after you apply the transformation.

Grouping layers into a Smart Object

Creating the Smart Object is a two-step process. First you have to merge the OLIO type layer and its clipping mask, then you will convert all of the label's layers into the Smart Object.

1 Select the OLIO layer in the Layers panel, and then Shift-click to also select the Olives layer. Choose Merge Layers from the Layers panel pop-up menu. Photoshop combines the layers into one layer, named Olives.

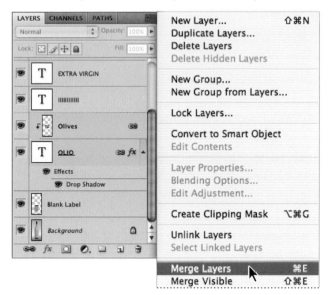

2 Select the Blank Label layer in the Layers panel, and then Shift-click the topmost layer in the stack, PRODUCT OF ITALY to select both layers and all of the layers between them. Then, choose Convert To Smart Object from the Layers panel menu.

▶ **Tip:** Right-click (Windows) or Control-click (Mac OS) to display the context menu with the Merge Layers and Convert To Smart Object commands.

Photoshop groups the selected layers into one Smart Object layer. The name for this new layer is the name of the top layer of the old stack, PRODUCT OF ITALY.

Warping with Smart Objects

Now you'll warp the Smart Object layer to match the contour of the bottle. To do this, it helps to have your guides visible.

1 Choose View > Show > Guides to display the guides you created earlier. Then, zoom in to the label.

2 With the PRODUCT OF ITALY layer selected, choose Edit > Transform > Warp.

Photoshop lays a 3-x-3 grid over the layer in the image window, with handles and lines that you can drag to warp the layer.

3 To help you apply the warp, drag out four horizontal guides, as follows: Place one guide at the top of the label, and one guide along the bottom of the label. Then, place two more guides one-quarter inch below each of those guides.

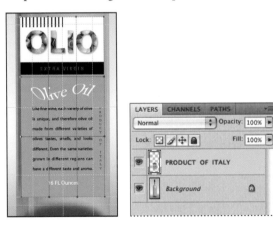

4 One at a time, click the center of each horizontal line of the grid and drag the line down one-quarter inch to create the curved label.

5 When you've finished, press Enter or Return to apply the warp transformation.

6 Choose View > Show > Guides to hide the guides. Then, click Fit Screen in the options bar to see the whole bottle composition on your screen.

7 Choose File > Save to save your work.

Congratulations! You've added and stylized all of the type on the Olio olive oil bottle. If you'd like to experiment further with the capabilities of Smart Objects, go on to the "Extra Credit" on the following page. Otherwise, in the real world, you would flatten and save this image file for printing.

8 Choose File > Save As, and rename the file **07Working_flattened**. Click OK if you see the Maximize Compatibility dialog box.

Keeping a layered version lets you return to the 07Working.psd file in the future to edit it—as you'll do if you complete the extra-credit section.

9 Choose Layer > Flatten Image.

10 Choose File > Save, and then close the image window.

Extra Credit

You can take full advantage of your Smart Object now by editing the label's content and letting Photoshop automatically update the bottle composition.

1   Double-click the PRODUCT OF ITALY Smart Object thumbnail in the Layers panel. (If you get a Smart Object alert dialog box, just click OK.) Photoshop opens the Smart Object in its own window.

2   Select the Horizontal Type tool, and in the Smart Object image window, change the "16 FL Ounces" text to **32 FL Ounces**. Then click the Commit Any Current Edits button.

3   Close the Product of Italy window, and when prompted, save your changes.

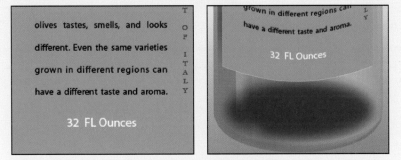

Photoshop returns to the 07Working.psd image file and applies the Smart Object updates to the label. You can repeat this process to make more edits as often as you'd like without compromising the quality of the image or the transformation. To edit the warp effect at any time, simply choose Edit > Transform > Warp in the 07Working.psd image file, and continue to edit the transformation nondestructively.

Review questions

1 How does Photoshop treat type?

2 How is a text layer the same as or different from other layers in Photoshop?

3 What is a clipping mask and how do you make one from type?

4 Describe two little-known ways to control type formatting in Photoshop.

Review answers

1 Type in Photoshop consists of mathematically defined shapes that describe the letters, numbers, and symbols of a typeface. When you add type to an image in Photoshop, the characters are composed of pixels and have the same resolution as the image file. However, Photoshop preserves the vector-based type outlines and uses them when you scale or resize type, save a PDF or EPS file, or print the image to a PostScript printer.

2 Type that is added to an image appears in the Layers panel as a text layer that can be edited and managed in the same way as any other kind of layer. You can add and edit the text, change the orientation of the type, and apply anti-aliasing as well as move, restack, copy, and change the options for layers.

3 A *clipping mask* is an object or group whose shape masks other artwork so that only areas that lie within the shape are visible. The letters on any text layer can be converted to a clipping mask by selecting both the text layer and the layer you want to show through the letters, and then choosing Create Clipping Mask from the Layers panel menu.

4 Select text in the image window, and in the Character panel or on the Type options bar you can do the following:

- Scrub the Size, Leading, Tracking, Kerning, Scaling, and Baseline Shift values.

- Select some type in the image window, click the font displayed in the Font Family pop-up menu, and press the Up and Down Arrow keys to cycle through the available fonts and watch them preview interactively in the image window.

8 VECTOR DRAWING TECHNIQUES

Lesson overview

In this lesson, you'll learn how to do the following:

- Differentiate between bitmap and vector graphics.

- Draw straight and curved paths using the Pen tool.

- Convert a path to a selection, and convert a selection to a path.

- Save paths.

- Draw and edit layer shapes.

- Draw custom layer shapes.

- Import and edit a Smart Object from Adobe Illustrator.

 This lesson will take about 90 minutes to complete. Copy the Lesson08 folder onto your hard drive if you haven't already done so. As you work on this lesson, you'll preserve the start files. If you need to restore the start files, copy them from the *Adobe Photoshop CS4 Classroom in a Book* CD.

Unlike bitmap images, vector images retain their crisp edges at any enlargement. You can draw vector shapes and paths in your Photoshop images and add vector masks to control what is shown in an image.

About bitmap images and vector graphics

Before working with vector shapes and vector paths, it's important to understand the basic differences between the two main categories of computer graphics: *bitmap images* and *vector graphics*. You can use Photoshop to work with either type of graphic; in fact, you can combine both bitmap and vector data in an individual Photoshop image file.

Bitmap images, technically called *raster images*, are based on a grid of colors known as pixels. Each pixel is assigned a specific location and color value. In working with bitmap images, you edit groups of pixels rather than objects or shapes. Because bitmap graphics can represent subtle gradations of shade and color, they are appropriate for continuous-tone images such as photographs or artwork created in painting programs. A disadvantage of bitmap graphics is that they contain a fixed number of pixels. As a result, they can lose detail and appear jagged when scaled up onscreen or printed at a lower resolution than they were created for.

Vector graphics are made up of lines and curves defined by mathematical objects called *vectors*. These graphics retain their crispness whether they are moved, resized, or have their color changed. Vector graphics are appropriate for illustrations, type, and graphics such as logos that may be scaled to different sizes.

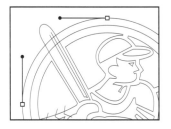

Logo drawn as vector art

Logo rasterized as bitmap art

About paths and the Pen tool

In Photoshop, the outline of a vector shape
is a *path*. A path is a curved or straight
line segment you draw using the Pen tool,
Magnetic Pen tool, or Freeform Pen tool. Of
these tools, the Pen tool draws paths with the
greatest precision; the Magnetic Pen tool and
Freeform Pen tool draw paths as if you were
drawing with a pencil on paper.

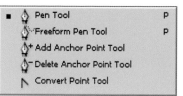

Julieanne Kost is an official Adobe Photoshop evangelist.

Tool tips from the Photoshop evangelist

Each tool in the Tools panel has a single-letter keyboard shortcut. Type the letter,
get the tool. For example, press P to select the Pen tool. Press Shift with the key to
cycle though any nested tools in a group. So press Shift+P to toggle between the
Pen and Freeform Pen tools.

Paths can be open or closed. Open paths (such as a wavy line) have two distinct
endpoints. Closed paths (such as a circle) are continuous. The type of path you draw
affects how it can be selected and adjusted.

Paths that have not been filled or stroked do not print when you print your artwork.
This is because paths are vector objects that contain no pixels, unlike the bitmap
shapes drawn by the Pencil tool and other painting tools.

Getting started

Before you begin, you'll view the image you'll be creating—a poster for a fictitious
toy company.

1   Start Adobe Photoshop, holding down Ctrl+Alt+Shift (Windows) or
    Command+Option+Shift (Mac OS) to restore the default preferences. (See
    "Restoring default preferences" on page 4.)

2   When prompted, click Yes to confirm that you want to reset preferences.

3   Click the Launch Bridge button (![Br]) in the application bar to open Adobe Bridge.

4   In the Favorites panel in the upper-left corner of Bridge, click the Lessons folder,
    and then double-click the Lesson08 folder in the Content panel.

5 View the 08End.psd file in the Content panel. To see larger thumbnails, drag the thumbnail slider at the bottom of the window.

● **Note:** If you open the 08End.psd file in Photoshop, you might be prompted to update type layers. If so, click Update. You may need to update type layers when files are transferred between computers, especially between operating systems.

To create this poster, you'll work with the image of the toy spaceship and practice making paths and selections using the Pen tool. As you create the background shapes and type, you'll learn advanced methods of using path and vector masks, as well as ways to use Smart Objects.

6 When you've finished looking at 08End.psd, double-click the Saucer.psd file to open it in Photoshop.

7 Choose File > Save As, rename the file **08Working.psd**, and click Save. Click OK in the Photoshop Format Options dialog box.

Using paths with artwork

You'll use the Pen tool to select the flying saucer. The saucer has long, smooth, curved edges that would be difficult to select using other methods.

You'll draw a path around the saucer and create two paths inside it. You'll convert the paths to selections, and then subtract one selection from the other so that only the saucer and none of the starry sky is selected. Finally, you'll make a new layer from the saucer image and change the image that appears behind it.

When drawing a freehand path using the Pen tool, use as few points as possible to create the shape you want. The fewer points you use, the smoother the curves are and the more efficient your file is.

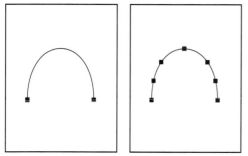

Correct number of points   Too many points

Creating paths with the Pen tool

You can use the Pen tool to create paths that are straight or curved, open or closed. If you're unfamiliar with the Pen tool, it can be confusing to use at first. Understanding the elements of a path and how to create them with the Pen tool makes paths much easier to draw.

To create a straight path, click the mouse button. The first time you click, you set the starting point. Each time that you click thereafter, a straight line is drawn between the previous point and the current point. To draw complex straight-segment paths with the Pen tool, simply continue to add points.

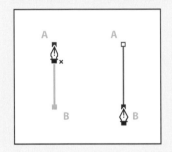

To create a curved path, click to place an anchor point, drag to create a direction line for that point, and then click to place the next anchor point. Each direction line ends in two direction points; the positions of direction lines and points determine the size and shape of the curved segment. Moving the direction lines and points reshapes the curves in a path.

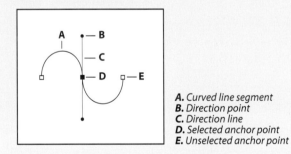

A. Curved line segment
B. Direction point
C. Direction line
D. Selected anchor point
E. Unselected anchor point

Smooth curves are connected by anchor points called *smooth points*. Sharply curved paths are connected by *corner points*. When you move a direction line on a smooth point, the curved segments on both sides of the point adjust simultaneously, but when you move a direction line on a corner point, only the curve on the same side of the point as the direction line is adjusted.

Path segments and anchor points can be moved after they're drawn, either individually or as a group. When a path contains more than one segment, you can drag individual anchor points to adjust individual segments of the path, or select all of the anchor points in a path to edit the entire path. Use the Direct Selection tool to select and adjust an anchor point, a path segment, or an entire path.

Creating a closed path differs from creating an open path in the way that you end the path. To end an open path, click the Pen tool in the Tools panel. To create a closed path, position the Pen tool pointer over the starting point and click. Closing a path automatically ends the path. After the path closes, the Pen tool pointer appears with a small x, indicating that your next click will start a new path.

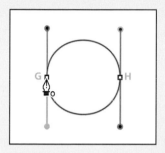

As you draw paths, a temporary storage area named Work Path appears in the Paths panel. It's a good idea to save work paths, and it's essential if you use multiple discrete paths in the same image file. If you deselect an existing Work Path in the Paths panel and then start drawing again, a new work path will replace the original one, which will be lost. To save a work path, double-click it in the Paths panel, type a name in the Save Path dialog box, and click OK to rename and save the path. The path remains selected in the Paths panel.

Drawing the outline of a shape

You'll use the Pen tool to connect the dots from point A to point N, and then back to point A. You'll set straight segments, smooth curve points, and corner points.

The first step is to configure the Pen tool options and the work area. Then you'll trace the outline of a flying saucer using a template.

1 In the Tools panel, select the Pen tool (✒).

2 In the options bar, select or verify the following settings:

   • Select the Paths (▨) option.

   • In the Pen Options pop-up menu, make sure that Rubber Band is not selected.

- Make sure that the Auto Add/Delete option is selected.
- Select the Add To Path Area option ().

A. Paths option **B.** Pen Options menu **C.** Add To Path Area option

3   Click the Paths tab to bring that panel to the front of the Layers panel group.

The Paths panel displays thumbnail previews of the paths you draw. Currently, the panel is empty because you haven't started drawing.

4   If necessary, zoom in so that you can easily see the lettered points and red dots on the shape template. Make sure you can see the whole template in the image window, and be sure to reselect the Pen tool after you zoom.

5   Click point A (the blue outlined box) and drag to the right to the red dot. Release the mouse. You've set the first anchor point and the direction of the curve.

6   Click point B (again, the blue outlined box) and drag down to the red dot. Release the mouse.

At the corner of the cockpit (point B), you'll need to convert the smooth point to a corner point to create a sharp transition between the curved segment and the straight one.

7   Alt-click (Windows) or Option-click (Mac OS) point B to convert the smooth point into a corner point and remove one of the direction lines.

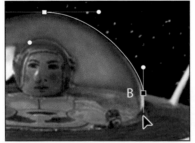

Setting a smooth point at B

Converting the smooth point to a corner point

8   Click point C to set a straight segment (don't drag).

If you make a mistake while you're drawing, choose Edit > Undo to undo the step. Then resume drawing.

9 Click point D and drag up from point D to its red dot. Then, click point E and drag down from point E to its red dot. Next, click point F.

10 Set curve points at G, H, and I by clicking each point and dragging from the point to its red dot, each in turn.

11 Click point J.

12 Set curve points at K and L by clicking each point and dragging from each one to its respective red dot.

13 Click point M.

14 Click point N and don't release the mouse button. Press Alt (Windows) or Option (Mac OS) and drag from point N to the red dot to add one direction line to the anchor point at N. Then, release the mouse button and the Alt or Option key.

15 Move the pointer over point A so that a small circle appears in the pointer icon, indicating that you are about to close the path. (The small circle may be difficult to see because the image is dark and the circle is faint.) Drag from point A to the red dot, and then release the mouse button to draw the last curved line.

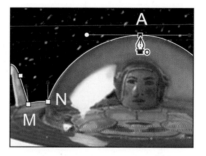

16 In the Paths panel, double-click the Work Path, type **Saucer** in the Save Path dialog box, and click OK to save it.

17 Choose File > Save to save your work.

Converting selections to paths

Now, you'll create a second path using a different method. First, you'll use a selection tool to select a similarly colored area, and then you'll convert the selection to a path. (You can convert any selection made with a selection tool into a path.)

1   Click the Layers tab to display the Layers panel, and then drag the Template layer to the Delete button at the bottom of the panel. You no longer need this layer.

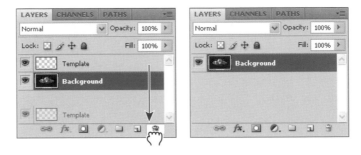

2   Select the Magic Wand tool (✎) in the tool box, hidden under the Quick Selection tool.

3   In the options bar, make sure the Tolerance value is **32**.

4   Carefully click the black area inside one of the saucer's vertical fins.

5   Shift-click inside the other fin to add that black area to the selection.

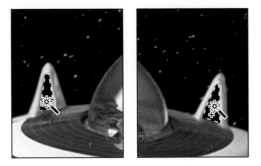

6 Click the Paths tab to bring the Paths panel forward. Then, click the Make Work Path From Selection button (⌐⌐) at the bottom of the panel.

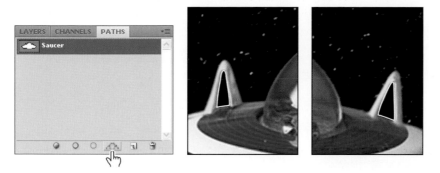

The selections are converted to paths, and a new work path is created.

7 Double-click the path named Work Path, name it **Fins**, and then click OK to save the path.

8 Choose File > Save to save your work.

Converting paths to selections

Just as you can convert selection borders to paths, you can convert paths to selections. With their smooth outlines, paths let you make precise selections. Now that you've drawn paths for the spaceship and its fins, you'll convert those paths to a selection and apply a filter to the selection.

1 In the Paths panel, click the Saucer path to make it active.

2 Choose Make Selection from the Paths panel menu, and then click OK to convert the Saucer path to a selection.

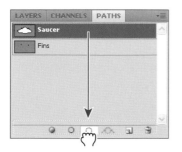

▶ **Tip:** You can also click the Load Path As Selection button at the bottom of the Paths panel to convert the active path to a selection.

Next, you'll subtract the Fins selection from the Saucer selection so that you can see the background through the vacant areas in the fins.

3 In the Paths panel, click the Fins path to make it active. Then, from the Paths panel menu, choose Make Selection.

4 In the Operation area of the Make Selection dialog box, select Subtract From Selection, and click OK.

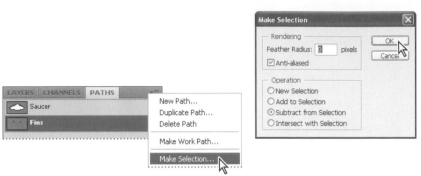

The Fins path is simultaneously converted to a selection and subtracted from the Saucer selection.

Leave the paths selected, because you'll use them in the next exercise.

Converting the selection to a layer

Now, you'll see how creating the selection with the Pen tool can help you achieve interesting effects. Because you've isolated the saucer, you can create a duplicate of it on a new layer. Then, you can copy it to another image file—specifically, to the image that is the background for the toy store poster.

1 Make sure that you can still see the selection outline in the image window. If you can't, repeat the previous exercise, "Converting paths to selections."

2 Choose Layer > New > Layer Via Copy.

3 Click the Layers tab to bring the Layers panel to the front. A new layer appears in the Layers panel, called Layer 1. The Layer 1 thumbnail shows that the layer contains only the image of the flying saucer, not the space background of the original layer.

4 In the Layers panel, rename Layer 1 **Saucer**, and press Enter or Return.

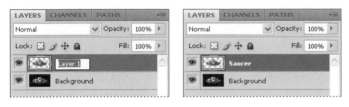

5 Choose File > Open, and double-click the 08Start.psd file in the Lessons/ Lesson08 folder.

The 08Start.psd file has a graduated blue background with a planet in the lower part of the image. You'll use this as the background for the flying saucer.

6 Click the Arrange Documents button in the application bar, and select a 2 Up layout so that you can see both the Saucer.psd and 08Start.psd files. Click the 08Working.psd image to make it active.

7 Select the Move tool (▶⊹), and drag the saucer from the 08Working.psd image window to the 08Start.psd image window so that the saucer appears to be hovering over the planet.

8 Close the 08Working.psd image without saving changes, leaving the 08Start.psd file open and active.

Now you'll position the flying saucer more precisely in the poster background.

9 Select the Saucer layer in the Layers panel and choose Edit > Free Transform.

A bounding box appears around the saucer.

Note: If you accidentally distort the saucer instead of rotating it, press Esc and start over.

10 Position the pointer near any corner handle until it turns into the rotate cursor (↱), then drag to rotate the saucer until it's at about a 20-degree angle. For precise rotation, you can enter the value in the Rotate box in the options bar. When you're satisfied, press Enter or Return.

11 Make sure that the Saucer layer is still selected, and then use the Move tool to drag the saucer so that it grazes the top of the planet, as in the following image.

12 Choose File > Save As, rename the file **08B_Working.psd**, and click Save. Click OK in the Photoshop Format Options dialog box.

Creating vector objects for the background

Many posters are designed to be scalable, either up or down, while retaining a crisp appearance. This is a good use for vector shapes. Next, you'll create vector shapes with paths, and use masks to control what appears in the poster. Because they're vectors, the shapes can be scaled in future design revisions without a loss of quality or detail.

Drawing a scalable shape

You'll begin by creating a white kidney-shaped object for the backdrop of the poster.

1 Choose View > Rulers to display the horizontal and vertical rulers.

2 Drag the tab for the Paths panel out of the Layers panel group so that it floats independently. Since you'll be using the Layers and Paths panels frequently in this exercise, it's convenient to have them separated.

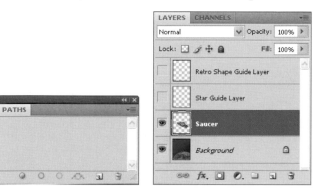

3 Hide all of the layers except the Retro Shape Guide layer and the Background layer by clicking the appropriate eye icons in the Layers panel. Select the Background layer to make it active.

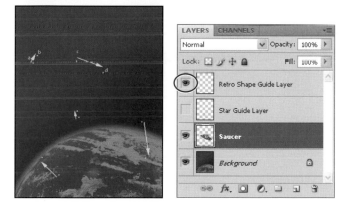

The guide layer will serve as a template as you draw the kidney shape.

A. Default Foreground And Background Colors button
B. Foreground Color button
C. Switch Foreground And Background Colors button
D. Background Color button

4 Set the foreground and background colors to their defaults (black and white, respectively) by clicking the Default Foreground And Background Colors button (▣) in the Tools panel (or type the keyboard shortcut D), and then swap the foreground and background colors by clicking the Switch Foreground And Background Colors button (↰) (or type X). Now the foreground color is white.

5 In the Tools panel, select the Pen tool (✎). Then, in the options bar, select the Shape Layers option.

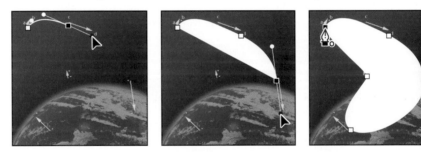

6 Create the shape by clicking and dragging as follows:

- Click point A and drag a direction line up and to the left of point B, and then release.

- Click point C and drag a direction line toward and above point D, and then release.

- Continue to draw curved segments in this way around the shape until you return to point A, and then click on A to close the path.

Notice that as you drew, Photoshop automatically created a new layer, Shape 1, just above the active layer in the Layers panel.

7 Double-click the Shape 1 layer name, rename the layer **Retro Shape**, and press Enter or Return.

● **Note:** If you have trouble, open the saucer image again and practice drawing the path around the saucer shape until you get more comfortable with drawing curved path segments. Also, be sure to read the sidebar, "Creating paths with the Pen tool."

LAYERS	CHANNELS	
Normal	Opacity:	100%
Lock: ☐ ⟋ ✛ 🔒	Fill:	100%
👁 ▨	Retro Shape Guide Layer	
☐ ▨	Star Guide Layer	
☐ ▨	Saucer	
👁	**Retro Shape**	

PATHS	
❯ *Retro Shape Vector Mask*	

8 Hide the Retro Shape Guide layer in the Layers panel.

9 Choose File > Save to save your work.

Deselecting paths

You may need to deselect paths to see the appropriate options in the options bar when you select a vector tool. Deselecting paths can also help you view certain effects that might be obscured if a path is highlighted.

Notice that the border between the white kidney shape and the blue background has a grainy quality. What you see is actually the path itself, which is a nonprinting item. This is a visual clue that the Retro Shape layer is still selected. Before proceeding to the next exercise, you'll make sure that all paths are deselected.

1 Select the Path Selection tool (▶), which may be hidden under the Direct Selection tool (▶).

2 In the options bar, click the Dismiss Target Path button (✔).

● **Note:** You can also deselect paths by clicking in the blank area below the paths in the Paths panel.

About shape layers

A shape layer has two components: a fill and a shape. The fill properties determine the color (or colors), pattern, and transparency of the layer. The shape is a layer mask that defines the areas in which the fill can be seen and those areas in which the fill is hidden.

In the layer you've just created, the fill is white. The fill color is visible within the shape you drew and is not visible in the rest of the image, so the background sky can be seen around it.

In the Layers panel, the Retro Shape layer sits above the Background layer because the background was selected when you started to draw. The shape layer has three items along with the layer name: two thumbnail images and a link icon between them.

A. Fill thumbnail
B. Layer mask link icon
C. Mask thumbnail

The Fill thumbnail on the left shows that the entire layer is filled with the white foreground color. The nonfunctioning small slider underneath the thumbnail symbolizes that the layer is editable.

The Mask thumbnail on the right shows the vector mask for the layer. In this thumbnail, white indicates the area where the image is exposed, and gray indicates the areas where the image is blocked.

The icon between the two thumbnails shows that the layer and the vector mask are linked.

Subtracting shapes from a shape layer

After you create a shape layer (vector graphic), you can set options to subtract new shapes from the vector graphic. You can also use the Path Selection tool and the Direct Selection tool to move, resize, and edit shapes. You'll add some interest to the retro shape by subtracting a star shape from it, allowing the outer space background to show through. To help you position the star, you'll refer to the Star Guide layer, which has been created for you. Currently, that layer is hidden.

1   In the Layers panel, show the Star Guide layer, but leave the Retro Shape layer selected. The Star Guide layer is now visible in the image window.

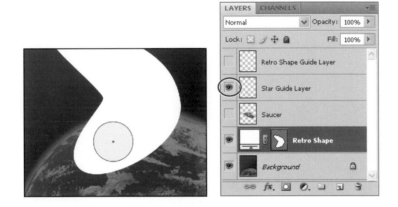

2   In the Paths panel, select the Retro Shape vector mask.

3   In the Tools panel, select the Polygon tool (⬡), hidden under the Rectangle tool (▢).

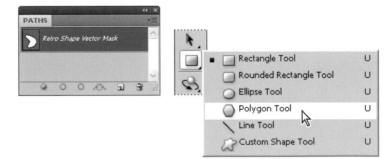

4 On the options bar, do the following:

- For Sides, type **11**.

- Click the arrow immediately to the left of the Sides option to display the Polygon Options window. Select Star, and type **50%** in the Indent Sides By box. Then click anywhere outside the Polygon Options window to close it.

- Select the Subtract From Shape Area option (⬚), or press either the hyphen or minus key to select it with a keyboard shortcut. The pointer now appears as cross hairs with a small minus sign (+.).

5 Click on the orange dot in the center of the orange circle in the image window, and drag outward until the tips of the star rays touch the circle's perimeter.

> ● **Note:** As you drag, you can rotate the star by dragging the pointer to the side.

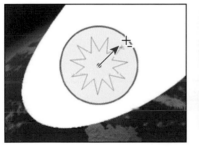 

When you release the mouse, the star shape becomes a cutout, allowing the planet to show through.

Notice that the star has a grainy outline, reminding you that the shape is selected. Another indication that the shape is selected is that the Retro Shape vector mask thumbnail is highlighted (outlined in white) in the Layers panel.

6 In the Layers panel, hide the Star Guide layer.

Notice how the thumbnails have changed in the panels. In the Layers panel, the left thumbnail for the Retro Shape layer is unchanged, but the mask thumbnails in both the Layers panel and Paths panel show the retro shape with the star-shaped cutout.

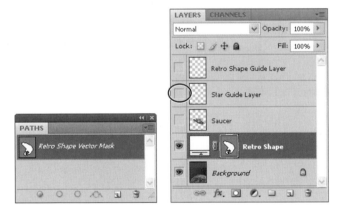

7 Select the Path Selection tool (⬏) and click the Dismiss Target Path button (✔) in the options bar to deselect the star and retro shape paths.

The paths are now deselected, and the grainy path lines have disappeared, leaving a sharp edge between the blue and white areas. Also, the Retro Shape Vector Mask path is no longer highlighted in the Paths panel.

8 Choose File > Save to save your work.

Working with defined custom shapes

Another way to use shapes in your artwork is to draw a custom or preset shape. Doing so is as easy as selecting the Custom Shape tool, picking a shape from the Custom Shape picker, and drawing in the image window. You'll do just that to add checkerboard patterns to the background of your poster for the toy store.

1   Make sure the Retro Shape layer is selected in the Layers panel. Then click the New Layer button (🖺) to add a layer above it. Rename the new layer **Pattern**, and then press Enter or Return.

2   In the Tools panel, select the Custom Shape tool (🔗), which is hidden under the Polygon tool (⬤).

3   In the options bar, select the Fill Pixels option.

4   In the options bar, click the arrow next to the Shape option to open the Custom Shape picker.

5   Double-click the checkerboard preset on the right side of the Custom Shape picker (you may need to scroll or drag the corner of the picker to see it) to select it. Click outside the picker to close it.

6 Make sure that the foreground color is white. Then press Shift and drag diagonally in the image window to draw and size the shape so that it's about 2 inches square. (Pressing Shift constrains the shape to its original proportions.)

7 Add five more checkerboards of various sizes until your poster resembles the following figure.

8 In the Layers panel, reduce the opacity of the Pattern layer to **20%**.

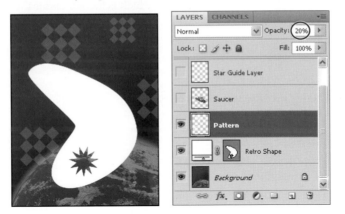

Your poster background is now complete.

9 In the Layers panel, show the Saucer layer so you can see the whole composition.

10 Choose File > Save to save your work.

Importing a Smart Object

Smart Objects are layers that you can edit in Photoshop nondestructively; that is, changes you make to the image remain editable and do not affect the actual image pixels, which are preserved. Regardless of how often you scale, rotate, skew, or otherwise transform a Smart Object, it retains its sharp, precise edges.

You can import vector objects from Adobe Illustrator as Smart Objects. If you edit the original object in Illustrator, the changes will be reflected in the placed Smart Object in your Photoshop image file. You learned a bit about Smart Objects in earlier lessons. You will explore them more now by placing text created in Illustrator into the toy store poster.

Adding the title

The toy store name was created in Illustrator. You'll add it to the poster now.

1   Select the Saucer layer and choose File > Place. Navigate to the Lessons/ Lesson08 folder, select the Title.ai file, and click Place. Click OK in the Place PDF dialog box that appears.

The Retro Toyz text is added to the middle of the composition, inside a bounding box with adjustable handles. A new layer, title, appears in the Layers panel.

2   Drag the Retro Toyz object to the upper-right corner of the poster, and then press Shift and drag a corner to make the text object proportionally larger— so that it fills the top portion of the poster, as in the following figure. When you've finished, either press Enter or Return, or click the Commit Transform button (✔) in the options bar.

When you commit to the transformation, the layer thumbnail icon changes to reflect that the title layer is a Smart Object.

Because the Retro Toyz title is a Smart Object, you can continue to edit its size and shape, if you'd like. Simply select the layer and choose Edit > Free Transform to access the control handles, and drag to adjust them. Or, select the Move tool (▶⊕), and check Show Transform Controls in the options bar. Then adjust the handles.

Adding a vector mask to a Smart Object

For a fun effect, you'll turn the center of each letter "O" in the title into a star that matches the cutout you created earlier. You'll use a vector mask, which you can link to a Smart Object in Photoshop CS4.

1 Select the title layer, and then click the Add Layer Mask button at the bottom of the Layers panel.

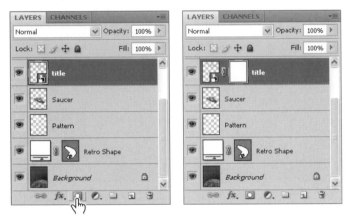

2 Select the Polygon tool (hidden beneath the Custom Shape tool). The options you used earlier to create the star should still be in effect. The Polygon tool holds your settings until you change them again. If you need to reset the options, refer to "Subtracting shapes from a shape layer."

3 Click the Switch Foreground And Background Colors button in the Tools panel, so that black is the foreground color.

4 Click in the center of the "O" in "Toyz" and drag the cursor outward until the star covers the center of the "O."

5 Repeat step 3 to add a star in the small "O" in Retro.

Rotating the canvas (OpenGL only)

You've been working with the image with "Retro Toyz" at the top of the work area and the planet at the bottom. But if your video card supports OpenGL, you can rotate the work area to draw, type, or position objects from a different perspective. You'll rotate the view as you add a copyright statement along the side of the image. (If your video card doesn't support OpenGL, skip this section.)

First, you'll type the text.

1 Choose Window > Character to open the Character panel. Select a serif font such as Myriad Pro with a small text size such as 10 pt, and set the color to white.

2 Select the Horizontal Type tool, and then click in the lower-left corner of the image. Type **Copyright YOUR NAME Productions**, substituting your own name.

You want the copyright to run along the left side of the image. You'll rotate the canvas to make it easier to place.

3 Select the Rotate View tool (⟳), hidden beneath the Hand tool (✋).

4 Press the Shift key as you drag the tool in an arc to rotate the canvas 90 degrees clockwise. Pressing the Shift key restrains the rotation to 45-degree increments.

▶ **Tip:** You can also enter a value in the Rotation Angle box in the options bar.

5   Select the Copyright text layer, and then choose Edit > Transform > Rotate 90 Deg CCW.

6   Use the Move tool to align the text along the top edge of the image, which will be the left edge when it is in its usual position.

7   Select the Rotate View tool again, and then click Reset View in the options bar.

8   Choose File > Save to save your work.

Finishing up

As a final step, clean up the Layers panel by deleting your guide template layers.

1   Make sure that the Copyright, title, Saucer, Pattern, Retro Shape, and Background layers are the only visible layers in the Layers panel.

2   Choose Delete Hidden Layers from the Layers panel pop-up menu, and then click Yes to confirm the deletion.

3   Choose File > Save to save your work.

Congratulations! You've finished the poster.

It should look similar to the following image. (The title text will only be stroked if you complete the Extra Credit task, which follows.)

Extra Credit

If you have Adobe Illustrator CS or later, you can go even further with the Retro Toyz text Smart Object—you can edit it in Illustrator, and it will update automatically in Photoshop. Try this:

1 Double-click the Smart Object thumbnail in the title layer. If an alert dialog box appears, click OK. Illustrator opens and displays the Retro Toyz Smart Object in a document window.

2 Using the Direct Selection tool, drag a marquee around the type to select all of the letters.

3 Double-click the Stroke button in the Tools panel to open the Color Picker. Select black, and click OK.

4 In Illustrator CS3 or later, in the options bar, choose 0.5 pt from the Stroke menu. If you are using an earlier version of Illustrator, open the Stroke panel and specify a 0.5 pt stroke.

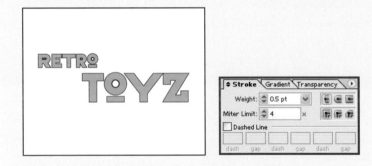

A 0.5-point black stroke appears around the Retro Toyz type.

5 Close the Vector Smart Object document, and click Save when prompted. Click OK if an alert box appears.

6 Switch back to Photoshop. The Retro Toyz poster image window updates to reflect the stroked type.

Review questions

1 How can the Pen tool be useful as a selection tool?

2 What is the difference between a bitmap image and a vector graphic?

3 What does a shape layer do?

4 What tools can you use to move and resize paths and shapes?

5 What are Smart Objects, and what is the benefit of using them?

Review answers

1 If you need to create an intricate selection, it can be easier to draw the path with the Pen tool and then convert the path to a selection.

2 Bitmap, or raster, images are based on a grid of pixels and are appropriate for continuous-tone images such as photographs or artwork created in painting programs. Vector graphics are made up of shapes based on mathematical expressions and are appropriate for illustrations, type, and drawings that require clear, smooth lines.

3 A shape layer stores the outline of a shape in the Paths panel. You can change the outline of a shape by editing its path.

4 You use the Path Selection tool and the Direct Selection tool to move, resize, and edit shapes. You can also modify and scale a shape or path by choosing Edit > Free Transform Path.

5 Smart Objects are vector objects that you can place and edit in Photoshop without a loss of quality. Regardless of how often you scale, rotate, skew, or otherwise transform a Smart Object, it retains sharp, precise edges. A great benefit of using Smart Objects is that you can edit the original object in the authoring application, such as Illustrator, and the changes will be reflected in the placed Smart Object in your Photoshop image file.

9 ADVANCED LAYERING

Lesson overview

In this lesson, you'll learn how to do the following:

- Import a layer from another file.

- Clip a layer.

- Create and edit an adjustment layer.

- Use Vanishing Point 3D effects with layers.

- Create layer comps to showcase your work.

- Manage layers.

- Flatten a layered image.

- Merge and stamp layers.

 This lesson will take about an hour to complete. Copy the Lesson09 folder onto your hard drive if you haven't already done so. As you work on this lesson, you'll preserve the start files. If you need to restore the start files, copy them from the *Adobe Photoshop CS4 Classroom in a Book* CD.

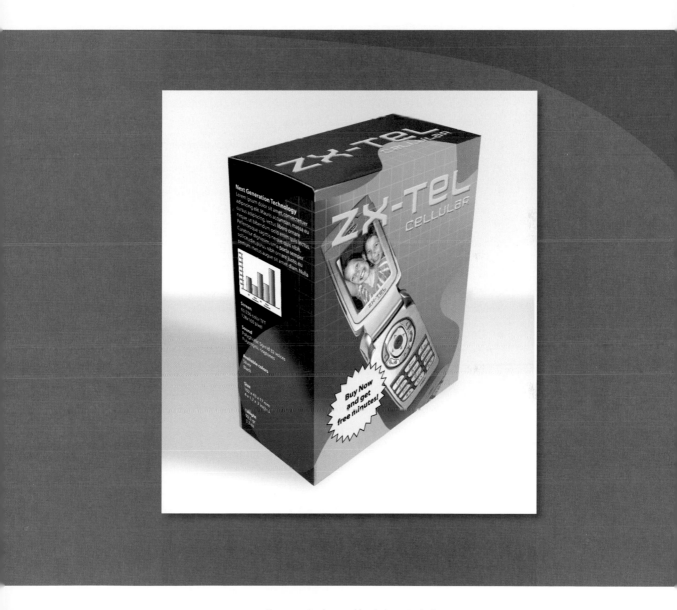

Once you've learned basic layer techniques, you can create more complex effects in your artwork using layer masks, adjustment layers, filters, and more layer styles. You can also add layers from other documents.

Getting started

In this lesson, you'll combine several images to create a cell phone package. You'll create three different, multilayered designs, which you can display selectively using layer comps. You'll gain more experience with adjustment layers, layer effects, layer masks, and layer filters. Beyond this lesson, the best way to learn how to work with layers is by experimenting with combinations of filters, effects, layer masks, and layer properties in new ways.

1 Start Photoshop and then immediately hold down Ctrl+Alt+Shift (Windows) or Command+Option+Shift (Mac OS) to restore the default preferences. (See "Restoring default preferences" on page 4.)

2 When prompted, click Yes to confirm that you want to reset preferences.

3 Click the Launch Bridge button (Br) in the application bar to open Adobe Bridge.

4 In the Favorites panel in the upper-left corner of Bridge, click the Lessons folder, and then double-click the Lesson09 folder in the Content panel.

5 Study the 09End.psd file in the Content panel. If necessary, drag the thumbnail slider at the bottom of the window to enlarge the thumbnail.

Your goal in this lesson is to create a package prototype by assembling artwork from various files, layering the artwork, adding perspective, and then refining the design. You'll create several layer comps to show the design to your client.

6 Double-click the 09Start.psd file to open it in Photoshop. Choose File > Save As, rename the file **09Working.psd**, and click Save. Click OK in the Photoshop Format Options dialog box.

7 Drag the Layers panel by its tab to the top of the work area. Drag its corner to expand the panel so that you'll be able to see about 10 layers without scrolling.

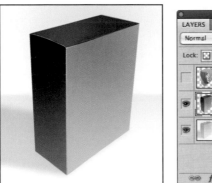

The panel lists three layers, two of which are visible—the gray three-dimensional box displayed in the image window, and the background stacked underneath it. The Full Art layer is hidden.

8 In the Layers panel, select the Full Art layer. Notice that even though the layer is selected, it remains hidden.

Clipping a layer to a shape

To start building a composite image, you'll add more artwork and clip it to a shape.

1 Click the Launch Bridge button (■) in the application bar to return to Bridge.

2 In the Bridge Content panel, double-click the Phone_art.psd file to open it.

This file has two layers: Phone Art and Mask. You will clip the phone art image so that it fits within the freeform shape in the Mask layer below it.

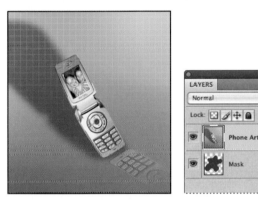

3 In the Layers panel, make sure that the Mask layer is below the Phone Art layer. A clipping shape must be below the image that you're clipping.

4 Select the Phone Art layer. Then press Alt (Windows) or Option (Mac OS) as you position the pointer between the Phone Art layer and the Mask layer until it becomes a double-circle icon (↤⊙), and click.

The thumbnail of the clipped layer, Phone Art, is indented in the Layers panel, and an arrow points to the layer beneath it, which is now underlined.

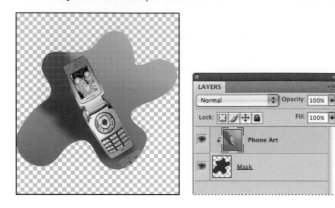

You will import this new image into the Start file. But first, you need to flatten the image to one layer.

5 Choose Merge Visible from the Layers panel menu.

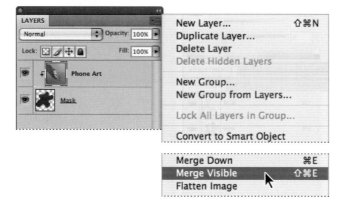

You can merge the layers in other ways. But don't choose Flatten Image because it would remove the transparency already set up in the file.

Now you'll add artwork from another file, simply by dragging and dropping.

6 Click the Arrange Documents button in the application bar, and select a 2 Up layout so you can see both images.

7 Drag the merged Phone Art layer from the Layers panel into the 09Working.psd image window. The layer appears above the active layer (Full Art) and at the top of the 09Working.psd Layers panel. The artwork covers the box.

8 In the 09Working.psd Layers panel, double-click the Phone Art layer name, and type **Shape Art** to rename it. Press Enter or Return.

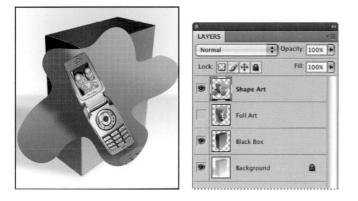

9 Choose File > Save to save your work so far.

10 Close the Phone_Art.psd file without saving your changes.

Setting up a Vanishing Point grid

The artwork you've added sits on top of the box—not exactly the effect you want. You'll fix that by making the artwork appear in perspective, wrapped around the box.

1 With the Shape Art layer selected in the Layers panel, press Ctrl+A (Windows) or Command+A (Mac OS) to select all of the layer's contents.

2 Press Ctrl+X (Windows) or Command+X (Mac OS) to cut the contents to the clipboard. Now only the box is visible, not the artwork.

3 Choose Filter > Vanishing Point. You'll use the Vanishing Point filter to draw a perspective plane that matches the dimensions of the box.

4 With the Create Plane tool (⊞), which is selected by default, click the upper-left corner of the front of the box to begin defining the plane. It's easiest to define planes when you can use a rectangular object in the image as a guide.

5 Continue drawing the plane by clicking each corner of the box side. Click the last corner to complete the plane. When you complete the plane, a grid appears on the front of the box and the Edit Plane tool (🖈) is automatically selected. You can adjust the size of this grid at the top of the dialog box using the Edit Plane tool.

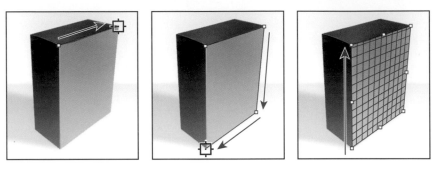

6 Use the Edit Plane pointer to adjust corner points to refine your plane, as needed.

Now you'll extend the grid to the front and top of the box to complete the perspective.

7 With the Edit Plane tool selected, press Ctrl (Windows) or Command (Mac OS) and drag the center point of the left side of the plane, extending the plane along the side of the box. As the grid displays on the side of the box, the grid on the front face disappears, but its blue border remains.

8 Use the Edit Plane pointer to adjust any corner points along the side plane, so that it more closely matches the shape of the box.

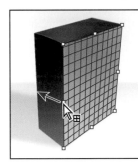  

9 When you are satisfied with the grid's placement, repeat steps 7 and 8 to extend the grid across the top of the box.

● **Note:** The final grid doesn't have to match the box dimensions exactly.

If you were applying perspective to many planes, you might want to create a separate layer for each plane. Putting the Vanishing Point results in a separate layer preserves your original image and lets you use the layer opacity control, styles, and blending modes.

You're ready to add the artwork and give it perspective.

10 Press Ctrl+V (Windows) or Command+V (Mac OS) to paste the contents of the clipboard onto the grid. This action automatically selects the Marquee tool in the Vanishing Point dialog box.

11 Using the Marquee tool (▢), select the contents and drag it to the center of the front perspective plane so that most of the artwork appears on the front panel, but wraps around the side and top. It's important to place the artwork on the front panel, so that it wraps correctly.

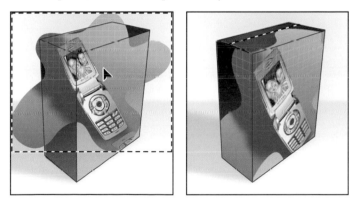

12 When you're satisfied with the positioning, click OK.

13 Choose File > Save to save your work so far.

Creating your own keyboard shortcuts

Photoshop comes with keyboard shortcuts for most common tools and commands. But you can customize shortcuts to fit your workflow. As you build the composite image, you'll place several images created in Adobe Illustrator. To make your work more efficient, create a keyboard shortcut for the Place command.

1 Choose Edit > Keyboard Shortcuts. The Keyboard Shortcuts and Menus dialog box appears.

2 Under Application Menu Command, click the triangle to the left of File to expand its contents. Scroll down to Place, and select it.

3 Press the F7 key on the keyboard to assign that key as a new shortcut. An alert appears, warning you that the F7 key is already in use. It's the keyboard shortcut for the Window > Layers command, which opens the Layers panel.

4 Click Accept, and then click OK.

Placing imported artwork

Now you'll take advantage of your new keyboard shortcut as you add more artwork to the package. The imported artwork contains the words *ZX-Tel cellular*, originally created with the Type tool in Illustrator, but then converted to a graphic. You can no longer edit the text with the Type tool. However, you don't have to worry about whether others working on the file can see the type correctly if they don't have the same font installed.

1 Press F7 to open the Place dialog box.

2 Select the ZX-Tel logo.ai file in the Lesson09 folder. Click Place. The Place PDF dialog box appears.

3 Leave the settings at their defaults, and click OK to place the file. The logo image opens in Free Transform mode, so you can modify it.

The Place command adds a photo, art, or any file Photoshop supports as a Smart Object to your document. You may remember from earlier lessons that Smart Objects preserve an image's source content with all its original characteristics, enabling you to edit the Smart Object layer nondestructively. However, when you're using a Smart Object, some filters and effects are not available.

4 Drag the logo over the front panel, and then drag the corner points to resize the logo to roughly the width of the box front. Don't worry about being exact: you'll use the Vanishing Point filter to position the logo in perspective soon.

5 When you are satisfied with the positioning, press Enter or Return to place the file.

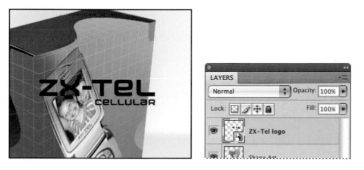

The placed image appears as the ZX-Tel logo layer at the top of the Layers panel. The icon in the lower-right corner of the layer thumbnail indicates that it is a Smart Object.

6 Choose File > Save to save your work so far.

Adding artwork in perspective

You'll apply the text you just placed to the three-dimensional box. Then, you'll transform and stylize it so that it looks realistic and in perspective. Because Smart Objects do not support the Vanishing Point filter, you'll start by converting the vector data in the Smart Object layer to pixels.

1   In the Layers panel, right-click (Windows) or Control-click (Mac OS) the ZX-Tel layer name, and choose Rasterize Layer from the context menu. This converts the Smart Object to a flat, raster layer.

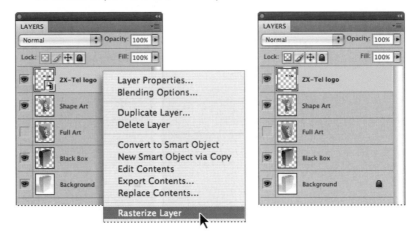

2   Choose Image > Adjustments > Invert to invert the color from black to gray. This will make it easier to read the text when it's added to the box.

3   With the ZX-Tel logo layer selected in the Layers panel, choose Select > All. The entire ZX-Tel logo layer is selected.

4   Choose Edit > Cut.

5   Choose Filter > Vanishing Point to return to the perspective plane. The 3D box with the cell phone artwork is already there.

6 Press Ctrl+V (Windows) or Command+V (Mac OS) to paste the logo onto the perspective plane, and drag it into position on the front of the box.

7 Press Ctrl+T (Windows) or Command+T (Mac OS) to access the free transform handles. Drag the handles to adjust the logo so that it matches the perspective of the box. You may need to rotate the logo.

8 Press the Alt (Windows) or Option (Mac OS) key, and drag a cloned copy of the logo directly upwards and onto the top of the box. When you are satisfied with the positioning, click OK.

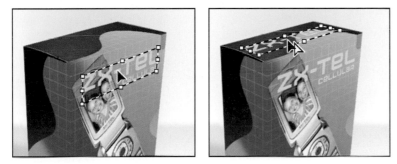

9 Choose File > Save to save your work.

Adding a layer style

Now you'll add a layer style to give the logo some depth. Layer styles are automated effects that you can apply to a layer.

1 In the Layers panel, select the ZX-Tel logo layer.

2 Choose Layer > Layer Style > Bevel And Emboss. Leave the settings at their default, and click OK.

Now the logo has sharp, deep edges, to give the box the appearance of more depth.

Placing the side panel artwork

To complete the package, you'll add product copy to the side panel of the box.

1 Press F7 and select the Side Box Copy.ai file. Click Place. In the Place PDF dialog box, leave the settings at their defaults, and click OK.

2 Press the Shift key and drag a corner to resize the placed image down to roughly the size of the side panel. Then press Enter or Return to place the artwork.

3 In the Layers panel, right-click (Windows) or Control-click (Mac OS) the side box copy layer name, and choose Rasterize Layer from the context menu.

You will select the type and change its color to make it more legible.

4 Select the Polygonal Lasso tool (⌇) in the Tools panel, hidden under the Lasso tool (⌇).

5 Using the Polygonal Lasso tool, click at each corner to draw a box around the top block of text. Then hold down the Shift key, and draw another box around the bottom block of text to add to the selection. You don't want to include the graph.

You used the Polygonal Lasso tool because the lines of text form a slightly irregular shape. You could also use the Rectangular Marquee tool.

6 Press Ctrl+I (Windows) or Command+I (Mac OS) to invert the color from black to white. Then, choose Select > Deselect.

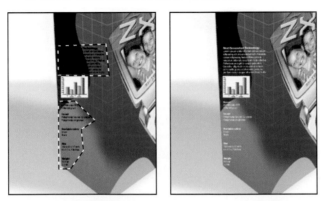

Adding more artwork in perspective

Now you'll add the copy from the side panel to your three-dimensional box.

1 Select the side box copy layer, and choose Select > All.

2 Press Ctrl+X (Windows) or Command+X (Mac OS) to cut the contents to the clipboard.

3 Choose Filter > Vanishing Point.

4 Press Ctrl+V (Windows) or Command+V (Mac OS) to paste the side copy artwork onto the perspective plane.

5 Position the artwork so that it fits along the side panel. If necessary, press Ctrl+T (Windows) or Command+T (Mac OS), and use the free transform handles to adjust the artwork so that it fits properly.

6 When you are satisfied with how the side copy artwork looks, click OK.

Now you'll repeat this procedure one more time to place the last piece of artwork and add it to the box in perspective.

7 Press F7, and double-click the Special Offer.ai file. Click OK to close the Place PDF dialog box. Resize the artwork to fit in the lower-left corner of the box front, and then press Enter or Return to place the file.

8 In the Layers panel, right-click (Windows) or Control-click (Mac OS) the special offer layer name, and choose Rasterize Layer from the context menu. The layer is no longer a Smart Object.

9 Place the special offer layer on the box in perspective, following the same procedure you used to add the box artwork, text, and side copy:

- With the special offer layer active, choose Select > All.

- Press Ctrl+X (Windows) or Command+X (Mac OS) to cut the contents to the clipboard.

- Choose Filter > Vanishing Point.

- Press Ctrl+V (Windows) or Command+V (Mac OS) to paste the contents from the clipboard.

- Position the artwork in the lower-left corner of the front panel, and then click OK.

10 Choose File > Save to save your work.

Adding an adjustment layer

To enhance the realism of the package, you'll add an adjustment layer to create a shadow over the side panel.

Adjustment layers can be added to an image to apply color and tonal adjustments without permanently changing the pixel values in the image. For example, if you add a Color Balance adjustment layer to an image, you can experiment with different colors repeatedly, because the change occurs only on the adjustment layer. If you decide to return to the original pixel values, you can hide or delete the adjustment layer.

You've used adjustment layers in other lessons. Here, you'll add a Levels adjustment layer to increase the tonal range of the selection, in effect increasing the overall contrast. An adjustment layer affects all layers below it in the image's stacking order, unless a selection is active when you create it.

1 In the Layers panel, select the side box copy layer.

2 Select the Polygonal Lasso tool (ᵧ) in the Tools panel, and click at each corner to draw a rectangular shape around the side panel.

3 Click the Levels button in the Adjustments panel to create an adjustment layer.

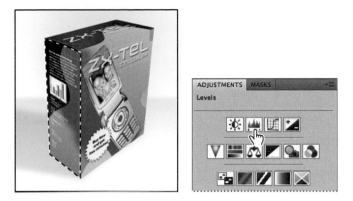

4 Double-click the name Levels 1 and rename it **Shadow**. Press Enter or Return.

5 In the Adjustments panel, drag the right (white) triangle in the Output Levels slider to about **210** to decrease the brightness. Then, click the Return To Adjustment List button at the bottom of the Adjustments panel.

6 Choose File > Save to save your work.

7 Experiment by clicking the Show/Hide Visibility button for the Shadow adjustment layer to see its effect. Because you made a selection before you created the adjustment layer, it affects only the selected area. When you finish, make sure that all layers but Full Art are visible.

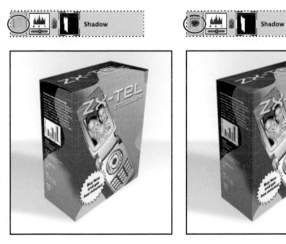

Working with layer comps

Next, you'll save this configuration as a layer comp. Layer comps let you easily switch between various combinations of layers and effects within the same Photoshop file. A layer comp is a snapshot of a state of the Layers panel.

1   Choose Window > Layer Comps.

2   At the bottom of the Layer Comps panel, click the New Layer Comp button. Name the new layer comp **Black Box**, and type a description of its appearance in the Comment box: **3D box, black top and side shape with full-color art**. Click OK.

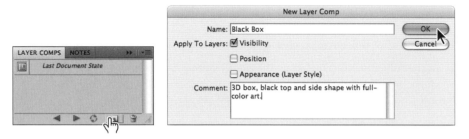

Now you'll make some changes and save the new look as a different layer comp.

3   In the Layers panel, hide the Black Box and Shape Art layers, and show the Full Art layer.

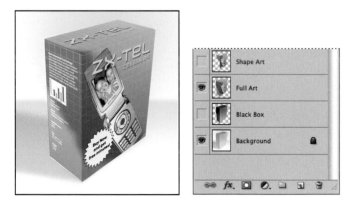

You'll save this version as a new layer comp.

4 In the Layer Comps panel, click the New Layer Comp button. Type **Full Image**, and enter a description: **3D box, blue top with full-color art**. Click OK.

5 In the Layer Comps panel, toggle the visibility icons to show and hide your two layer comps and view the differences.

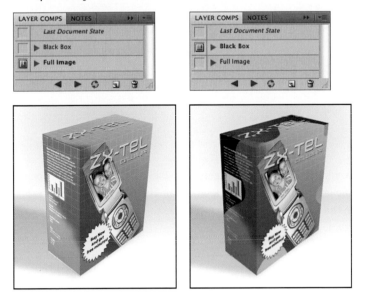

You can also use layer comps to record the layer position in the document or the layer appearance, including layer styles and blending modes.

6 Choose File > Save to save your work.

Managing layers

With layer comps, you learned a great way to present different design options for a package. It is also helpful to be able to group your layers by content. You'll organize your type and art elements by creating a separate group for each.

1 In the Layers panel, Control-click (Windows) or Command-click (Mac OS) to select the special offer, side box copy, and ZX-Tel logo layers.

2 From the Layers panel menu, choose New Group From Layers. Type **Box Type** for the name, and click OK.

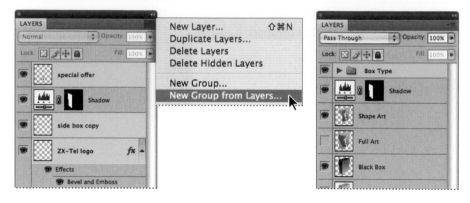

3 Select the Shadow adjustment layer, and then Shift-click the Full Art layer to select them and the layer (Shape Art) between them. Then, choose New Group From Layers from the Layers panel menu, and name this group **Box Artwork**. Then click OK.

Layer groups help you organize and manage individual layers. You can expand a layer group to view its layers, or collapse the group to simplify your view. You can change the stacking order of layers within a layer group.

4 Hide each layer group to see how the layers are grouped together. Then show the layer groups again.

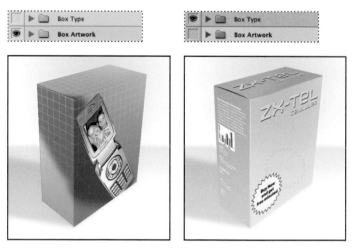

Layer groups can function like layers in a number of ways. You can select, duplicate, and move entire groups, as well as apply attributes and masks to the entire layer group. Any changes you make at the group level apply to all the layers within the group.

Flattening a layered image

As you've done in previous lessons of this book, you'll now flatten the layered image. When you flatten a file, all layers are merged into a single background, greatly reducing the size of the file. If you plan to send a file out for proofs, it's a good idea to save two versions of the file—one containing all the layers so that you can edit the file if necessary, and one flattened version to send to the print shop.

1   First, note the values in the lower left corner of the image or application window. If the display does not show the file size (such as "Doc: 5.01M/43M"), click the arrow and choose Show > Document Sizes.

The first number is the printing size of the image, which is about the size that the saved, flattened file would be in Adobe Photoshop format. The number on the right indicates the approximate document size of the file as it is now, including layers and channels.

2   Choose Image > Duplicate, name the duplicate file **09Final.psd**, and click OK.

3   From the Layers panel menu, choose Flatten Image. Click OK when prompted to discard hidden layers.

The layers for the 09Final.psd file are combined onto a single background layer. Now the file sizes in the lower-left area of the work area are similar to the smaller number that you saw earlier. Note that flattening fills transparent areas with white.

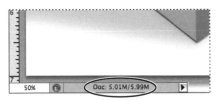

4   Choose Edit > Undo Flatten Image.

You'll try another way to merge layers and reduce the file size.

Merging layers and layer groups

Unlike flattening a layered image, merging layers allows you to select which layers to flatten or leave unflattened.

You'll merge all the elements of the box, while keeping the Box Type layer group and Background layer untouched. This way, you could return to the file and reuse the Background and Box Type layers at any time.

1   In the Layers panel, hide the Box Type layer group to hide all of its layers.

2   Select the Box Artwork layer group in the Layers panel.

3   Choose Layer > Merge Visible. Any layers that aren't visible in the layer group will remain, unmerged, in the Layers panel.

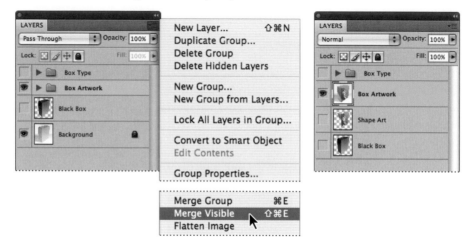

4   Choose Edit > Undo Merge Visible.

You'll try another way to merge layers and reduce the file size.

Stamping layers

You can combine the benefits of flattening an image while keeping some layers intact by stamping the layers. Stamping flattens two or more layers and places the flattened image into a new layer, while leaving other layers intact. This is useful if you need to use a flattened image but also need to keep some layers intact for your work.

1   In the Layers panel, select the Box Artwork group.

2 Press Alt (Windows) or Option (Mac OS) while you choose Layer > Merge Group. The Layers panel displays a new layer that includes your merged image. To reduce the file size, you could delete the original layers from the file.

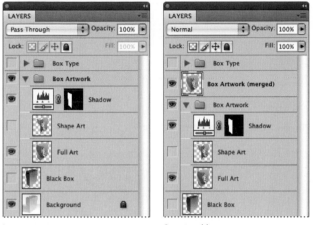

Layer group   Stamped layer

3 Choose File > Save. In the Save As dialog box that appears, click Save to save the file in Photoshop format. Click OK if the Photoshop Format Options dialog box appears.

You've created a three-dimensional composite image and explored multiple ways to save final artwork.

Review questions

1   Why would you use layer groups?

2   How can you clip a layer to a shape?

3   How do adjustment layers work, and what is the benefit of using them?

4   What are layer styles, and why would you use them?

5   What is the difference between flattening, merging, and stamping layers?

Review answers

1   Layer groups let you organize and manage layers. For example, you can move all the layers in a layer group and then apply attributes or a mask to the entire group.

2   Position the layer you want to clip above the layer you want to use as a clipping path. Select the first layer, and then press Alt or Option as you position the pointer between the layers, and click. The clipped layer is indented, with an arrow pointing down to the clipping path layer.

3   An adjustment layer applies color and tonal adjustments without changing the underlying pixels. You can show or hide, edit, delete, or mask adjustment layers without permanently affecting the image.

4   Layer styles are customizable effects that you can apply to layers. You can use them to apply changes to a layer, and you can modify or remove them at any time.

5   Flattening an image merges all layers into a single background, greatly reducing the size of the file. Merging layers lets you choose which layers to flatten; this technique combines all selected or visible layers in one layer. Stamping combines the benefits of flattening an image with the benefits of keeping some layers intact; it flattens two or more layers and places the flattened image into a new layer, while leaving other layers intact.

10 ADVANCED COMPOSITING

Lesson overview

In this lesson, you'll learn how to do the following:

- Add guides to help you place and align images precisely.

- Save selections and load them as masks.

- Apply color effects only to unmasked areas of an image.

- Apply filters to selections to create various effects.

- Add layer styles to create editable special effects.

- Record and play back an action to automate a series of steps.

- Blend images to create a panorama.

 This lesson will take about 90 minutes to complete. Copy the Lesson10 folder onto your hard drive if you haven't already done so. As you work on this lesson, you'll preserve the start files. If you need to restore the start files, copy them from the *Adobe Photoshop CS4 Classroom in a Book* CD.

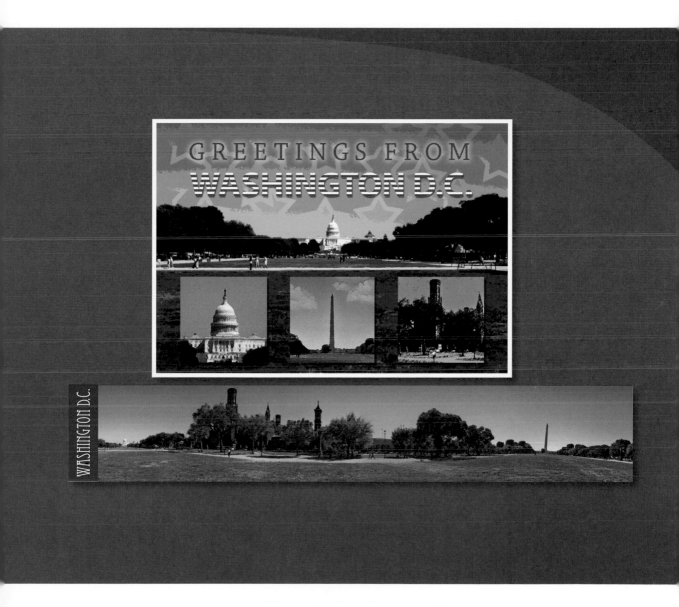

Filters can transform ordinary images into extraordinary digital artwork. Choose from filters that blur, bend, sharpen, or fragment images, or that simulate a traditional artistic medium, such as watercolor. You can also use adjustment layers and painting modes to vary the look of your artwork.

Getting started

In this lesson, you'll create souvenirs from a vacation to Washington, D.C. You'll assemble a montage of images for a postcard, and then stitch together a panorama to create a poster. First, look at the final projects to see what you'll be creating.

1   Start Photoshop and then immediately hold down Ctrl+Alt+Shift (Windows) or Command+Option+Shift (Mac OS) to restore the default preferences. (See "Restoring default preferences" on page 4.)

2   When prompted, click Yes to confirm that you want to reset preferences.

3   Click the Launch Bridge button (![Br icon]) in the application bar to open Adobe Bridge.

4   In the Favorites panel in the upper-left corner of Bridge, click the Lessons folder, and then double-click the Lesson10 folder in the Content panel.

5   View the 10A_End.psd thumbnail in the Content panel. If necessary, move the thumbnail slider to increase the size of the thumbnail so that you can see the image clearly.

This file is a postcard that comprises four photos. Each image has had a specific filter or effect applied to it.

6   View the 10B_End.psd thumbnail.

This file is a poster with a panoramic image and text. You'll create the postcard first.

7   Double-click the 10A_Start.jpg thumbnail to open the file in Photoshop.

Assembling a montage of images

The postcard is a montage of four different images. You'll crop each image, and add them as separate layers to a composite image. Using guides, you'll align the images precisely without much effort. Before you make additional changes to the images, you'll add the text and apply effects to it.

Opening and cropping the images

The images you'll use in the insets are larger than you need, so you'll crop them before combining them in a composite file. Cropping images involves aesthetic choices about where and how much of the image to crop. The 10A_Start.jpg file is already open, so you'll start with it.

1   Select the Crop tool (⊟). In the options bar, enter **500 px** for the Width and **500 px** for the Height. Enter **300** ppi for the Resolution.

The crop box will be a fixed size of 500 pixels by 500 pixels.

2   Drag a crop box around the right side of the image, so that the Smithsonian Institution is the focus of the cropped area. You can use the Right Arrow and Left Arrow keys on your keyboard to nudge the crop box into position if necessary.

● **Note:** Be sure to enter 500 pixels, not 500 inches!

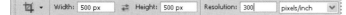

3   When you are satisfied with the crop area, double-click inside the crop area, or press Enter or Return to apply it.

Because you're working with several files, you'll give the 10A_Start.jpg file a descriptive name so that it will be easy to identify. You'll also save the file in the Photoshop format, because each time you edit and then resave a JPEG file, its quality degrades.

4   Choose File > Save As, choose Photoshop for the Format, and save the cropped image as **Museum.psd** in the Lesson10 folder.

5   Choose File > Open, navigate to the Lesson10 folder, and select the Capitol_Building.jpg and Washington_Monument.jpg files. (Control-click or Command-click to select discontiguous files.) Then, click Open.

The image files open in Photoshop, each with its own tab.

6   Select the Washington_Monument.jpg file, and choose File > Save As. Choose Photoshop for the Format, and rename the file **Monument.psd**. Then, click Save.

7   Select the Capitol_Building.jpg tab. Choose File > Save As, choose Photoshop for the Format, and rename the file **Capitol.psd**. Then, click Save.

8   Follow steps 1–3 to crop the Capitol.psd and Monument.psd files. Then, save each file.

Cropped versions of Museum.psd, Capitol.psd, and Monument.psd

9   Choose File > Open, navigate to the Lesson10 folder, and double-click the Background.jpg file to open it in Photoshop.

10 Choose File > Save As. Choose Photoshop for the Format, and rename the file **10A_Working.psd**. Then, click Save.

Leave all four files open for the next exercise.

Positioning images using guides

Guides are nonprinting lines that help you align elements in your document, either horizontally or vertically. If you choose a Snap To command, the guides behave like magnets: When you drag an object close to a guide and then release the mouse button, the object snaps into place along the guide. You'll add guides to the background image that you'll use as the basis for the composite.

1   Click the Show Extras button (▣) in the application bar, and choose Show Rulers. Rulers appear along the top and left edges of the window.

2   Choose Window > Info to open the Info panel.

3   From the horizontal ruler, drag a guide to the middle of the image, and release the mouse when the Y coordinate value in the Info panel is 3.000 inches. A blue guide line appears across the image.

● **Note:** If the ruler units are marked in a unit other than inches, right-click or Control+click a ruler, and choose Inches from the context menu.

 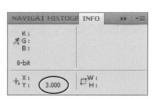

4   Drag another guide, this time from the vertical ruler, and release the mouse when X = 3.000 inches.

▶ **Tip:** If you need to adjust a ruler guide, use the Move tool.

5   Choose View > Snap To, and make sure Guides is selected.

6   Drag another guide from the vertical ruler to the middle of the image. Though you could move it further, it snaps into place at the exact midpoint of the image.

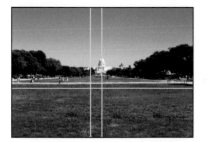

7   Click the Arrange Documents button (▣) on the application bar, and select the Tile All In Grid option. All four images are visible, each in its own window.

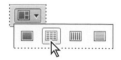

8 Select the Move tool (⤧), and then drag the Museum.psd image onto the 10A_Working.psd image. Photoshop places the Museum.psd image on its own layer in the 10A_Working.psd file.

9 Drag the Monument.psd and Capitol.psd images onto the 10A_Working.psd file.

10 Close the Monument.psd, Capitol.psd, and Museum.psd files without saving them.

11 Rename the layers in the Layers panel to correspond with the appropriate images: **Musuem**, **Monument**, and **Capitol**. If you dragged them in the order listed above, rename Layer 1 **Museum**, Layer 2 **Monument**, and Layer 3 **Capitol**.

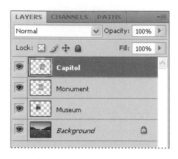

12 Select the Monument layer, and then select the Move tool (⤧) in the Tools panel. Move the Monument layer to the center of the canvas, with its top edge aligned to the horizontal guide.

13 Select the Capitol layer, and then drag it to the left of the monument so that the top of the image snaps onto the horizontal guide. Space it evenly between the image of the monument and the left edge of the postcard. Do the same for the Museum layer, placing it to the right of the monument image.

14 Choose View > Show > Guides to hide the guides. Then, choose View > Rulers to hide them.

15 Choose File > Save to save your work so far. Click OK if the Photoshop Format Options dialog box appears.

Extra Credit

It was easy to align the images using centered guides, but for greater precision, Smart Guides are an excellent way to align photos and objects. Using your working file as it is after the "Positioning images using guides" exercise, you can try another way to align these photos; or continue with the lesson and try this technique some other time.

1   Select the Museum layer in the Layers panel. In the image window, use the Move tool to move the image out of alignment.

2   Choose View > Show > Smart Guides.

3   Using the Move tool, drag the Museum image in the image window to align its top edge with the top edge of the monument

4   Choose View > Show > Smart Guides to hide the Smart Guides.

Adding text to a montage

You'll add text to the postcard, and then apply some effects to it.

1   Select the Text tool (T). Then, click in the sky area and type **Greetings From**. Click the Commit Edits button in the options bar to accept the text. Photoshop creates a new text layer.

2   With the Greetings From text layer selected, choose Window > Character, and
    then enter the following settings in the Character panel:

    • Font: Chapparal Pro, Regular

    • Font size: **36 pt**

    • Tracking: **220**

    • Color: Red

    • All Caps (**TT**)

    • Anti-Aliasing: smooth

3   Select the Move tool (▶⊕), and then move the text across the center of the top
    of the canvas. It snaps into place when it's centered even though the guides are
    hidden because Snap To Guides is still selected.

4   Select the Text tool again, click on the canvas, and type **Washington, D.C.** Then,
    click the Commit Edits button.

Photoshop used the current settings in the Character panel for the new text.

5   Enter the following settings in the Character panel:

    • Font: Myriad Pro, Bold

    • Font Size: **48 pt**

    • Tracking: **0**

    • Color: White

(Leave All Caps selected, and Anti-Aliasing set to smooth.)

6 Use the Move tool to drag the Washington, D.C. text to the center of the canvas, just below the other text.

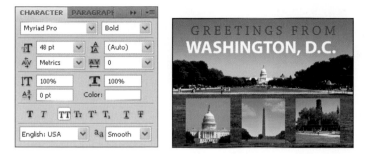

7 Select the Greetings From text layer in the Layers panel. Click the Add A Layer Style button (*fx*) at the bottom of the Layers panel, and choose Outer Glow.

8 Apply these settings in the Outer Glow area of the Layer Style dialog box:

- Blend Mode: Screen
- Opacity: **40**%
- Color: White
- Spread: **14**%
- Size: **40** px

9 Click OK to accept the layer style.

10 In the Tools panel, click the Foreground Color swatch, and then select red from the Color Picker dialog box. Click OK.

You'll use the foreground color to create stripes in the lower text.

11 Select the Washington, D.C. text layer, click the Add A Layer Style button (*fx*), and choose Gradient Overlay.

12 In the Gradient Overlay area of the Layer Style dialog box, click the arrow next to the Gradient swatch to open the Gradient pop-up menu. Select the gradient that looks like red and transparent stripes (the last one in the menu). You'll use the defaults for the other settings.

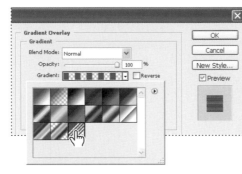

13 Click Drop Shadow in the list on the left to add another effect to the same text. In the Drop Shadow area of the dialog box, change the Opacity to **45**% and the Distance to **9** px. Leave the other settings unchanged.

14 Click OK to apply the effects and close the Layer Style dialog box. Then, choose File > Save to save your work so far.

Applying filters

Photoshop includes many filters for creating special effects. The best way to learn about them is to test different filters with various options on your files. You can use the Filter Gallery to preview a filter's effect on your image without committing to it.

You've used filters in some earlier lessons. In this lesson, you'll apply the Graphic Pen filter to the museum image for a hand-sketched effect.

Improving performance with filters

Some filter effects can be memory-intensive, especially when applied to a high-resolution image. You can use these techniques to improve performance:

- Test filters and settings on a small portion of an image.

- Apply the effect to individual channels—for example, to each RGB channel—if the image is large and you're having problems with insufficient memory. (Note, however, that some filters may produce different results when you apply them to individual channels rather than the composite image, especially if the filter randomly modifies pixels.)

- Free up memory before running the filter by using the Purge commands (in the Edit menu).

- Close other open applications to free more memory for Photoshop. If you're using Mac OS, allocate more RAM to Photoshop.

- Try changing settings to improve the speed of memory-intensive filters such as Lighting Effects, Cutout, Stained Glass, Chrome, Ripple, Spatter, Sprayed Strokes, and Glass filters. For example, with the Stained Glass filter, you might increase cell size. With the Cutout filter, try increasing Edge Simplicity, decreasing Edge Fidelity, or both.

- If you plan to print to a grayscale printer, convert a copy of the image to grayscale before applying filters. However, applying a filter to a color image and then converting to grayscale may not have the same effect as applying the filter to a grayscale version of the image.

1 Select the Museum layer in the Layers panel.

2 In the Tools panel, click the Default Foreground And Background Colors button to return the foreground color to black.

The Graphic Pen filter uses the foreground color.

3 Choose Filter > Filter Gallery.

The Filter Gallery includes a preview window, lists of available filters, and the settings for the selected filter. This is a great place to test filter settings on your image before you decide which settings to apply.

4 Click the triangle next to Sketch to expand the section. Then, select Graphic Pen. The image preview immediately changes to reflect the default values for that filter.

5 In the rightmost pane, set the Light/Dark Balance to **25**. Leave the other options at their default settings. (Stroke Length should be 15, and the Stroke Direction should be Right Diagonal.) The preview updates.

6 Click OK to apply the filter and close the Filter Gallery.

7 Choose File > Save to save your work so far.

Using filters

As you consider which filter to use and the effect it might have, keep in mind the following:

- The last filter chosen appears at the top of the Filter menu.

- Filters are applied to the active, visible layer.

- Filters cannot be applied to bitmap-mode or indexed-color images.

- Some filters work only on RGB images.

- Some filters are processed entirely in RAM.

- To apply more than one filter in the Filter Gallery, click the New Filter button at the bottom of the filters list, and then select a filter.

- See "Using filters" in Photoshop Help for a list of filters that can be used with 16- and 32-bit-per-channel images.

- Photoshop Help provides specific information on individual filters.

Julieanne Kost is an official Adobe Photoshop evangelist.

Tool tips from the Photoshop evangelist

Using filter shortcuts

These powerful shortcuts can save time when working with filters:

- To reapply the most recently used filter with its last values, press Ctrl+F (Windows) or Command+F (Mac OS).

- To display the dialog box for the last filter you applied, press Ctrl+Alt+F (Windows) or Command+Option+F (Mac OS).

- To reduce the effect of the last filter you applied, press Ctrl+Shift+F (Windows) or Command+Shift+F (Mac OS).

Hand-coloring selections on a layer

Before the days of color photography, artists painted color onto black-and-white images. You can create the same effect by hand-coloring selections on a layer. In this exercise, you'll hand-color the museum image, and then add stars to the sky in the background image.

Applying painting effects

You'll use different brushes, with varying opacities and blending modes, to add color to the sky, grass, and building in the museum image.

1   In the Layers panel, Control-click (Windows) or Command-click (Mac OS) the image thumbnail on the Museum layer. The contents of the layer are selected.

You can paint only within the selection, so you don't need to worry about painting the background image or the other images. Just make sure you see the selection border around the image before you start painting.

▶ **Tip:** You can change the brush opacity by pressing a number on the keypad from 0 to 9 (where 1 is 10%, 9 is 90%, and 0 is 100%).

2   Zoom into the museum image so that you can see it clearly.

3   Select the Brush tool (🖌). In the options bar, select a **90**-pixel brush with a Hardness of **0**. Select Darken from the Mode menu. Set the brush opacity to **20**%.

4   Click the Foreground Color swatch in the Tools panel, and select a color of bright blue (not too light). You'll use this color to paint the sky.

5   Paint the sky in the museum image. Because the opacity is set to 20%, you can paint over the same area again to darken it. Don't be afraid to paint near the borders; nothing outside the image border is affected by the paintbrush. You can change the brush size and opacity as you paint; for example, you may need a smaller brush to paint the areas between tree tops. If you make a mistake, press Ctrl+Z (Windows) or Command+Z (Mac OS) to undo it. But remember that you're going for a handpainted look; it doesn't need to be perfect.

▶ **Tip:** To change the brush size as you paint, press the bracket keys on your keyboard. The Left Bracket key ([) decreases the brush size; the Right Bracket (]) increases it.

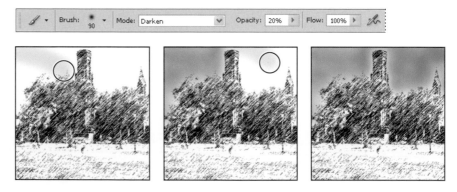

6 Paint the trees and grass the same way. Change the foreground color to green, and then set up a **70**-pixel soft brush, using the Darken blending mode, and **80%** opacity. It's fine to paint over the black sketched areas; only the white areas show much color.

▶ **Tip:** When hand-coloring an image, work from the background forward, so that you can overpaint any stray marks.

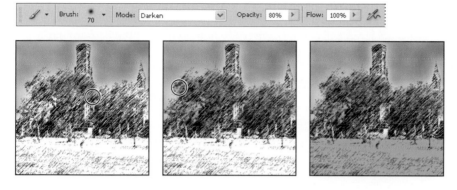

7 Next, paint the museum façade a dark red color. Start with a **40**-pixel brush, using the Lighten blending mode, and **80%** opacity.

Using the Lighten blending mode affects the black lines rather than the white areas.

8 When you're satisfied with the painting, choose Select > Deselect to deselect the image. Then, choose File > Save to save your work.

Saving selections

In order to fill the background sky with handpainted stars, you need to save a selection of the sky. First, you'll save the background image as a Smart Object so that you can apply Smart Filters to it later.

1   In the Layers panel, right-click (Windows) or Control-click (Mac OS) the Background layer, and choose Convert To Smart Object. (The Background layer is at the bottom of the layer stack.)

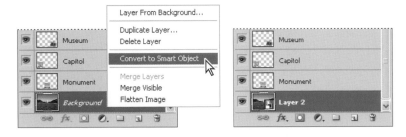

The layer name changes to Layer 2. An icon appears in the layer thumbnail, indicating that the layer is now a Smart Object. Filters, called *Smart Filters*, are applied to Smart Objects nondestructively, so that you can continue to edit them later.

2   Rename Layer 2 **Capitol and Mall**.

3   Double-click the image thumbnail on the Capitol and Mall layer; click OK in the informational message.

The Smart Object opens in its own image window. You can edit it without affecting any other objects.

4   Select the Quick Selection tool (🖌) and then use it to select the sky. If you need to remove an area of the selection, click the Subtract From Selection button in the options bar, and then click the area you need to deselect. Don't worry about making the selection perfect.

For help using the Quick Selection tool and other selection tools, see Lesson 3, "Working with Selections."

5 With the sky selected, click Refine Edge in the options bar. Change the following settings, and click OK:

- Smooth: **25**

- Feather: **30**

- Contract/Expand: **-20**

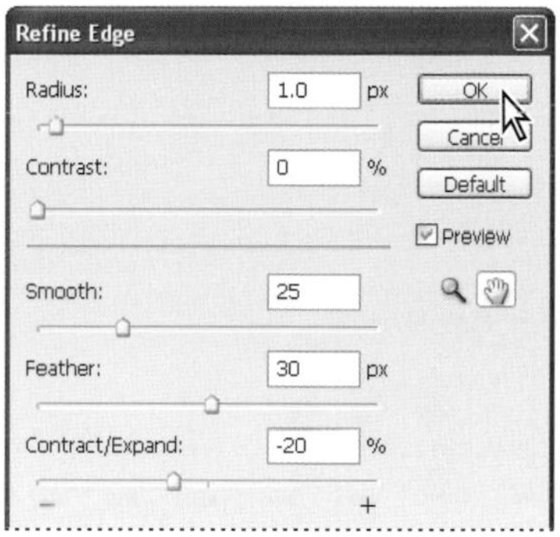

These settings will feather the edge of the skyline so that the selection will not have a hard edge.

6 Choose Select > Save Selection. In the Save Selection dialog box, name the selection **Sky**, and click OK.

7 Choose Select > Deselect.

Painting with a special effects brush

You'll add stars to the sky you just selected, using a star-shaped brush.

1 Press D to restore the default foreground and background colors to the Tools panel. Then press X to switch them, so that white is the foreground color.

You'll paint white stars on the sky, so the foreground color needs to be white.

2 Select the Brush tool (✐). In the options bar, open the Brush Preset picker.

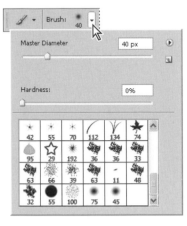

3 Scroll down in the Brush Preset picker and select the Star brush. Increase its size to **300** pixels, choose Normal from the Mode menu, and select **100%** opacity.

Now that you have your brush set up, you need to load the selection you saved.

4 Choose Select > Load Selection. In the Load Selection dialog box, choose Sky from the Channel menu, and click OK.

5 In the Layers panel, click the New Layer button. Rename the layer **Paint**.

6 Paint stars in the sky. You can paint near the edges, because only the selection will be affected. Just make sure the selection remains active.

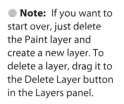
● **Note:** If you want to start over, just delete the Paint layer and create a new layer. To delete a layer, drag it to the Delete Layer button in the Layers panel.

7 When you are satisfied with the arrangement of the stars, change the Opacity of the Paint layer to **50**% in the Layers panel. Then, in the Layers panel, choose Overlay from the Blending Mode menu.

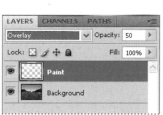

8 Choose File > Save, and then close the Smart Object. When Photoshop returns you to the 10A_Working.psd image, choose View > Fit On Screen so you can see the entire postcard.

The stars have been added to your postcard. You can edit the stars at any time by double-clicking the image thumbnail in the Layers panel to open the Smart Object.

9 Choose File > Save to save your work.

Applying Smart Filters

Unlike regular filters, which permanently change an image, Smart Filters are non-destructive: they can be adjusted, turned off and on, and deleted. However, you can apply Smart Filters only to a Smart Object.

You already converted the Capitol and Mall layer to a Smart Object. You'll apply several Smart Filters to the layer, and then add some layer styles.

1 Select the Capitol and Mall layer in the Layers panel. Then, choose Filter > Artistic > Cutout.

Photoshop opens the Filter Gallery, with the Cutout filter selected and applied to the preview. The Cutout filter makes an image appear as if it were constructed from roughly cut pieces of colored paper.

2 On the right side of the dialog box, change the Number of Levels to **8**, leave Edge Simplicity at **4**, and move the Edge Fidelity slider to **3**. Then, click OK.

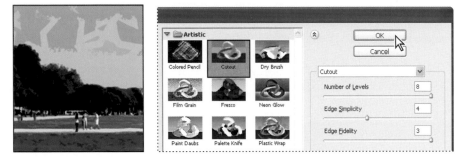

Smart Filters appear with the Smart Object in the Layers panel. An icon appears to the right of a layer name if filter effects are applied to a layer.

3 Double-click the Cutout filter in the Layers panel to open the Filter Gallery again. Click the New Effect Layer button at the bottom of the applied filters list, and then select any filter. Experiment with the settings until you're satisfied, but don't click OK yet.

We chose Film Grain from the Artistic folder, and used the following settings: Grain 2, Highlight Area 6, and Intensity 1.

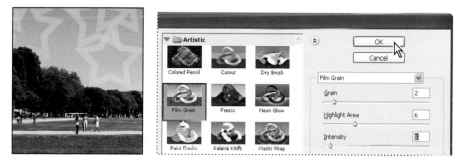

You can mix and match Smart Filters and turn them off and on.

4 In the applied filters list in the Filter Gallery, drag the Cutout filter above the second filter you applied to see how the effect changes. Click OK to close the Filter Gallery.

The order in which you apply filters can change the effect. You can also hide an effect by clicking the eye icon (👁) next to its name in the filter list.

You'll use filters to give the other inset images a handpainted look without going to all the trouble of painting them manually. First, you'll convert them to Smart Objects.

5 Select the Capitol layer, and then choose Filter > Convert For Smart Filters. Click OK in the informational dialog box. The Capitol layer is now a Smart Object.

6 Select the Monument layer, and choose Filter > Convert For Smart Filters to convert it to a Smart Object, too.

7 Select the Capitol layer, and then choose Filter > Filter Gallery, and select a filter you like. Experiment with the settings until you find an effect you like. Then click OK to apply the filter.

We chose the Crosshatch filter (in the Brush Strokes folder), with a Stroke Length of 12, Sharpness of 9, and Strength of 1.

8 Select the Monument layer, and choose Filter > Filter Gallery. Select a filter you like, and then click OK to apply it.

You can apply almost any filter, including third-party filters, as a Smart Filter. The only exceptions are the Extract, Liquify, Pattern Maker, and Vanishing Point filters, because those require access to the original image pixels. In addition to filters, you can apply the Shadows/Highlights and Variations adjustments to Smart Objects.

9 Choose File > Save to save your work.

Adding drop shadows and a border

You're almost done with the postcard. To make the inset images stand out a little more, you'll add drop shadows to them. Then, you'll add a border around the entire postcard.

1 Select the Capitol layer, and click the Add A Layer Style button (*fx*) at the bottom of the Layers panel. Choose Drop Shadow.

2 In the Layer Style dialog box, change the Opacity to **40**%, Distance to **15** px, Spread to **9**%, and the Size to **9** px. Then, click OK.

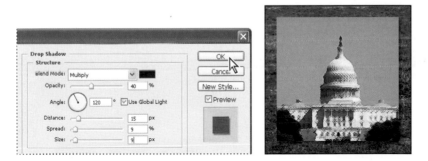

3 In the Layers panel, press Alt (Windows) or Option (Mac OS) as you drag the Drop Shadow effect from the Capitol layer onto the Monument layer.

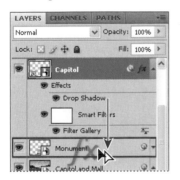

4 Alt-drag or Option-drag the same Drop Shadow effect onto the Museum layer.

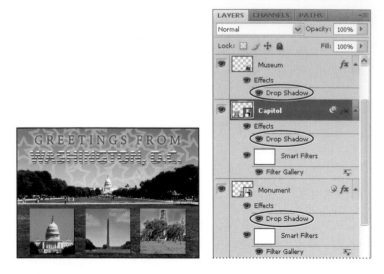

Now you'll expand the canvas so that you can add a border without covering any of your image.

5 Choose Image > Canvas Size, and enter **7** inches for the Width and **5** inches for the Height. Click OK.

A transparent border appears around the image. You'll make that border appear white.

6 Press D to return the foreground and background colors to the defaults in the Tools panel, so that the background layer is white.

7 In the Layers panel, click the Create A New Layer button, and then drag the new layer to the bottom of the layer stack. Name it **Border**.

8 With the Border layer selected, choose Select > All.

9 Choose Edit > Fill. In the Fill dialog box, choose Background Color from the Use menu, and click OK.

10 Choose File > Save to save the postcard.

The postcard is ready to print and mail. It's a standard U.S. Postal Service postcard size.

11 Close the 10A_Working.psd file. You'll use different files to create the panorama.

Matching color schemes across images

You'll be combining four images into a panorama for the poster. To provide continuity in the panorama, you'll harmonize the color schemes in the images by matching the target image to the dominant colors in a source. First, you'll open the document that you'll use as the source for the color matching.

1   In Photoshop, choose File > Open. Navigate to the Lesson10 folder, and double-click the IMG_1441.psd file to open it.

There are four sequentially numbered images in the same folder. You'll match the colors for these files.

2   Choose File > Open, navigate to the Lesson10 folder, and double-click the IMG_1442.psd file to open it.

The IMG_1442.psd file is overexposed in some areas, and a little washed out. You'll use the Match Color feature to match its colors to those in the source file.

3   With IMG_1442.psd active, choose Image > Adjustments > Match Color. In the Match Color dialog box, do the following:

   • Select the Preview option, if it is not already selected.

   • Choose IMG_1441.psd from the Source menu.

   • Choose the Background layer from the Layer menu. You can select any layer in the source image, but this image has only one layer.

- Experiment with the Luminance, Color Intensity, and Fade settings.
- When the color scheme unifies the colors in the images, click OK.

4 Choose File > Save to save the IMG_1442.psd file with the new colors.

You can use Match Color with any source file to create interesting and unusual effects. The Match Color feature is also useful for certain color corrections (such as skin tones) in some photographs. The feature can also match the color between different layers in the same image. See Photoshop Help for more information.

Automating a multistep task

An *action* is a set of one or more commands that you record and then play back to apply to a single file or a batch of files. In this exercise, you'll use actions to color match, sharpen, and save the images you'll combine in a panorama.

Using actions is one of several ways that you can automate tasks in Adobe Photoshop. To learn more about recording actions, see Photoshop Help.

You've already matched the color for one of the images. Now, you'll sharpen one image using the Unsharp Mask filter and save it to a new Ready For Panorama folder.

1   With the IMG_1442.psd file active, choose
    Filter > Sharpen > Unsharp Mask.

2   In the Unsharp Mask dialog box, change
    the Radius to **1.2**, and leave the other
    settings unchanged, and click OK.

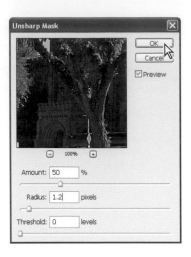

3   Choose File > Save As. Choose TIFF for the Format, use the same name
    (IMG_1442), and save it to a new folder called Ready For Panorama. Then, click
    Save.

4   In the Image Compression area of the TIFF Options dialog box, select LZW, and
    click OK.

5   Close the IMG_1442.tif file.

Preparing to record an action

You use the Actions panel to record, play, edit, and delete individual actions. You also use the Actions panel to save and load action files. First, you'll open the Actions panel and open the additional files you'll be using.

1   Choose Window > Workspace > Automation to display the Automation workspace.

The Actions panel is prominent in this workspace, as is the Layers panel.

2   In the Actions panel, click the Create New Set button (📁). Name the new set **My Actions**, and click OK.

3   Choose File > Open. In the Open dialog box, navigate to the Lesson10 folder. Shift-select the IMG_1443.psd, IMG_1444.psd, IMG_1445.psd, and IMG_1446. psd files. Then, click Open.

Now there are five tabs, representing five open files in Photoshop.

Recording actions

You'll record the steps for matching colors, sharpening, and saving the images as an action.

1   Select the IMG_1443.psd tab. Then, in the Actions panel, click the New Action button (🔲).

2   In the New Action dialog box, name the action **color match and sharpen**, and make sure that My Actions is selected in the Set menu. Then click Record.

> **Note:** You must finish all steps in this procedure without interruption. If you need to start over, skip ahead to step 8 to stop the recording; then drag the action onto the Delete button in the Actions panel. Use the History panel to delete any states after you opened the files. Then start again at step 1.

Don't let the fact that you're recording rush you. Take all the time you need to do this procedure accurately. The speed at which you work has no influence on the amount of time required to play a recorded action.

3   Choose Image > Adjustments > Match Color.

4 In the Match Color dialog box, select IMG_1441.psd from the Source menu, select Background from the Layer menu, and make any other changes that you made when you matched color for IMG_1442.psd. Click OK.

5 Choose Filter > Sharpen > Unsharp Mask. The settings in the Unsharp Mask dialog box should be the settings you used for the IMG_1442.psd file. Click OK.

Photoshop preserves your most recent settings in filter dialog boxes until you change them again.

6 Choose File > Save As. In the Save As dialog box, choose TIFF for the Format, keep the same name (IMG_1443), and save the file to the Ready For Panorama folder. Click Save. In the TIFF Options dialog box, make sure LZW is selected, and click OK.

7 Close the image.

8 Click the Stop button (■) at the bottom of the Actions panel to stop recording.

The action you just recorded is now saved in the Actions panel. Click the arrows to expand different sets of steps. You can examine each recorded step and the specific selections you made.

Playing an action

You'll apply the color match and sharpen action to one of the other three image files that you opened.

1 Click the IMG_1444.psd tab to make that image active.

2 In the Actions panel, select the color match and sharpen action in the My Actions set, and then click the Play button (▶).

The IMG_1444.psd image is automatically color matched, sharpened and saved as a TIFF so that it now matches the IMG_1443.tif image for these properties. Because you recorded closing the file, the file has also been closed.

Batch-playing an action

Applying actions is a time-saving process for performing routine tasks on files, but you can streamline your work even further by applying actions to all open files. Two more files in this project need to be prepared for the panorama, so you'll apply your automated action to them simultaneously.

● **Note:** If the IMG_1441.psd file is not the third tab, it will close before the color can be matched for one or both of the other images. Match Color requires that the source file be open.

1   Make sure that the IMG_1445.psd and IMG_1446.psd files are open. Close the IMG_1441.psd file, and then open it again to ensure that it is the third tab.

2   Choose File > Automate > Batch.

3   In the Play area of the Batch dialog box, choose My Actions from the Set menu, and choose color match and sharpen from the Action menu.

4   Choose Opened Files from the Source menu. Leave Destination set to None, and click OK.

The action is applied to both IMG_1445.psd and IMG_1446.psd, so the files have the same color matching and sharpening and are saved as TIFF files. The same action was applied to IMG_1441.psd, even though its color was matched with itself.

In this exercise, you batch-processed three files instead of making all the same changes in each of them; this was a mild convenience. But creating and applying actions can save significant amounts of time and tedium when you have dozens or even hundreds of files that require any routine, repetitive work.

Stitching a panorama

The files have been color matched, sharpened, and saved to prevent unsightly inconsistencies in your panorama. Now you're ready to stitch the images together! Then, you'll add a border with lettering to complete the poster.

1 With no files open in Photoshop, choose File > Automate > Photomerge.

2 In the Layout area, select Auto. Then, in the Source Files area, click Browse and navigate to the Lesson10/Ready For Panorama folder. Select the first image, then press Shift and select the last so that all the images are selected, and click Open.

3 At the bottom of the Photomerge dialog box, select Blend Images Together, Vignette Removal, and Geometric Distortion Correction. Then, click OK.

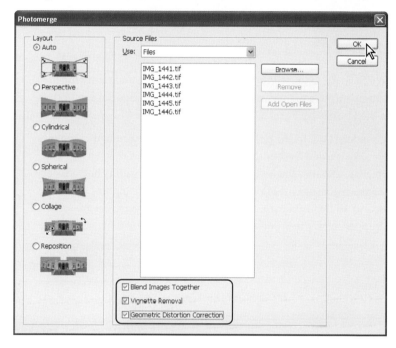

Photoshop creates the panorama image. It's a complex process, so you may have to wait several minutes while Photoshop works. When it is finished, you should see an image that looks similar to the one below, with six layers in the Layers panel: one for each of the images. Photoshop has found the overlapping areas of the images and matched them, correcting any angular discrepancies. In the process, it left some empty areas. You'll make the panorama tidy by adding a little sky to fill in some of the empty area, and by cropping the image.

4 Select all the layers in the Layers panel, and then choose Layer > Merge Layers.

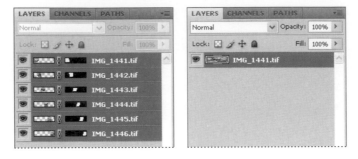

5 Choose File > Save As. Choose Photoshop for the Format, and name the file **10B_Working.psd**. Save the file in the Lesson10 folder. Click Save, and then click OK in the Photoshop Format Options dialog box.

6 Select the Crop tool (⌗). In the options bar, click Clear to remove any values in the Height, Width, and Resolution boxes so that you can crop to any size. Then draw a crop selection from the edge of the grass (where its bottom edge is highest) to the highest point of the image (just above the highest museum tower). Crop out all the transparent areas on the sides. When you are satisfied with your cropped area, press Enter or Return.

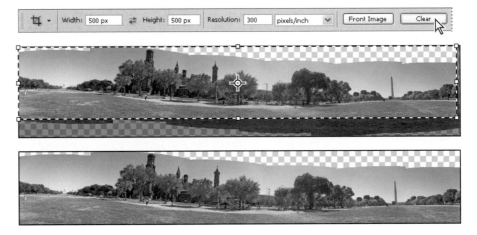

7 In the Layers panel, click the Create A New Layer button (⬚).

8 Select the Rectangular Marquee tool ([]), and then draw a selection across the top of the image, where you want to add sky. It's fine to overlap trees and buildings; just make to cover all of the transparent areas (represented by a checkerboard pattern).

9 Select the Eyedropper tool ( ), and then select a dark blue from the sky for your foreground color. Select a light blue color for the background color.

10 With the selection still active, select the Gradient tool ([]). In the options bar, select the Foreground To Background gradient in the Gradient preset picker. Then, drag the gradient tool vertically from the top to the bottom of the selection.

11 Choose Select > Deselect. Then, select both layers in the Layers panel, and choose Edit > Auto-Blend Layers. In the Blend Method area, select Panorama, and click OK.

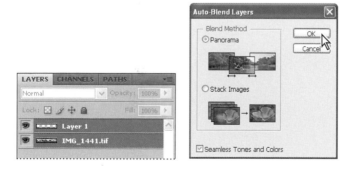

Photoshop blends the layers together based on their content. When it's done, the selected area is filled with sky, and it's no longer blocking the buildings or trees.

12 With both layers selected, choose Layer > Merge Layers.

The poster needs only the lettering on the side to be complete.

13 Choose File > Open, navigate to the Lesson10 folder, and double-click the DC_Letters.psd file to open it.

14 Click the Arrange Documents button in the application bar, and choose a 2 Up layout option so that you can see both files. Then, use the Move tool (➤⊕) to drag the DC_Letters.psd image onto the Panorama image. Close the DC_Letters.psd file without saving it.

15 With the Move tool, position the lettering and red background along the left side of the image.

Because you're preparing this poster for printing, you'll convert it to CMYK.

16 Choose Image > Mode > CMYK Color. Click Merge to merge layers. Click OK if you see a color profile informational dialog box.

17 Choose Layer > Flatten Image to reduce the image size.

18 Choose File > Save to save your work.

You've created two photographic souvenirs by combining images. You created a montage of several images, and you blended images into a panorama. You're ready to create montages and panoramas from your own images.

Review questions

1 What is the purpose of saving selections?

2 How can you preview filter effects before you commit to them?

3 What are the differences between using a Smart Filter and a regular filter to apply effects to an image?

4 Describe one use for the Match Color feature.

Review answers

1 By saving a selection, you can create and reuse time-consuming selections and uniformly select artwork in an image. You can also combine selections or create new selections by adding to or subtracting from existing selections.

2 Use the Filter Gallery to test different filters with different settings to see the effect they'll have on your image.

3 Smart Filters are nondestructive: they can be adjusted, turned off and on, and deleted, at any time. In contrast, regular filters permanently change an image; once applied, they cannot be removed. Smart Filters can be applied only to a Smart Object layer.

4 You can use the Match Color feature to match color between different images, such as to adjust the facial skin tones in photographs—or to match color between different layers in the same image. You can also use the feature to create unusual color effects.

11

PREPARING FILES FOR THE WEB

Lesson overview

In this lesson, you'll learn how to do the following:

- Slice an image in Photoshop.

- Distinguish between user slices and auto slices.

- Link user slices to other HTML pages or locations.

- Define rollover states to reflect mouse actions.

- Preview rollover effects.

- Create simple animated GIFs using a layered file.

- Use the Layers and Animation panels to create animation sequences.

- Tween frames to create smooth transitions.

- Preview animations in a web browser.

- Optimize images for the web and make good compression choices.

- Export large, high-resolution files that tile for zooming and panning.

- Showcase your images in a Media Gallery.

 This lesson will take about 90 minutes to complete. Copy the Lesson11 folder onto your hard drive if you have not already done so. As you work on this lesson, you'll preserve the start files. If you need to restore the start files, copy them again from the *Adobe Photoshop CS4 Classroom in a Book* CD.

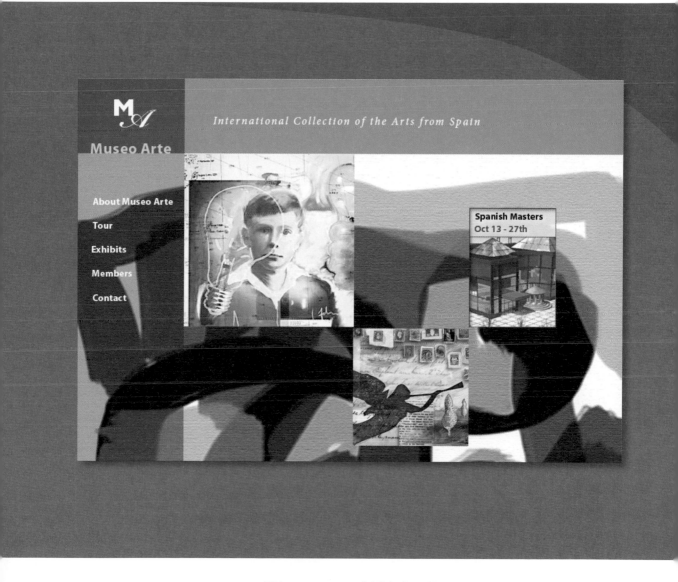

Web users expect to click linked graphics to jump to
another site or page, and activate built-in animations.
You can prepare a file for the web in Photoshop by
adding slices to link to other pages or sites, and
creating rollovers and animations.

Getting started

For this lesson, you will need to use a web browser application such as Firefox, Netscape, Internet Explorer, or Safari. You do not need to connect to the Internet.

In this lesson you'll fine-tune graphics for the home page of a Spanish art museum's website. You'll add hypertext links to the topics, so that website visitors can jump to other prebuilt pages on the site. You'll also add rollovers to alter how the web page looks, and you'll animate the Museo Arte logo in the upper-left corner.

First, you'll explore the final HTML page that you will create from a single Photoshop file. Several areas of the artwork react to mouse actions. For example, some areas of the image change appearance when you hover the pointer over them, or when you click a link.

1 Start Adobe Photoshop, holding down Ctrl+Alt+Shift (Windows) or Command+Option+Shift (Mac OS) to restore the default preferences. (See "Restoring default preferences" on page 4.)

2 When prompted, click Yes to confirm that you want to reset preferences.

3 Click the Launch Bridge button (■) in the application bar to open Adobe Bridge.

4 In Bridge, click Lessons in the Favorites panel. Double-click the Lesson11 folder in the Content panel, and then double-click the 11End folder, and finally, double-click the Site folder.

The Site folder contains the contents of the website that you'll be working with.

5 Right-click (Windows) or Control-click (Mac OS) the home.html file, and choose Open With from the context menu. Choose a web browser to open the HTML file.

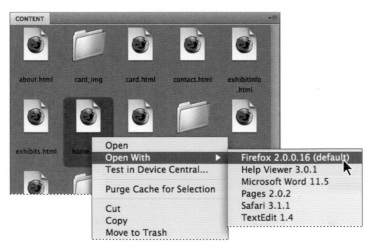

As the website opens, notice the logo animate in the upper-left corner. If you missed it, click the Refresh button in your browser to load the page again.

6 Move the pointer over the topics on the left side of the web page and over the images. When the pointer hovers over a link, it changes from an arrow to a pointing hand.

7 Click the angel in the lower center of the image to view the Zoomify window. Click the Zoomify controls to see how they change the magnification and reposition the image.

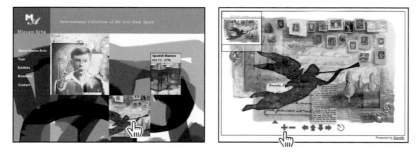

8 To return to the home page, close the Zoomify window.

9 Click one of the other images to get a closer look at it in its own window. Close its browser window when you have finished.

10 On the home page, click the topics on the left side to jump to their linked pages. To return to the home page, click *Museo Arte* just below the logo in the upper-left corner of the window.

11 When you have finished viewing the web page, quit the web browser and return to Bridge.

In the preceding steps, you used two different types of links: slices (the topics on the left side of the page) and images (the boy, Spanish Masters page, and angel).

Slices are rectangular areas in an image that you define based on layers, guides, or precise selections in the image, or by using the Slice tool. When you define slices in an image, Photoshop creates an HTML table or Cascading Style Sheet (CSS) layers to contain and align the slices. If you want to, you can generate and preview an HTML file that contains the sliced image along with the table or cascading style sheet.

You can also add hypertext links to images. A website visitor can then click the image to open a linked page. Unlike slices, which are always rectangular, images can be any shape.

Selecting a web design workspace

As the leading application for preparing images for websites, Photoshop also has some basic, built-in HTML creation tools. To make it easier to get to these tools for your web design tasks, you can customize the default arrangement of panels, tool-bars, and windows, using one of the predefined workspaces in Photoshop.

1 In Bridge, click the Lesson11 folder in the breadcrumbs at the top of the window to display the Lesson11 folder contents. Double-click the 11Start folder in the Content panel, and then double-click the 11Start.psd thumbnail to open the file in Photoshop.

You'll take advantage of the predefined Web workspace in Photoshop.

2   Choose Web from the workspace switcher in the application bar.

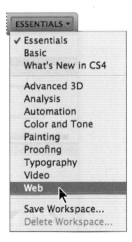

Photoshop displays only the panels you're most likely to need when designing for the web.

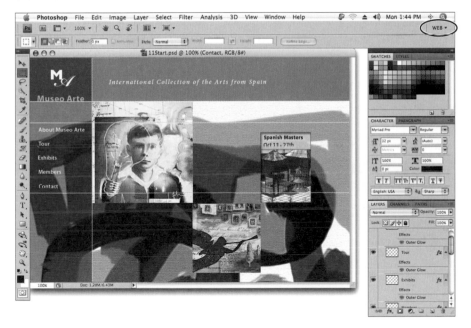

3   Choose File > Save As, and rename the file **11Working.psd**. Click OK in the Photoshop Format Options dialog box. Saving a working copy preserves the original start file in case you need to return to it later.

Creating slices

When you define a rectangular area in an image as a slice, Photoshop creates an HTML table to contain and align the slice. Once you create slices, you can turn them into buttons and then program those buttons to make the web page work.

You can't create just one slice—unless you create a slice that includes the whole image, which would be fairly useless. Any new slice you create within an image (a *user slice*) automatically creates other slices (*auto slices*) that cover the entire area of the image outside the user slice.

Selecting slices and setting slice options

You'll start by selecting an existing slice in the start file. We created the first slice for you, so that it exactly matches the pixel size of the animation you'll add to the slice at the end of the lesson.

1 In the Tools panel, select the Slice Select tool (🔪) tool, hidden under the Crop tool (✄).

When you select the Slice or Slice Select tool, Photoshop displays the slices, with their slice numbers, on the image.

The slice numbered 01 includes the upper-left corner of the image; it also has a small icon, or *badge*, that resembles a tiny mountain. The blue color means that the slice is a user slice, a slice we created in the start file.

Also notice the gray slices—02 to the right, and 03 just below slice 01. The gray color indicates that these are auto slices, automatically created by making a user slice. The symbol indicates that the slice contains image content. See "About slice symbols" for a description of the slice symbols.

About slice symbols

The blue and gray slice symbols, or *badges*, in the Photoshop image window and Save For Web And Devices dialog box can be useful reminders if you take the time to learn how to read them. Each slice can contain as many badges as are appropriate. These badges indicate the following:

(▣) The number of the slice. Numbers run sequentially from left to right and top to bottom of the image.

(⊠) The slice contains image content.

(⊠) The slice contains no image content.

(▥) The slice is layer-based; that is, it was created from a layer.

(▤) The slice is linked to other slices (for optimization purposes).

2   In the upper-left corner of the image, click the slice numbered 01 with the small blue rectangle. A gold bounding box appears, indicating that the slice is selected.

3   Using the Slice Select tool, double-click slice 01. The Slice Options dialog box appears. By default, Photoshop names each slice based on the filename and the slice number—in this case, 11Start_01.

Slices aren't particularly useful until you set options for them. Slice options include the slice name and the URL that opens when the user clicks the slice.

4   In the Slice Options dialog box, name the slice **Logo Animation**. For URL, type #. The pound sign (#) lets you preview a button's functionality without programming an actual link. It's very helpful in the early stages of website design, when you want to see how a button will look and behave.

5   Click OK to apply the changes. Later in the lesson, you will create an animated version of this sliced image to replace it on the final website.

Note: You can set options for an auto slice, but doing so automatically promotes the auto slice to a user slice.

Creating navigation buttons

Now you'll slice the navigation buttons on the left side of the page, so that you can turn them into rollovers. You could select one button at a time and add navigation properties to it. But you can do the same thing a faster way.

1 In the Tools panel, select the Slice tool (✗) or press Shift+C. (The Crop tool, Slice tool, and Slice Select tool share the key C as their keyboard shortcut. To change which of the three tools is selected, press Shift+C.)

Notice the guides above and below the words on the left side of the image.

2 Using the guides on the left side of the image, drag the Slice tool diagonally from the upper-left corner above *About Museo Arte*, to the bottom guide below *Contact*, so that all five lines are enclosed.

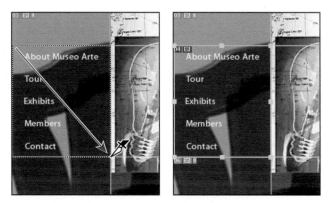

A blue rectangle, similar to the one for slice 01, appears in the upper-left corner of the slice you just created, numbered slice 04. The blue color tells you that this is a user slice, not an auto slice.

The original gray rectangle for auto slice 03 remains unchanged, but the area included in slice 03 is smaller, covering only a small rectangle above the text. Another auto slice, numbered 05, appears below the slice you created.

The gold bounding box indicates the bounds of the slice and that it's selected.

3 With the Slice tool still selected, press Shift+C to toggle to the Slice Select tool (✗). The options bar above the image window changes, and it includes a series of alignment buttons.

Now you'll slice your selection into five separate buttons.

4 Click the Divide button in the options bar.

5 In the Divide Slice dialog box, select Divide Horizontally Into, and type **5** for Slices Down, Evenly Spaced. Click OK.

You'll name each slice and add a corresponding link.

6 Using the Slice Select tool, double-click the top slice, labeled *About Museo Arte*.

7 In the Slice Options dialog box, name the slice **About**; type **about.html** for URL; and type **_self** for Target. (Be sure to include the underscore before the letter *s*.) Click OK.

The Target option controls how a linked file opens when the link is clicked. The _self option displays the linked file in the same frame as the original file.

8 Repeat steps 6 and 7 for the remaining slices in turn, starting from the second slice, as follows:

- Name the second slice **Tour**; type **tour.html** for URL; and type **_self** for Target.

- Name the third slice **Exhibits**; type **exhibits.html** for URL; and type **_self** for Target.

● **Note:** Type the HTML file names in the URL box exactly as shown, to match the names of the existing pages to which you will link the buttons.

▶ **Tip:** If you find the indicators for the auto slices distracting, select the Slice Select tool and then click the Hide Auto Slices button in the options bar. You can also hide the guides by choosing View > Show > Guides, because you won't need them again.

- Name the fourth slice **Members**; type **members.html** for URL; and type **_self** for Target.

- Name the fifth slice **Contact**; type **contact.html** for URL; and type **_self** for Target.

9 Choose File > Save to save your work so far.

Creating slices based on layers

In addition to using the Slice tool, you can create slices based on layers. The advantage of using layers for slices is that Photoshop creates the slice based on the dimensions of the layer and includes all its pixel data. When you edit the layer, move it, or apply a layer effect to it, the layer-based slice adjusts to encompass the new pixels.

1 In the Layers panel, select the Image 1 layer. If you can't see all of the contents of the Layers panel, drag the panel from its dock and expand it by dragging the lower-right corner.

2 Choose Layer > New Layer Based Slice. In the image window, a slice numbered 04, with a blue badge, appears over the image of the boy. It is numbered according to its position in the slices, starting from the top-left corner of the image.

3 Using the Slice Select tool (📐), double-click the slice and name it **Image 1**. For URL, type **image1.html** for URL. Type **_blank** for Target. The _blank Target option opens the linked page in a new instance of the web browser. Click OK.

Be sure to enter these options exactly as indicated, to match the pages you'll be linking the slices to.

Now you'll create another slice for the Exhibit Info layer.

4 Repeat steps 1 through 3 for the remaining images, as follows:

- Create a slice from the Exhibit_info layer; name it **Exhibit Info**; for URL, type **exhibitinfo.html** for URL; and type **_blank** for Target. Click OK.

- Create a slice from the Image 2 layer; name it **Card**; type **card.html** for URL, and type **_blank** for Target. Click OK.

You may have noticed that the dialog box contains more options than the three you specified for these slices. For more information on how to use these options, see Photoshop Help.

5 Choose File > Save to save your work so far.

About creating slices

Here are other methods for creating slices that you can try on your own:

- You can create No Image slices, and then add text or HTML source code to them. No Image slices can have a background color and are saved as part of the HTML file. The primary advantage of using No Image slices for text is that the text can be edited in any HTML editor, saving you the trouble of having to go back to Photoshop to edit it. However, if the text grows too large for the slice, it will break the HTML table and introduce unwanted gaps.

- If you use custom guides in your design work, you can instantly divide up an entire image into slices with the Slices From Guides button on the options bar. Use this technique with caution, however, because it discards any previously created slices and any options associated with those slices. Also, it creates only user slices, and you may not need that many of them.

- When you want to create identically sized, evenly spaced, and aligned slices, try creating a single user slice that precisely encloses the entire area. Then, use the Divide button on the Slice Select options bar to divide the original slice into as many vertical or horizontal rows of slices as you need.

- If you want to unlink a layer-based slice from its layer, you can convert it to a user slice. Simply double-click it with the Slice Select tool, and select options for it.

Adding animation

In Photoshop, you can create animations from a single image using animated GIF files. An *animated GIF* is a sequence of images, or frames. Each frame varies slightly from the preceding frame, creating the illusion of movement when they are viewed in quick succession—just like movies. You can create animation in several ways:

- By using the Duplicate Selected Frames button in the Animation panel to create animation frames, and then using the Layers panel to define the image state associated with each frame.

- By using the Tween feature to quickly create new frames that warp text or vary a layer's opacity, position, or effects to create the illusion of an element in a frame moving or fading in and out.

- By opening a multilayer Adobe Photoshop or Adobe Illustrator file for an animation, with each layer becoming a frame.

In this lesson, you'll use the first two techniques.

Files for animations must be saved in GIF format or as QuickTime movies. You cannot create animations as JPEG or PNG files.

Creating an animated GIF

To add interest to the web page, you'll animate the Museo Arte logo so that it seems to dance across the left corner. You'll animate the type using the Animation and Layers panels in tandem, as you continue to work in the Web workspace.

1 In the Layers panel, click the triangle next to the Logo Animation group to expand its contents, if they aren't already displayed. The group consists of three components—an *M*, an *A*, and the text *Museo Arte*—on separate layers.

You will create an animation showing the two letters appearing and moving into their final position. At the end, they will glow, and the text *Museo Arte* will fade in.

2 Choose Window > Animation to display the Animation panel at the bottom of the image window.

3 In the Animation panel, click the Duplicate Selected Frames button (⬛).
This creates a new frame based on the previous one.

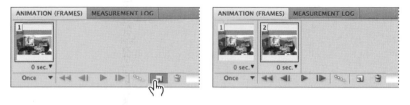

4 In the Layers panel, select the M layer.

5 Select the Move tool (▸⊕) in the Tools panel. In the image, drag the *M* to the left
side of the image window, holding down the Shift key to keep the movement
perfectly horizontal. Press the Left Arrow key on the keyboard to nudge the *M* to
the left until it is barely visible.

Be careful not to drag the letter completely out of the image window.

6 In the Layers panel, select the A layer.

7 In the image window, use the Move tool to drag the *A* directly upward—hold
down the Shift key to constrain the move—until the letter is just out of the
frame.

Another way to animate objects is by changing their opacity, so that they gradually appear or fade away.

8 In the Layers panel, select the Museo Arte layer. Reduce its Opacity to **0%**.

9 In the Layers panel, select the M layer and reduce its opacity to **10%**. Then select the A layer and reduce its opacity to **10%**.

10 Choose File > Save to save your work so far.

Tweening the position and opacity of layers

Next, you'll add frames that represent transitional image states between the two existing frames. When you change the position, opacity, or effects of any layer between two animation frames, you can instruct Photoshop to *tween,* which automatically creates as many intermediate frames as you specify.

You'll begin by making frame 2 the starting state of the animation.

1 In the Animation panel, drag frame 2 to the left of frame 1. The frames are instantly renamed in sequence. To see the state you've recorded for each frame, click each one.

Now you'll tween between these two frames.

2 In the Animation panel, make sure that frame 1 is selected, and then click the Tween button (⁂) at the bottom of the panel.

3 In the Tween dialog box, set the following options (if they are not already selected):

-   Choose Tween With: Next Frame.

-   For Frames to Add, type **5**.

-   Under Layers, select All Layers.

-   Under Parameters, make sure that all of the options are selected.

4 Click OK to close the dialog box.

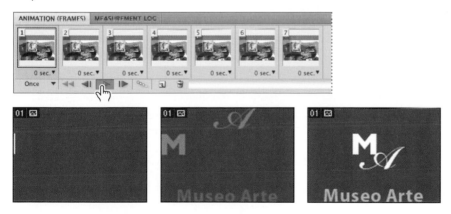

5 To test the animation, click the the Play button at the bottom of Animation panel. This previews the animation; it may be a bit jerky, but it will play fine in your browser.

Tweening frames

You use the Tween command to automatically add or modify a series of frames between two existing frames—varying the layer attributes (position, opacity, or effect parameters) evenly between the new frames to create the appearance of movement. For example, if you want to fade out a layer, set the opacity of the layer in the starting frame to 100%, and then set the opacity of the same layer in the ending frame to 0%. When you tween between the two frames, the opacity of the layer is reduced evenly across the new frames.

The word *tweening* is derived from "in betweening," the term used in traditional animation to describe this process. Tweening significantly reduces the time required to create animation effects such as fading in or fading out, or moving an element across a frame. You can edit tweened frames individually after you create them.

If you select a single frame, you choose whether to tween the frame with the previous frame or the next frame. If you select two contiguous frames, new frames are added between the frames. If you select more than two frames, existing frames between the first and last selected frames are altered by the tweening operation. If you select the first and last frames in an animation, these frames are treated as contiguous, and tweened frames are added after the last frame. (This tweening method is useful when the animation is set to loop multiple times.)

Note: You cannot select discontiguous frames for tweening.

Animating a layer style

In addition to animating the position or opacity of an object, you can also animate a layer effect, or *layer style*. The final result will be a little flash of light that appears and then disappears behind the letters *M* and *A*.

1 In the Animation panel, select frame 7, and then click the Duplicate Selected Frames button (▣) to create a new frame with all the same settings as frame 7. Leave frame 8 selected.

2 In the Layers panel, select the M layer. Click the Add A Layer Style button (*fx*) at the bottom of the panel, and choose Outer Glow. In the Layer Style dialog box, set the following options:

- Choose Screen for Blend Mode.

- Set the Opacity to **55**%. Set the Spread to **0**%.

- Set the size to **5** px.

- For color, click the color swatch and choose a light yellow in the color picker.

3 Click OK to apply the style to the M layer. Now you'll copy this effect to the A layer.

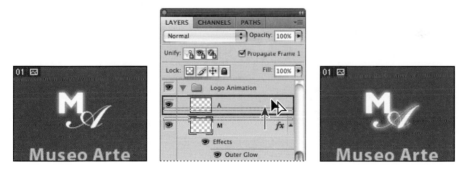

4 In the Layers panel, press Alt (Windows) or Option (Mac OS), and drag the effects icon from the M layer to the A layer. This copies the effect to the A layer.

Now you'll tween this copied effect, so that the letters glow at the end of the animation.

5 In the Animation panel, select frame 7. Click the Tween button (⌐⌐⌐) at the bottom of the panel.

6 In the Tween dialog box, type **2** for Frames To Add. Make sure that Effects is selected in the Parameters area, and click OK.

7 In the Animation panel, select frame 7, and then click the Duplicate Selected Frames button to create a new frame with all the same settings as frame 7.

8 Drag this new frame 8 to the end of the animation, where it becomes frame 11.

You'll set this animation to play only once on the website.

9 At the bottom-left corner of the Animation panel, make sure that Once is selected in the pop-up menu.

10 Click the Play button at the bottom of the Animation panel to preview the animation.

11 Choose File > Save to save your work.

Exporting HTML and images

You're ready to make your final slices, define your links, and export your file so that it creates an HTML page that will display all of your slices as one unit.

It's important to keep web graphics as small as possible so that web pages open quickly. Photoshop has built-in tools to help you gauge how small you can export each slice without compromising image quality. A good rule of thumb is to use JPEG compression for photographic, continuous-tone images, and GIF compression for broad areas of color—in the case of this lesson's site, all of the areas around the three main art images on the page.

You'll use the Save For Web & Devices dialog box to compare settings and compression options for different image formats.

1   Choose File > Save For Web & Devices.

2   Select the 2-Up tab at the top of the Save For Web & Devices dialog box.

3   Choose the Slice Select tool (✄) in the dialog box, and select slice 04 (the portrait of the boy) from the slices in the top image. Note the file size displayed beneath the image.

4   If necessary, use the Hand tool (✋) in the dialog box to move the image within the window and adjust your view.

5 On the right side of the dialog box, choose JPEG Medium from the Preset pop-up menu. Notice the file size displayed beneath the image; the file size changes dramatically when you choose JPEG Medium.

Now you'll look at a GIF setting for the same slice in the lower image.

6 With the Slice Select tool, select slice 04 in the lower image. On the right side of the dialog box, choose GIF 32 No Dither from the Preset pop-up menu.

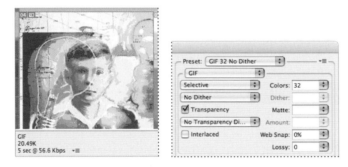

Notice that the color area in the portrait in the lower image looks flatter and more posterized, but the image size is roughly the same.

Based on what you've just learned, you will choose which compression to assign to all of the slices on this page.

7 Select the Optimized tab at the top of the dialog box.

8 With the Slice Select tool, Shift-click to select the three main art images in the preview window. From the Preset menu, choose JPEG Medium.

9 Shift-click to select all of the remaining slices in the preview window, and then choose GIF 64 Dithered from the Preset menu.

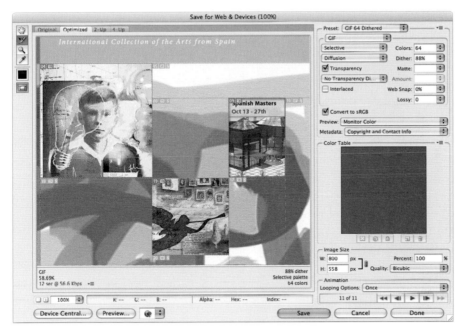

10 Click Save. In the Save Optimized As dialog box, navigate to the Lesson11/ 11Start/Museo folder, which contains the rest of the site, including the pages that your slices will link to.

11 For format, choose HTML And Images. Use the default settings, and choose All Slices for Slices. Name the file **home.html**, and click Save. If you're prompted to replace images, click Replace.

12 In Photoshop, click the Launch Bridge button (![Br]) to switch to Bridge. Click Lessons in the Favorites panel. Double-click the Lesson11 folder in the Content panel; double-click the 11Start folder; then double-click the Museo folder.

13 Right-click (Windows) or Control-click (Mac OS) the home.html file, and choose Open With from the context menu. Choose a web browser to open the HTML file.

14 In your web browser, move around the HTML file:

- Position your mouse over some of the slices you created. Notice that the pointer turns into a pointing finger to indicate a button.

- Click the portrait of the boy to open a new window with the full image.

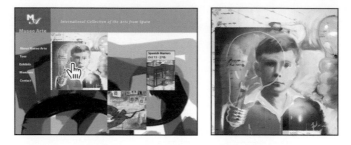

- Click the Spanish Masters link to open its window.

- Click the text links on the left to jump to other pages in the site.

15 When you have finished exploring the file, close your browser.

Using the Zoomify feature

With the Zoomify feature, you can publish high-resolution images on the web that viewers can pan and zoom to see more detail. The basic-size image downloads in the same time as an equivalent-size JPEG file. Photoshop exports the JPEG files and HTML file that you can upload to your website. The Zoomify capabilities work with any web browser.

1 In Bridge, click the 11Start folder in the breadcrumbs at the top of the window. Then, double-click the card.jpg file to open it in Photoshop.

The card is a large bitmap image that you'll export to HTML using the Zoomify feature. You'll convert the angel image into a file that will be linked to one of the links that you've just created in the home page.

2 Choose File > Export > Zoomify.

3 In the Zoomify Export dialog box, click Folder, and select the Lesson11/11Start/ Museo folder. For Base Name, type **Card**. Set the quality to **12**; set the Width to **600** and set the Height to **400** for the base image in the viewer's browser. Make sure that the Open In Web Browser option is selected.

4 Click OK to export the HTML file and images. Zoomify opens them in your web browser.

5 Use the controls in the Zoomify window to test your Zoomify link on the angel image.

6 When you have finished, close the browser.

Creating a web gallery

Using Bridge, you can easily showcase your images in an online gallery, so that visitors can view individual images or a slide show of your work. You'll create a media gallery linked to the exhibits.html file in the museum website.

1 In Bridge, double-click the Watercolors folder. (The Watercolors folder is in the Lesson11/11Start folder.)

You'll create a slide show from the images in the Watercolors folder.

2 Select the first image, and then Shift-select the last, so that all the images are selected. Remember that you can use the Thumbnails slider at the bottom of the Bridge window to reduce the size of the thumbnails, so that more fit in the Content panel at a time.

3 Click Output at the top of the Bridge window to display the Output workspace. If there is no Output button, choose Window > Workspace > Output.

4 In the Output panel, click the Web Gallery button.

5 Click the triangle next to Site Info if its contents aren't already displayed. In the Site Info area of the Output panel, enter **Watercolors** for the Gallery Title, **Paintings from the Watercolors exhibit** for the Gallery Caption, and **Now showing at Museo Arte** in the About This Gallery box. You can add contact name and information if you want to, as well.

6 Click the triangle next to Site Info to collapse its contents. Scroll down to the Create Gallery area. Expand its contents if they aren't already visible.

7 Name the gallery **Watercolors.** Select Save To Disk, click Browse, and navigate to the Lesson11/11Start/Museo folder. Click OK or Choose to close the dialog box, and then click Save in Bridge.

> ▼ Create Gallery
>
> Gallery Name:
>
> Watercolors
>
> ⊙ Save to Disk
>
> /Lessons/Lesson11/11Start/Museo
>
> [Browse...]   [Save]

Bridge creates a gallery folder named Watercolors that contains an index.html file and a resources folder containing the watercolor images.

8 Click OK when Bridge reports that the gallery has been created. Then, in Bridge, click the Essentials button at the top of the window to return to the default workspace.

9 Navigate to the Lesson11/11Start/Museo folder. Double-click the Watercolors folder, which is the gallery folder Bridge created. Right-click or Control-click the index.html file, choose Open With, and select a browser.

10 If you see a security warning, click OK or follow the instructions to change settings.

The gallery opens. One image is displayed on the right side, and thumbnails of the others are shown on the left.

11 Click the View Slideshow button beneath the larger image to start the slide show. Click the View Gallery button beneath the featured image to return to gallery view.

12 Close the browser application.

The exhibits.html file already contains a link to the folder you created, as long as you named the folder exactly as specified in step 7. Now you'll open your website and use the link to view the gallery.

13 In Bridge, navigate to the Lesson11/11Start/Museo folder. Right-click (Windows) or Control-click (Mac OS) the home.html file, and choose Open With from the context menu. Choose a web browser to open the HTML file.

14 In the website, click the Exhibits link in the navigation area. Then, on the Exhibits page, click the link to the Watercolors gallery. The gallery opens.

15 Explore the gallery and the website further, if you'd like. When you're finished, close the browser application, Bridge, and Photoshop.

You're on your way to building engaging websites from Photoshop images. You've learned how to add animation and interactivity to your web page with slices, rollovers, Zoomify, and the Web Gallery feature in Bridge.

Extra Credit

Creating slices for rollovers is an easy way to make buttons more obvious. When creating content for the web, it's always good practice to clearly communicate to users when they've encountered a button. In this lesson, the only clue to buttons is that they change from a pointer to a pointing finger when you move the mouse over them. This hint may be too subtle for many people.

Here's how to make buttons stand out: you create a second state for the navigation slices, to appear when the mouse hovers over each slice. You'll do that here by making layers visible, exporting them to a separate folder, and then dropping them into a file with HTML code already written to make the rollovers work.

1   Return to the 11Working.psd file in Photoshop.

2   In the Layers panel, click the triangle to expand the Menu Color Bkgds group and display its layers. Currently, all the layers in this group are hidden.

3   Show the Cell_1 layer. The background in slice 06 lightens.

4   Toggle the visibility on and off for the Cell_1 through Cell_5 layers, and observe the changes in the slices.

You want the buttons to change color when the mouse hovers over them.

5   Make all the Cell_1 through Cell_5 layers visible, and then choose File > Save For Web & Devices.

6   In the preview window, select the Slice Select tool, and Shift-select the five navigation buttons.

7   In the Save For Web & Devices dialog box, make sure that the GIF file type is selected. Click Save.

8   In the Save Optimized As dialog box, navigate to the Lesson11 folder, and create a new folder named Over States. For format, select Images Only. Leave the default settings, and choose Selected Slices from the Slices menu. Click Save.

9   In Bridge, navigate to the Over States folder you just created, double-click the Images folder, and open one of the image files you just exported.

If you were creating a real web page, you would import these files into an HTML editor such as Adobe Dreamweaver® CS4. In Dreamweaver, you would program the page so that the images in the Over States folder would swap with the first image slices whenever the mouse hovered over those slices.

We've built a mock-up to show you what a finished version of this web page might look like.

10 In Bridge, click the Lesson11 folder in the breadcrumbs at the top of the window. Double-click the 11 End folder, and then double-click the site folder to open it.

11 Right-click (Windows) or Control-click (Mac OS) the home.html file, and choose Open With from the context menu. Choose a web browser to open the HTML file. Move the mouse over the navigation buttons. The background changes for each button as the mouse moves over it.

Review questions

1 What are slices? How do you create them?

2 Describe a rollover.

3 Describe a simple way to create an animation.

4 What file formats can you use for animations?

5 What is image optimization and how do you optimize images for the web?

Review answers

1 Slices are rectangular areas of an image that you define for individual web optimization and to which you then can add animated GIFs, URL links, and rollovers. You can create image slices with the Slice tool or by converting layers into slices using the Layer menu.

2 A rollover is a web effect that alters a web page's appearance without switching the user to a different web page—such as a button that changes color when the mouse rolls over it.

3 A simple way to create an animation is to start with a layered Photoshop file. Use the Duplicate Selected Frames button in the Animation panel to create a new frame, and then use the Layers panel to alter the position, opacity, or effects of selected frames. Add intermediate frames between two frames manually using the Duplicate Selected Frames button, or add them automatically using the Tween command.

4 Files for animations must be saved in GIF format or as QuickTime movies. You cannot create animations as JPEG or PNG files.

5 Image optimization is the process of choosing a file format, resolution, and quality settings for an image to keep it small, useful, and visually appealing when published to the web. Continuous-tone images are typically optimized in JPEG format; solid-color images or those with repetitive color areas typically are optimized as GIF. To optimize images, choose File > Save For Web & Devices.

12 WORKING WITH 3D IMAGES

Lesson overview

In this lesson, you'll learn how to do the following:

- Create a 3D shape from a layer.

- Manipulate 3D objects using the 3D Orbit tool.

- Adjust the position of lighting using the Rotate Light tool.

- Configure options in the 3D panel.

- Adjust light sources.

- Import 3D objects.

- Manipulate objects using the 3D Axis tool.

- Paint on a 3D object.

- Apply the 3D postcard effect.

- Animate a 3D file.

 This lesson will take about 90 minutes to complete. Copy the Lesson12 folder onto your hard drive if you have not already done so. As you work on this lesson, you'll preserve the start files. If you need to restore the start files, copy them again from the *Adobe Photoshop CS4 Classroom in a Book* CD.

Traditional 3D artists spend hours, days, and weeks creating images with photo-realism. Photoshop's 3D capabilities allow you to create sophisticated precision 3D images easily—and you can change them easily, too.

Getting started

This lesson explores 3D features, which are only available in Adobe Photoshop CS4 Extended. If you are not using Photoshop CS4 Extended, skip this lesson and proceed to Lesson 13.

In this lesson, you'll create and fine-tune the CD cover art for a fictitious band named *Brick Hat*. Then, you'll use create a 3D postcard from that cover art for use in an advertisement.

Working with 3D artwork can be processor-intensive. For better performance, enable OpenGL in the Photoshop Preferences dialog box, if your video card supports OpenGL. Additionally, some tools designed to assist you in working with 3D images aren't available if your video card doesn't support OpenGL or if it isn't enabled. However, you should be able to complete the lesson regardless.

First, you'll view the finished CD cover art.

1 Start Adobe Photoshop, holding down Ctrl+Alt+Shift (Windows) or Command+Option+Shift (Mac OS) to restore the default preferences. (See "Restoring default preferences" on page 4.)

2 When prompted, click Yes to confirm that you want to reset preferences.

3 Click the Launch Bridge button (Br) in the application bar to open Adobe Bridge.

4 In Bridge, click Lessons in the Favorites panel. Double-click the Lesson12 folder in the Content panel, and then double-click the 12End folder.

5 View the 12End.psd file and the 12End_Layers.psd file in the Content panel. If your video card supports Open GL, you should see both images. Both files are CD cover art.

   The 12End_Layers.psd file includes all the layers, before the file was flattened. You may find it useful to refer to it as you work through the lesson.

Creating a 3D shape from a layer

Photoshop includes several 3D shape presets, representing geometric shapes and the shapes of everyday objects, such as a wine bottle or ring. When you create a 3D shape from a layer, Photoshop wraps the layer onto the 3D object preset. You can then rotate, reposition, and resize the 3D object—you can even light it from various angles with a number of colored lights.

You'll start by creating a 3D hat using the layer that contains the image of a brick wall.

1 In Bridge, double-click the 12Start.psd thumbnail to open the file in Photoshop. The 12Start.psd file contains several layers with the contents of the final CD cover: type, music notes, sky, and a brick wall texture.

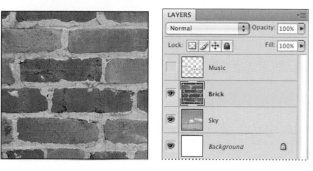

2 Choose Window > Workspace > Advanced 3D to display the 3D and Layers panels, which you'll use in this lesson.

3 Select the Brick layer, and then choose 3D > New Shape From Layer > Hat.

Photoshop creates a 3D object, wrapping the two-dimensional image of bricks around the shape of a hat.

Manipulating 3D objects

The advantage to working with 3D objects is, obviously, that you can work with them in three dimensions. Photoshop CS4 Extended includes several basic tools that make it easy to rotate, resize, and position 3D objects. The 3D Rotate tool and the other tools grouped with it in the Tools panel all let you manipulate the object itself. In addition, the 3D Orbit tool and its group let you change the camera positions and angles, which can have a dramatic effect on your object.

You can use the 3D tools whenever a 3D layer is selected in the Layers panel. A 3D layer behaves like any other layer—you can apply layer styles, mask it, and so on. However, a 3D layer can be quite complex.

Unlike a regular layer, a 3D layer contains one or more *meshes*. A mesh defines the 3D object. In the layer you just created, the mesh is the hat shape. Each mesh, in turn, includes one or more *materials*, the appearance of a part or all of the mesh. Each material includes one or more *maps*, which are the components of the appearance. There are nine typical maps, including the Bump map, and there can be only one of each kind; however, you can also use custom maps. Each map contains one *texture,* the image that defines what the maps and materials look like. The texture may be a simple bitmap graphic or a set of layers. The same texture might be used by many different maps and materials. In the layer you just created, the image of the brick wall composes the texture.

In addition to meshes, a 3D layer also includes one or more *lights*, which affect the appearance of 3D objects and remain in a fixed position as you spin or move the object. A 3D layer also includes *cameras*, which are saved views, with the objects in a particular position. The *shader* creates the final appearance based on the materials, object properties, and renderer.

That may all sound complicated, but the most important thing to remember is that some tools move objects in 3D space and some tools move the cameras that view the object.

1   In the Tools panel, select the 3D Orbit tool (◌). When you select the 3D Orbit tool, several other 3D tools become available in the options bar.

2   In the options bar, choose Top from the View pop-up menu. You're now viewing the top of the hat.

● **Note:** If OpenGL is enabled, a three-dimensional widget, called the 3D Axis, appears on the screen, with red, blue, and green representing different axes. You can use the 3D Axis to position and move the object.

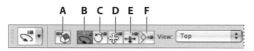

A. Return to initial camera position **B.** 3D Orbit tool
C. 3D Roll View tool **D.** 3D Pan View tool **E.** 3D Walk
View tool **F.** 3D Zoom tool

Options in the View menu determine the angle from which you see the object.

3   In the Tools panel, select the 3D Rotate tool (◌).

4   Click in the center of the hat and drag outward, in a circle, around the edge of the composition. Drag diagonally, as well, to get a feel for how the 3D Rotate tool moves the object on the x and y axes.

5 Select the 3D Roll tool (🔄) in the options bar. Drag the hat. Notice that you can flip the hat around, but you're constrained to movement on a single axis.

6 Select the 3D Pan tool (✛) in the options bar. Drag the hat from side to side, vertically, or horizontally. With the 3D Pan tool you can move the object on the plane, but you cannot rotate it.

7 Select the 3D Scale tool (📦) in the options bar. Click just above the hat, and drag toward the center of the hat until the X, Y, and Z values in the options bar are each **0.75**. The hat is 75% of its original size.

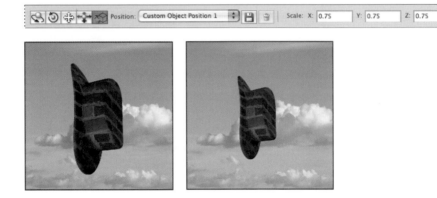

You've used several tools to manipulate the hat. Now, you'll enter values to position the hat precisely.

8 Select the 3D Rotate tool (⟲) in the options bar. Then, in the Orientation area of the options bar, enter **11** for X, **45** for Y, and **-37** for Z.

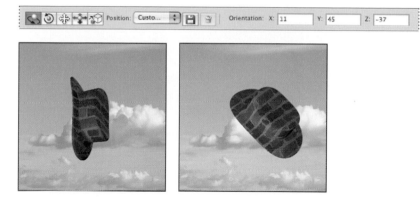

You can use the 3D tools to reposition and rotate a 3D object manually, or, if you know where you want the object to be, select the 3D Rotate tool (⟲) and type values in the options bar.

9 Choose File > Save As. Navigate to the Lesson12 folder, and save the file as **12Working.psd**. Click OK if the Photoshop Format Options dialog box appears.

Using the 3D panel to adjust lighting and surface texture

One of the benefits of working with a three-dimensional object is that you can adjust the lighting angles and the surface texture on the object. The 3D panel gives you quick access to settings for the scene, mesh, materials, and lighting.

1 In the 3D (Scene) panel, select the Hat Material component. The options in the lower area of the panel change.

2 Enter **80%** for Glossiness.

Photoshop adds shine to the hat, as if it's lit from the front.

3 Click the Filter By Light button (🔆) at the top of the 3D panel. The 3D (Lights) panel displays options for lighting.

4 Select the Infinite Light 2 component in the 3D panel.

5 Select the Rotate The Light tool (🔄) in the 3D (Lights) panel.

● **Note:** If your video card does not support OpenGL, the Toggle Lights button isn't available. However, you can rotate the light without the guide.

6 If you're using a video card that supports OpenGL, click the Toggle Lights button (💡) at the bottom of the panel to view the light guide.

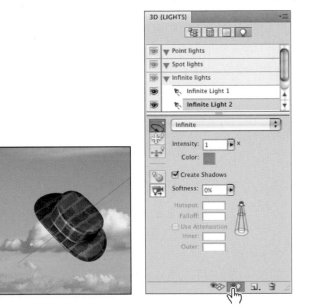

7 If light guides are displayed, drag the bulb end of the guide that appears to be entering the top of the hat. As you drag the bulb down, the light shifts over the hat. If guides aren't displayed, move the cursor down on the screen to shift the light.

Because you've selected Infinite Light 2 in the 3D (Lights) panel, only that light changes as you move the cursor across the screen. If you select a different light, the same cursor movement moves the selected light and creates a different effect.

8 With Infinite Light 2 selected, click the swatch next to Color in the 3D (Lights) panel, and select a light yellow color. As you select a color for the light, you can preview it in the image window. When you're satisfied with the color, click OK to close the Select Light Color dialog box. Click the Toggle Lights button again to hide the light guides.

9 Choose File > Save to save your work.

Viewing 3D cross-sections

You can rotate 3D objects, change their lighting, and move the camera positions. But what about seeing what's going on inside? Product designers, medical professionals, and engineers often need to work with 3D objects both outside and in. It's easy to see a cross-section of a 3D object in Photoshop CS4 Extended.

Take a peek under the hood of this lovely old car to see how cross-sections work.

The 3D car was created in a 3D application and imported into Photoshop. You can view a cross-section of any 3D layer in Photoshop Extended, but how much information you see in the cross-section depends on how the object was created and which details the creator included.

To view a cross-section, select Cross-Section in the 3D panel.

In this example, selecting Cross-Section cuts the car in half so that the interior is visible. It's pretty dark, though, and hard to see details. You can adjust the lighting for cross-sections using the 3D panel.

Just as you can change the lighting when you're viewing the exterior of an object, you can change the intensity, direction, or other attributes of lights when you're viewing a cross-section. It's particularly useful to rotate the light so that you can emphasize different portions of the interior.

To return to viewing the full object, deselect Cross-Section in the 3D panel.

Merging two-dimensional layers onto 3D layers

You created the three-dimensional layer by wrapping a two-dimensional image around a shape. But you can wrap additional 2D layers onto the same shape. Just position them where you want them, and then merge them; they'll follow the shape of the 3D object. You'll merge a layer of musical notes onto the hat.

1 In the Layers panel, select the Music layer and make it visible. The Music layer is a two-dimensional layer of musical notes. It should be the top layer in the Layers panel, so that it appears in front of the hat and the sky.

2 Select the Move tool (▶⊕) in the Tools panel, and then position the Music layer so that the notes are centered over the hat.

3 Choose Layer > Merge Down. The musical notes wrap around the hat, and the Music layer is no longer listed in the Layers panel.

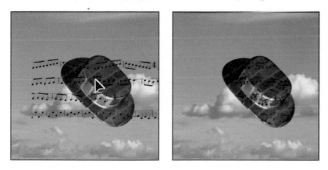

When you use the Merge Down command, Photoshop merges the selected layer with the layer directly beneath it in the Layers panel. The two layers become a single layer, keeping the name of the bottom layer.

Importing 3D files

In Photoshop CS4 Extended, you can open and work with 3D files created by applications such as Adobe Acrobat 9 Professional Extended, 3D Studio Max, Alias, Maya, and Google Earth. You can also work with files saved in Collada format, a file interchange format that is supported by Autodesk, for example. When you add a 3D file as a 3D layer, it includes the 3D model and a transparent background. The layer uses the dimensions of the existing file, but you can resize it.

You'll create a new 3D layer from the 3D file of a pyramid and scale it down.

1 In the Layers panel, hide the Brick layer so that only the sky is visible.

2 Select the Sky layer, and choose 3D > New Layer From 3D File. Navigate to the Lesson12 folder and then double-click the Pyramid.obj file. (In Windows, choose All Formats from the File Type pop-up menu to see the file listed.)

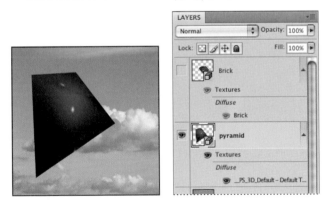

A pyramid appears in the image window, and Photoshop adds a 3D layer named pyramid above the Sky layer in the Layers panel. When you create a 3D layer from an imported file, it's always added above the selected layer.

3   In the Layers panel, make sure the pyramid layer is selected, and then choose Linear Light from the Mode pop-up menu. Lower the Opacity value to **85%**.

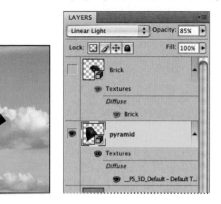

4   Select the 3D Scale tool (⬡), hidden under the 3D Rotate tool (◈) in the Tools panel.

5   Click above the pyramid and drag toward its center until it's half its original size. The X, Y, and Z values in the options bar should each be 0.5.

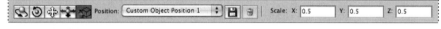

Merging 3D layers to share the same 3D space

You can include multiple 3D meshes in the same 3D layer. Meshes in the same layer can share lighting effects and be rotated in the same 3D space (also called the *scene*), creating a more realistic 3D effect.

You'll duplicate the pyramid layer, and then merge the two layers into the same 3D layer.

1 In the Layers panel, make sure the pyramid layer is selected, and then choose Duplicate Layer from the Layers panel menu. Click OK in the Duplicate Layer dialog box.

A second pyramid appears directly in front of the first one.

● **Note:** To merge 3D layers, their cameras must match. In this case, because the layer was essentially duplicated, the cameras already match.

2 Select the pyramid and pyramid copy layers, and then choose 3D > Merge 3D Layers.

The merged layers are in exactly the same position. To position and rotate a mesh individually, you must select the mesh in the 3D (Scene) panel.

3 Select the top objMesh component in the 3D (Scene) panel.

4 Select the Drag The Mesh tool ( ) in the 3D (Mesh) panel.

5 Drag the pyramid to the upper-right corner of the image.

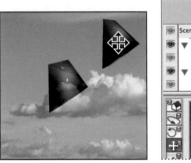 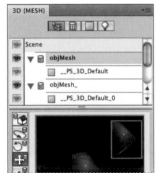

6 Select the objMesh_ component in the 3D (Mesh) panel. The objMesh_ component is the second mesh listed, and it represents the duplicate pyramid.

7 Drag the second pyramid to the lower-left corner of the image window.

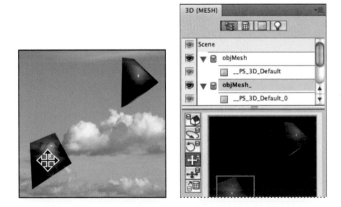

8 With the objMesh_component still selected, select the Roll The Mesh tool in the 3D (Mesh) panel. Then, click in the bottom-center of the image window, and drag to the left to roll the pyramid upright. It doesn't need to be perfect.

You can use the mesh tools to move a selected mesh independently of other meshes in the same layer. However, if you selected the standard 3D Roll tool in the Tools panel, all the meshes in the layer would move at the same time.

9 Select the Drag The Mesh tool in the options bar, and drag the upright pyramid back down to the lower-left corner of the image window.

10 Select the objMesh component (the first mesh) in the 3D (Mesh) panel to return to the pyramid in the upper-right corner. Then, select the Scale The Mesh tool in the 3D (Mesh) panel, click in the center of the pyramid, and drag down until the X, Y, and Z values are each 0.**6**, so that the pyramid is 60% its original size.

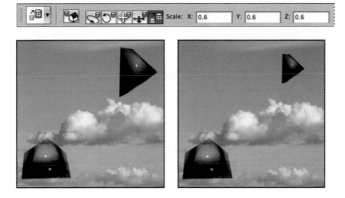

11 Select the Rotate The Mesh tool in the 3D (Mesh) panel, and then rotate the pyramid to match the image below. We dragged the right tip of the upper pyramid toward the upper-left corner of the canvas. You may need to use the Drag The Mesh tool to reposition the pyramid after you've rotated it.

12 Select Infinite Light 1 in the 3D panel, and then select the Rotate The Light tool (⟳) in the 3D (Lights) panel, and click the Toggle Lights button (🔦). (The Toggle Lights button is available only if OpenGL is enabled.)

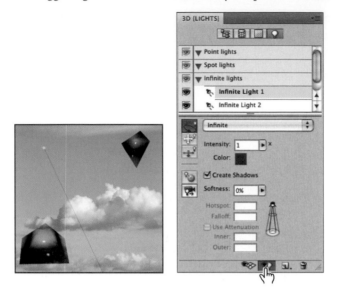

13 Drag the light source (represented by the bulb in the light guide if OpenGL is enabled) to the lower-right corner to change the lighting for both pyramids.

Though the pyramids are different meshes, they can share the same light source because they occupy the same 3D layer.

14 Click the Toggle Lights button again to hide the light guides, and then choose File > Save.

Adding a spot light

So far, you've manipulated the infinite light sources for 3D objects. You can also intensify the light for a specific area of an object using a spot light. You'll use a spot light to add color to one of the pyramids.

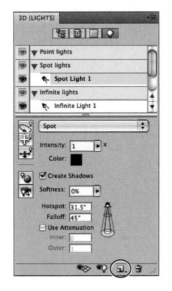

1   Make sure the 3D panel is displaying lighting options; its title should be 3D (Lights). If it isn't, click the Filter By Lights button.

2   Click the Create A New Light button (◫) at the bottom of the 3D (Lights) panel, and choose New Spot Light.

Spot Light 1 appears in the 3D (Lights) panel in the Spot Lights category, but nothing has changed in the image window.

3   Click the Color swatch in the 3D (Lights) panel, and select a magenta color. (We used RGB 215, 101, 235.) Click OK to close the Select Light Color dialog box.

4   In the 3D (Lights) panel, change the Intensity to 0.7.

5   Select the Rotate The Light tool (◔) in the 3D (Lights) panel, and then click on the image and drag down until the top pyramid has a magenta spot light on it.

▶ **Tip:** If OpenGL is enabled, click the Toggle Lights button to see the light source shift as you drag.

6 In the Layers panel, make the Brick layer visible so you can see all the elements of your image. Then, choose File > Save.

● **Note:** If your video card does not support OpenGL, you won't see the 3D Axis. You can skip this exercise and complete the lesson.

Using the 3D Axis to manipulate 3D objects

Manipulating objects in a 3D environment can be tricky and confusing at times. To help you more accurately control the *x*, *y*, and *z* axes, Adobe provides a 3D Axis widget. If OpenGL is enabled, the 3D Axis automatically appears in the upper-left corner of the image when a 3D layer is selected.

The box at the base of the 3D Axis scales the 3D object. Each of the colored arrows represents an axis: red for the *x* axis, green for the *y* axis, and blue for the *z* axis. Click the tip of an arrow to move the object on that axis; click the arc to rotate on that axis; click the block to resize on that axis only.

1 In the Layers panel, select the Brick layer.

2 Select the 3D Rotate tool in the Tools panel, and then move the cursor over the 3D Axis. Notice the gray bar that appears above the 3D Axis as the cursor approaches it. This bar lets you resize, reposition, or even hide the 3D Axis.

3 Drag the gray bar above the 3D Axis to another area on the image. The 3D Axis moves with the gray bar.

4 Click the magnifying glass on the right side of the gray bar, and then move the cursor to the right to enlarge the 3D Axis. Move the cursor to the left to reduce the size of the 3D Axis.

Moving the 3D Axis

Enlarging the 3D Axis

5 Click the center block at the base of the 3D Axis, and then drag
   it up to enlarge the hat.

6 Click the block on the blue arrow and drag down to resize the object on the *z*
   axis.

Resizing the object on all axes   *Resizing the object on the z axis*

7 Move the cursor over the arc on the blue arrow until you see a yellow circle.
   Then, drag around that circle to rotate the object on the *z* axis.

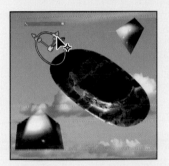

8 Hover over the point of the blue arrow and drag diagonally to reposition the hat
   along the *z* axis.

9 If you're satisfied with the changes you've made, choose File > Save. To return to
   the hat's previous position, choose File > Revert. Photoshop reverts back to the
   last version you saved.

Painting on a 3D object

You can paint directly onto 3D objects in Photoshop CS4 Extended using any Photoshop paintbrush, and the paint follows the object's contours.

1 Select the pyramid layer, and then select the Brush tool ( ) in the Tools panel.

2 Click the Foreground Color swatch in the Tools panel, and select a bright green color. (We used RGB 25, 207, 16.)

3 Select a soft, 65-pixel brush, and then paint the tip of the lower pyramid. The green paint follows the edges of the object, and affects nothing else.

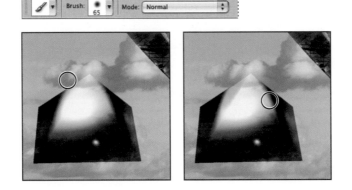

Adding 3D text

You can import three-dimensional files that contain text into Photoshop CS4 Extended, as well. Rotating and manipulating text in a 3D scene can give you fun and interesting results.

You'll import the CD cover art title as a 3D object and then position it in the image.

1 Select the Brick layer, and then choose 3D > New Layer From 3D File.

2 Navigate to the Lesson12 folder, and double-click the title.obj file. Photoshop imports the text and adds a 3D layer named title just above the Brick layer.

3 With the title layer selected, choose Vivid Light from the Mode menu in the Layers panel, and lower the Opacity to **80%**.

4 Select the 3D Pan tool (✥) in the Tools panel, and drag the text to the upper-left corner of the canvas.

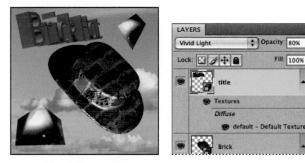

5 Select the 3D Rotate tool (◈), and rotate the text so that it's a little easier to read.

6 Choose File > Save to save your work so far.

Creating a 3D postcard

In Photoshop CS4 Extended, you can transform a 2D object into a 3D postcard that you can manipulate in perspective in a 3D space. It's called a 3D postcard, because it's as if your image became a postcard you could turn over in your hand. To create a 3D postcard, you must flatten all layers in Photoshop.

You'll use a 3D postcard to prepare the CD cover art for use in a larger advertisement.

1 In the Layers panel, choose Flatten Image from the panel menu. Click OK when asked whether you want to flatten layers.

All the layers become a single Background layer.

2 Choose 3D > New 3D Postcard From Layer.

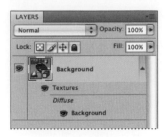

The Background layer becomes a 3D layer. The image doesn't appear to have changed, but when you add a background, it will become more obvious that it's a 3D object. Now, you'll resize it.

3 Select the 3D Scale tool (🎡) in the Tools panel. In the options panel, type **.75** for the X and Y values. Press Enter or Return to apply the values.

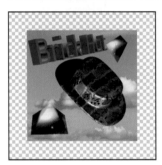

Adding a gradient background

You'll add a gradient in the background to help the postcard stand out.

1 Click the Create A New Layer button in the Layers panel.

2 Rename the new layer **Gradient**, and drag it below the Background layer in the Layers panel.

3 Click the Default Foreground And Background Colors button in the Tools panel to restore the foreground color to black and the background color to white.

4 Select the Gradient tool (▬) in the Tools panel.

5 Drag the Gradient tool from the top center directly to the bottom of the image.

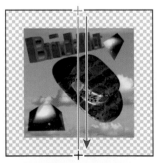

Animating a 3D layer

Now you're ready to have some fun with your 3D postcard. Not only can you swivel it in 3D space, but you can record its movement over time in an animated QuickTime movie. To see the finished animation, play the Lesson12_end.mov file in the Lesson 12 folder. You must have Apple QuickTime installed to view the animation.

1 Rename the Background layer **CD Cover**.

2 Choose Window > Animation to open the Animation panel. The Animation panel lists both layers.

3 In the Animation panel, click the triangle next to the CD Cover layer to display its keyframe attributes. You may need to resize the panel to see the attributes.

4 Click the stopwatch icon (⏱) next to 3D Object Position to create an initial keyframe. The initial keyframe marks the position of the object at 0 seconds.

5 Drag the current-time indicator to 3:00f. This is where you'll set the next keyframe, which will record the object's position at that point in the timeline.

6 Select the 3D Rotate tool (⟳) in the Tools panel.

7 Hold down the Shift key as you click on the center-left edge of the canvas and drag the cursor all the way to the right of the canvas. The postcard flips so that you're seeing its back. Photoshop adds a keyframe to 3:00f to mark the new position.

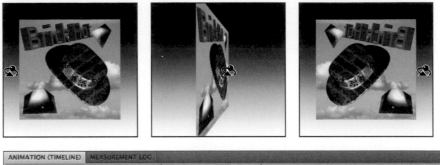

8 Move the current-time indicator back to the beginning of the timeline, and then press Play. Press the space bar to stop the playback.

It's a catchy little animation, and it's ready to export.

9 Drag the end point of the work area to 3:00f, so that the entire work area is from 0:00 to 3:00f. Photoshop will render the frames included in the work area.

10 Choose File > Export > Render Video.

11 In the Render Video dialog box, select QuickTime Export, and choose QuickTime Movie from the pop-up menu. Then click Settings.

12 Click Settings again in the Movie Settings dialog box. From the Compression Type menu, choose H.264. Choose 15 from the Frame Rate menu. Set Quality to Medium, and select Faster Encode for Encoding. Click OK, and click OK again to return to the Render Video dialog box.

13 In the Render Video dialog box, make sure Currently Selected Frames is selected in the Range area. Change the Size to **700** x **700**. Then, click Render.

```
┌─────────────────────────────────────────────────────────┐
│                      Render Video                         │
│ ┌─ Location ──────────────────────────────┐   ⟨ Render ⟩ │
│ │ Name: 12Flat.mov                         │   ⟨ Cancel ⟩ │
│ │ ⟨ Select Folder... ⟩ Macintosh HD:Users:...:Desktop:Lessons:Lesson12: │
│ │ ☐ Create New Subfolder: [            ]   │             │
│ └──────────────────────────────────────────┘             │
│ ┌─ File Options ──────────────────────────┐              │
│ │ ⦿ QuickTime Export: [ QuickTime Movie ▼] ⟨ Settings... ⟩│
│ │      H.264 (Low Quality, RGB 24 bits)    │              │
│ │ ◯ Image Sequence: [ Photoshop ▼] ⟨ Settings... ⟩        │
│ │    Starting #: [0]  Digits: [4 ▼]  Ex: File0000.psd     │
│ │ Size: [ Custom          ▼] [700] x [700] │              │
│ └──────────────────────────────────────────┘             │
│ ┌─ Range ─────────────────────────────────┐              │
│ │ ◯ All Frames                             │              │
│ │ ◯ In Frame: [0]   Out Frame: [299]       │              │
│ │ ⦿ Currently Selected Frames:  0 to 89    │              │
│ └──────────────────────────────────────────┘             │
└─────────────────────────────────────────────────────────┘
```

Photoshop renders the movie to your Lesson12 folder.

EXTRA CREDIT: Rendering art for 3D glasses

Remember those 3D movies you saw as a kid (or maybe even as an adult)? Photoshop CS4 Extended makes it easy to create images that come to life with traditional red/blue 3D glasses. You can't make the glasses themselves in Photoshop, but if you don't have a pair lying around, you can find them using a quick Internet search or visit to your local novelty shop.

For extra credit, you can render this CD cover art for a 3D viewing effect.

1   Choose 3D > Render Settings.

2   In the 3D Render Settings dialog box, select the last option. From the Stereo Type menu, choose Red/Blue. For Focal Plane, enter **50**. For Parallax, enter **50**.

3   Click OK, and then render the movie again, using the same settings you used to create the previous QuickTime movie.

When you've created the 3D movie, put on some 3D glasses and watch the objects on the postcard appear to pop out of the screen!

Review questions

1 How does a 3D layer differ from other layers in Photoshop?

2 What's the difference between the 3D Rotate tool and the 3D Orbit tool?

3 What do you use the 3D panel for?

4 Why would you merge two 3D layers?

5 How can you add a spot light to a 3D object?

Review answers

1 A 3D layer behaves like any other layer—you can apply layer styles, mask it, and so on.
   However, unlike a regular layer, a 3D layer also contains one or more meshes, which
   define 3D objects. You can work with meshes and the materials, maps, and textures
   they contain. You can also adjust the lighting for a 3D layer.

2 The 3D Rotate tool adjusts the position of the 3D object itself. The 3D Orbit tool
   changes the camera angle from which the object is viewed.

3 You use the 3D panel to select components in the 3D layer and to set options for
   modifying meshes, lighting, textures, and other components of the 3D scene.

4 Merging two 3D layers lets you work with the 3D objects in the same 3D space. In a
   single layer, multiple 3D objects can share lighting sources, for example, but you can
   continue to manipulate each of the meshes independently, as well.

5 To add a spot light to a 3D object, select its layer in the Layers panel. Then, click the
   Create A New Light button at the bottom of the 3D panel, and choose New Spot Light.
   Use the options in the 3D (Lights) panel to change the color and intensity of the light.
   Finally, click on the image and drag the light to position it.

13 WORKING WITH SCIENTIFIC IMAGES

Lesson overview

In this lesson, you'll learn how to do the following:

- Use Adobe Bridge to add metadata and keywords.

- Search across a collection of files with Bridge.

- Label, rank, and sort images in Bridge.

- Enhance images for analysis and presentation.

- Create a custom dashed-line border.

- Use the Measurement tool.

- Record measurement data in the Measurement Log panel.

- Export spreadsheet data from the Measurement Log panel.

- Measure in perspective using the Vanishing Point feature.

- Animate a presentation.

This lesson will take about 90 minutes to complete. Copy the Lesson13 folder onto your hard drive if you have not already done so. As you work on this lesson, you'll preserve the start files. If you need to restore the start files, copy them again from the *Adobe Photoshop CS4 Classroom in a Book* CD.

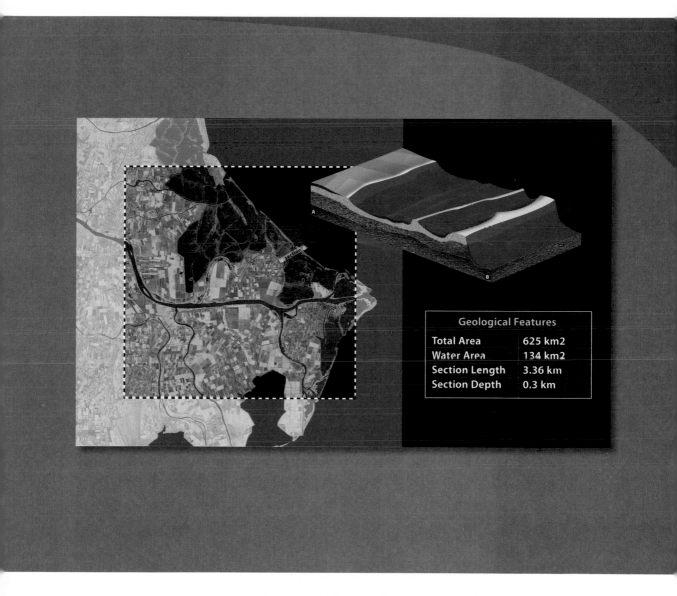

Geological Features	
Total Area	625 km2
Water Area	134 km2
Section Length	3.36 km
Section Depth	0.3 km

Creating spiffy infographics is a snap with Photoshop tools and Adobe Bridge—even with very large images. Bridge organizes and ranks images so you can see and search for exactly the ones you need. Measurement and image analysis tools in Photoshop Extended give your images additional dimension.

Getting started

Many professionals use Photoshop for highly technical, precise work. In this lesson, you will assemble an informational graphic on water levels and land masses using graphics provided by the U.S. Geological Survey. You will learn how Bridge is a valuable tool for organizing and identifying images as well as creating a presentation.

1 Start Photoshop and then immediately hold down Ctrl+Alt+Shift (Windows) or Command+Option+Shift (Mac OS) to restore the default preferences. (See "Restoring default preferences" on page 4.)

2 When prompted, click Yes to confirm that you want to reset preferences.

3 Choose File > Browse In Bridge to open Adobe Bridge.

In this lesson, you'll work with very large files, selecting only the area you need to make measurements and comparisons of data. You'll learn that working with very large files in Photoshop is really no different than editing other, smaller images.

This lesson also introduces you to Photoshop Extended, a version of Photoshop CS4 that includes all the features in the standard edition of Photoshop, plus functions for specialized markets—technical image analysis, film and video work, and three-dimensional design. Some exercises in this lesson require Photoshop Extended measurement and data analysis tools. If you don't have Photoshop Extended, you can complete this lesson up to "Measuring objects and data,", and then read through the remaining lesson or skip to the review questions.

Viewing and editing files in Adobe Bridge

As you've seen in previous lessons, Adobe Bridge helps you navigate your image files and folders. But Bridge is much more than a navigator. A cross-platform application included with Adobe Creative Suite components, Bridge also helps you organize and browse the assets you need to create print, web, video, and audio content. You can start Bridge from any Creative Suite component (except Adobe Acrobat), and use it to access both Adobe and non-Adobe assets.

You'll try out some of these management capabilities as you explore and customize the Bridge browser window. You'll also organize map sections for use in your infographics project.

Customizing Adobe Bridge views and workspaces

The panels in Adobe Bridge help you navigate, preview, search, and manage information for your image files and folders. The ideal arrangement and relative sizes of items and areas of Bridge depend on your work style and preferences. Depending on the tasks you're doing, it may be important to see which images are in a file; at other times, viewing information about the file may take priority. You can customize Bridge to increase your efficiency in these different situations.

In this procedure, you'll try out some of the custom views you can use in Adobe Bridge. The following figure shows the default configuration of Adobe Bridge areas, although you won't see these particular thumbnails on your screen yet.

1   In the upper-left corner of the Bridge browser window, click the Folders tab, and navigate to the Lessons/Lesson13/Maps folder that you copied to your hard disk from the *Adobe Photoshop CS4 Classroom in a Book* CD. To navigate, either click the arrows to open nested folders or double-click the folder icons in the Folders panel.

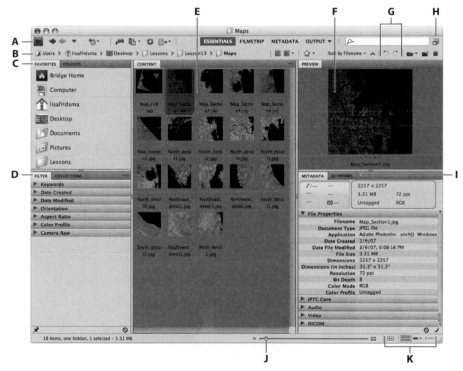

A. Menu bar **B.** Breadcrumbs **C.** Favorites and Folders panels **D.** Filter and Collections panels
E. Content panel **F.** Thumbnail preview panel **G.** Rotation buttons **H.** Compact mode button
I. Metadata and Keywords panels **J.** Thumbnail slider **K.** View option buttons

2 In the upper-right corner of the Bridge window, click the arrow to expand the Workspace pop-up menu, and choose Light Table.

Bridge displays only the Content panel, with thumbnails of the images in the Maps folder.

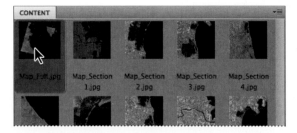

3 At the top of the Bridge window, click Essentials. Bridge returns to the original workspace.

The Bridge Preview panel updates interactively, showing you thumbnail previews of selected asset files. Adobe Bridge displays previews of image files such as those in PSD, TIFF, and JPEG formats as well as Adobe Illustrator vector files, multipage Adobe PDF files, and Microsoft Office documents.

4 In the Content panel, select the Map_Full.jpg thumbnail.

This is one of a series of aerial photographs taken of the northeastern coast of Italy, near Venice. Other images show section details from this map.

5 On the right side of the browser window, review the information at the top of the Metadata panel, including the image file size and resolution.

6 In the Metadata panel, review the contents of the File Properties area. It displays additional information about the image, including the file type, date it was created and modified, dimensions, bit depth, and color mode.

This 3600-x-3244-pixel image is relatively compact in file size (5.75 MB), but physically very large: the image measures 50 inches by 45.1 inches. You'll see how easily you can work with very large images using the precision tools in Photoshop.

7 At the bottom right of the Bridge window, drag the thumbnail slider to the right to enlarge the thumbnail previews. Enlarging the preview acts as a loupe, letting you zoom in on an image and inspect it more closely. Drag the slider to the left to reduce the size of the thumbnails.

▶ **Tip:** To see a full-screen preview of an image, select its thumbnail and press the spacebar. To review all the images in a folder, press Ctrl+B (Windows) or Command+B (Mac OS) to enter Review Mode.

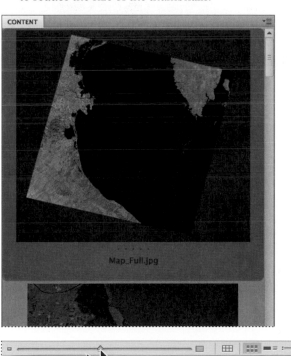

8   Select different workspaces using the workspace buttons at the top of the Bridge window (such as Essentials and Filmstrip) and the Workspace pop-up menu. Each workspace emphasizes different information, such as the Metadata panel or the Preview panel, so that you can easily access the information you need for a particular task.

9   Click the Essentials button at the top of the Bridge window to return to the default workspace.

Using Bridge to organize and search your elements

▶ **Tip:** In Bridge CS4, you can quickly search your entire computer for specific files. Enter a keyword or file name in the search box in the upper-right corner of the Bridge window.

You can quickly see file information in one of several ways: by keywords, by filtered information, or by metadata. Now you will look more closely at the metadata information. Metadata is a set of standardized information about a file, such as author name, resolution, color space, copyright, and keywords applied to it. You can use metadata to streamline your workflow and organize your files.

1   Make sure that you're using the Essentials workspace.

2   In the Content panel, select the Map_Section1.jpg thumbnail.

▶ **Tip:** Enlarging the Metadata panel reduces the amount of scrolling you need to do to review and edit the information.

3   Drag the right panel's splitter bar to the left, to expand the Preview and Metadata panels.

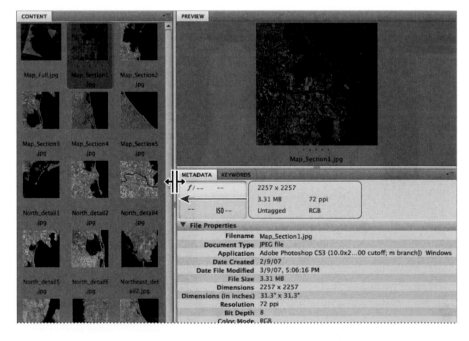

4   In the Metadata panel, click the triangle (▶) next to the IPTC Core heading to expand it, if it isn't already expanded.

The information in the Metadata panel is nested under headings that you can expand or collapse. In Bridge, you can directly edit only some of the IPTC metadata.

METADATA	KEYWORDS			
f / --	--	2257 x 2257		
--	--	3.31 MB	72 ppi	
--	ISO --	Untagged	RGB	

▼ IPTC Core

Creator	Andrew Faulkner	🖉
Creator: Job Title	Digital Image Consultant	🖉
Creator: Address	1435 C Street	🖉
Creator: City	San Rafael	🖉
Creator: State/Province	California	🖉
Creator: Postal Code	94901	🖉
Creator: Country	USA	🖉
Creator: Phone(s)	1-800-000-0000	🖉
Creator: Email(s)	andrew@432email.com	🖉
Creator: Website(s)	www.afstudio.com	🖉
Headline	Map Coast Section 1	🖉
Description	This map section of Northeast coast of Italy Near Ferrara	🖉
Keywords	Italy; coast; survey; area; digital	🖉
IPTC Subject Code	43453-827346-234	🖉
Description Writer	Rachel Lightfoot	🖉
Date Created	2/9/07	🖉

5   Review the information under the IPTC Core heading. Information has been entered about the file, including the file creator's name and address, a description of the image, and keywords. Pencil icons (🖉) appear on the right side of items that you can edit.

Now you'll add some metadata to a different image.

6   In the Content panel, select the Map_Section3.jpg thumbnail. You may have to scroll down to see it.

7   In the IPTC Core area of the Metadata panel, click the pencil icon (✐) next to the first field, named Creator. White fields appear, indicating that you can enter information.

8   For Creator, type your name. Then enter information in the following fields, pressing Tab to advance to the next text box:

   •   For Job Title, type your professional title.

   •   For Address, type your address.

   •   For Keywords, type **coast**.

9   Click the Apply button (✔) at the bottom of the Metadata panel to apply the changes you made.

METADATA	KEYWORDS			
f / --	--	1080 x 1080		
--	--	1.21 MB	72 ppi	
--	ISO --	Untagged	RGB	

▼ IPTC Core

Creator	Andrew Faulkner	✐
Creator: Job Title	Digital Image Consultant	✐
Creator: Address	1010 B Street	✐
Creator: City	San Rafael	✐
Creator: State/Province	CA	✐
Creator: Postal Code		✐
Creator: Country		✐
Creator: Phone(s)		✐
Creator: Email(s)		✐
Creator: Website(s)		✐
Headline		✐
Description		✐
Keywords	coast	✐
IPTC Subject Code		✐

You'll search for other images containing the same keyword.

10 Drag the splitter bar to the right to restore the size of the Metadata and Preview panels.

11 To search all images with the keyword "coast," choose Edit > Find. In the Find dialog box, choose Maps from the Look In pop-up menu. Then, in the Criteria area, choose Keywords from the first pop-up menu, Contains from the second pop-up menu, and type **coast** in the text box. Leave the other settings unchanged, and click Find.

Two images with the keyword "coast" appear in the Content panel.

12 On the right side of the Bridge window, click the Keywords tab to show the Keywords panel. Then click an image in the Content panel to display the keywords assigned to it in the Keywords panel.

Ranking and stacking images

You can organize images in Bridge using labels, including stars or colors, or by stacking related images.

1 In the Content panel, Shift-click to select both images with the keyword "coast."

2 Choose Label > Approved. A green bar appears below the images to indicate their status. You can also rank images in ascending or descending order using the star labels (1 through 5 stars).

3 In the top-left corner of the Bridge window, click the Go Back button (◀) to display all the images in the Maps folder again.

Now you'll label the best images in the group.

4 In the Content panel, Control-click (Windows) or Command-click (Mac OS) to select the North_detail5.jpg, South_detail2.jpg, and West_detail1.jpg thumbnails. Remember that you can resize the thumbnails in the Content window to see more images.

5 Choose Label, and select five stars to label all of the images with five stars.

On the left side of the Bridge window, notice that the Filter panel displays three images with 5-star ratings.

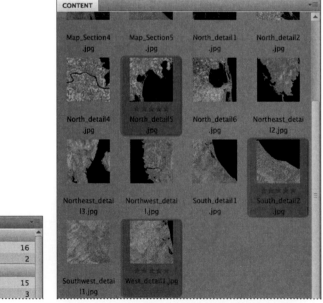

6 Click the 5-star rating under the Filter heading to display only the three ranked images in the Content panel. Once you've ranked images, it's easy to filter your view of the pertinent images for your work.

7 Click the Clear Filter button (⊘) at the bottom of the Filter panel to display all of the images in the Maps folder again, including those marked with the 5-star rating. You can also just click the 5-star rating again to deselect it and return to the view of all the images.

Rating images helps you sort through a large number of images quickly.

Now you'll group related images into stacks, so that you can view and retrieve them more easily. Stacks are a convenient way to group files together visually.

8 Shift-click to select all five of the North_detail thumbnails—North_detail1.jpg through North_detail6.jpg (there's no North_detail3.jpg thumbnail). Then choose Stacks > Group As Stack. Click in a blank area of the Content panel to deselect the group you just created.

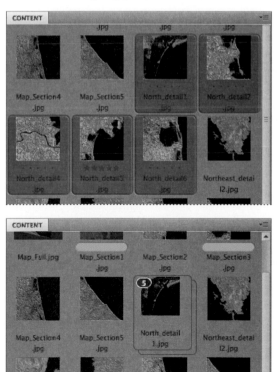

The number in the upper-left corner of the thumbnail indicates the number of files in the stack.

9 Repeat Step 8 for the two Northeast and one Northwest_detail thumbnails. You can use the keyboard shortcut to create the stack quickly: select the thumbnails and press Ctrl+G (Windows) or Command+G (Mac OS) to group them.

10 Create a third stack that includes the two South_detail and one Southwest_detail thumbnails.

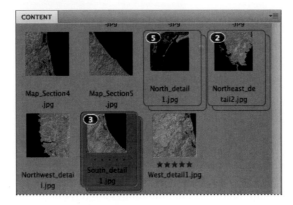

Now you can easily identify the map sections by region when you need to locate them for your work. To open a stack, click the number in the upper-left corner; to collapse the stack, click the number again.

Viewing file information

You'll view information about the file you're about to open, to find out what you'll be working with.

1 In the Content panel, select the Map_Section1.jpg thumbnail.

Bridge lists myriad information about a selected file in the File Properties area of the Metadata panel.

2 Select the Metadata tab, and view the File Properties area. (Expand File Properties or scroll to see the area if it's not visible.)

As you review the information about the file, you can see that it is a JPEG image, 31.3 inches square, with a 72-ppi resolution, bit depth of 8, in RGB mode. You can find this same information in Photoshop, but Bridge displays it more concisely.

3 In the Content panel, double-click the Map_Section1.jpg thumbnail to open the image in Photoshop. Although it's very large in dimension—almost 3 feet square—this image appears like any other image onscreen, though it opens at a 25% to 33% view.

Another way to view file information is using the status bar in Photoshop.

4 In the status bar at the bottom of the image window, click the triangle to display the pop-up menu, and choose Show > Document Dimensions.

Photoshop displays the dimensions in the status bar.

5   Select other options from the Show menu to display additional file information, including the document profile (untagged RGB), measurement scale (currently set at the default of 1:1 pixels), scratch sizes (representing the amount of memory currently used by Photoshop to display all open images, and the total amount of RAM available for processing images, respectively), and the current tool.

6   Choose File > Save As. For Format, choose Photoshop, rename the file **13Working.psd**, navigate to the Lesson13 folder, and click Save.

Brightening and boosting color in an image

Before you dive into your measuring project, you'll spruce up the image that you'll work with throughout this exercise. This image is a bit dark and lacks detail. You want to brighten it to bring out more of the details, and boost the color so that it doesn't look so washed out.

1   Click the Levels button in the Adjustments panel to create an adjustment layer.

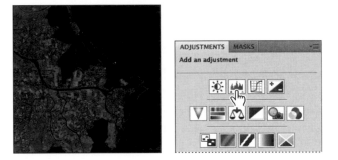

The histogram shows most of the image's pixels clustered in the shadows and midtones.

▶ **Tip:** Instead of moving sliders, you can select the appropriate eyedropper and drag it across the image window to adjust shadows, highlights, or midtones.

2   Drag the white Input Levels slider to the left, to about the point where the pixels begin clustering, or a value of about **142**. We used Input Levels of 0, 1.00, and 142.

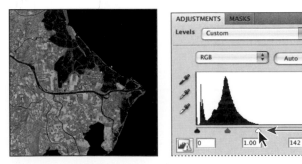

The image still looks a little washed out. You'll correct that.

3 Click the Return To Adjustment List button (◀) at the bottom of the Adjustments panel.

4 Click the Hue/Saturation button in the Adjustments panel to create another adjustment layer.

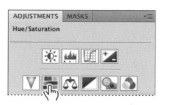

5 Increase the Saturation to +**20**, and then click the Return To Adjustment List button again.

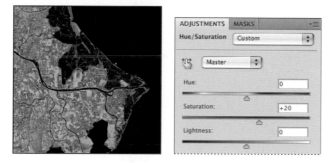

6 Choose File > Save to save your work so far. Click OK in the Photoshop Format Options dialog box.

Creating a map border and work area

To begin creating an infographic from this map segment, you'll select a specific, 25-kilometer-square quadrant in the map using a fixed-size selection marquee, and add a border to it.

The map you'll work on has a predetermined scale of 1605 pixels to 25 kilometers. First, you need to set the proper unit of measure, and then you can find the center of the image using rulers.

1   Choose Edit > Preferences > Units And Rulers (Windows) or Photoshop > Preferences > Units And Rulers (Mac OS). In the Units area, choose Pixels from the Rulers pop-up menu. Click OK.

You'll add guides to help you measure.

2   Choose Window > Info to open the Info panel.

Note: If you position the guide in the wrong spot, press Control (Windows) or Command (Mac OS) and drag the guide out of the image window. Then drag a new guide to the correct location.

3   Choose View > Rulers to display rulers across the top and left side of the image window. Drag a guide from the top ruler down until the Y value in the Info panel reads 326 pixels. (Zoom in if you have difficulty moving to exactly 326 pixels.)

The 326-pixel border plus 1605-pixel-square inset equals the size of the 2257-pixel-square image. You can verify this measurement by selecting the image in the Content section of Bridge and reviewing its metadata.

4   Drag a guide from the left ruler to the right until the X value in the Info panel reads 326 pixels.

5   Select the Rectangular Marquee tool (⬚) in the Tools panel. In the options bar, choose Fixed Size from the Style pop-up menu. Type **1605 px** in both the Width and Height boxes. According to the map's scale, this value is equivalent to 25 kilometers.

6 At the top-left corner where the guides intersect, click the Rectangular Marquee tool to set a selection marquee 1605 pixels square. Now your selection area is exactly centered within the image.

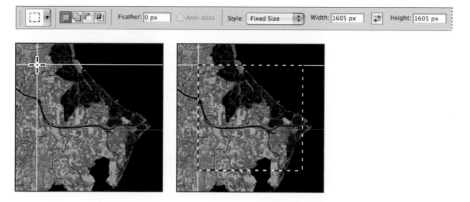

You'll lighten the area around the centered square to bring focus to your work area. First, you will invert the selection, so that it's the border area that's selected.

7 Choose Select > Inverse.

8 Select the Background layer in the Layers panel. Then click the Hue/Saturation button in the Adjustments panel to create an adjustment layer. Increase the Lightness to **+31**, and click the Return To Adjustment List button (◄) at the bottom of the Adjustments panel.

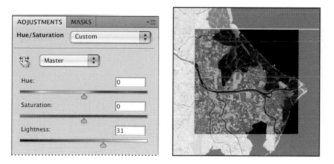

9 Choose File > Save to save your work.

Making a custom border

You'll add a custom border to the selection to make the image pop a bit.

1   Select the Background layer again, and click the Marquee tool in the corner of the inset to select it again.

2   In the Layers panel, select the top Hue/Saturation adjustment layer, and then click the New Layer button (■) at the bottom of the panel. A new, empty layer appears at the top of the panel. Select the layer name and rename it **Border**.

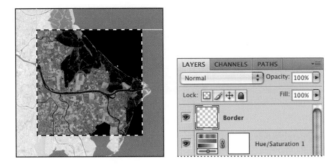

First you'll outline the border, so that you can apply a dashed line to the outline.

3   Choose Edit > Stroke, type **10 px** for Width. Then, click the Color swatch, and click the upper-left corner of the color picker to select white. Click OK to close the color picker. For Location, select Inside. Click OK.

You'll complete the border by applying a dashed-line pattern to the white outline.

4   Choose File > Open, navigate to the Lesson13 folder, and open the Dashed Line.psd file.

5 Choose Edit > Define pattern. In the Pattern Name dialog box, the default pattern name is **Dashed Line.psd**. Delete **.psd** so that the pattern name is **Dashed Line**. Click OK. Then close the Dashed Line.psd file.

6 Select the 13Working.psd tab to make the image active. With the border selection active, choose Blending Options from the Layers panel menu.

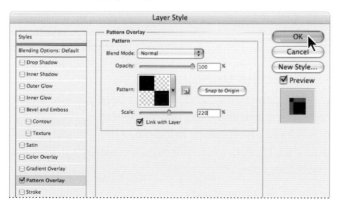

7 In the Blending Options dialog box, click Pattern Overlay in the list on the left. The Pattern Overlay options appear in the center of the Layer Style dialog box.

8 Click the arrow next to the Pattern swatch to display the pattern picker. Select the Dashed Line pattern you just created, and then click away from the pattern picker to close it. Set the Scale to **220**%.

9 Click OK to apply the pattern to the border.

▶ **Tip:** You can use this same technique to add a different colored dashed line. Just vary the Stroke color and the Dashed Line color so that they contrast well. Before you convert artwork to a pattern, make sure that it is on a transparent background.

10 Zoom in on the dashed line in the image window to examine it more closely by pressing Ctrl+spacebar (Windows) or Command+spacebar (Mac OS) and clicking the image.

11 Zoom back out by pressing Alt+spacebar (Windows) or Option+spacebar (Mac OS) and clicking the image.

12 Choose File > Save to save your work. Do not deselect.

Measuring objects and data

You may already be familiar with the Ruler tool in Photoshop, which lets you calculate the distance between any two points in the workspace. The Measurement feature in Photoshop Extended is much more sophisticated: it lets you measure any area defined with the Ruler tool or with a selection tool, including irregular areas selected with the lasso, Quick Selection, or Magic Wand tools. You can also compute the height, width, area, and perimeter, or track measurements of one image or multiple images. Measurement data is recorded in the Measurement Log panel.

The Measurement tool is available only in Photoshop Extended, a version of Photoshop CS4 with additional functionality. If you don't have this version of Photoshop, you can read the next sections to learn about the tool or skip to the review questions.

Working with the Measurement tool

The first step in working with measurements and the Measurement tool is to set the scale. A measurement scale sets a specified number of pixels in the image equal to a number of scale units, such as inches, millimeters, or microns—or, in this case, kilometers. Once you've created a scale, you can measure areas and receive calculations and log results in the selected scale units.

1 In the Layers panel, select the Background layer.

2 Choose Analysis > Set Measurement Scale > Custom.

This map has a scale of 1605 pixels equal to 25 kilometers. You'll use those values now to create a custom scale.

3 In the Measurement Scale dialog box, type **1605** for Pixel Length, **25** for Logical Length, and **Kilometers** for Logical Units.

4 Click OK to set your scaling.

▶ **Tip:** If you're not sure which numbers to use, drag the Ruler tool across the area you want to set. For example, in this image, you'd drag it across the distance you know to be 25 kilometers to determine the pixel length.

Measurement Scale	
Presets: Custom	OK
	Cancel
Pixel Length: 1605	Save Preset...
Logical Length: 25	Delete Preset...
Logical Units: Kilometers	
1605 pixels = 25.0000 Kilometers	
⚠ The Ruler tool has been activated while this dialog is open. You may use it to measure the pixel length for use in your scale.	

Another way to set the scale is to use either the overall dimensions of your image or a measurement from within the image. You then enter these values in the boxes in the Measurement Scale dialog box. Or, you can select a preset scale from the Presets menu.

You're ready to begin measuring the map. You'll start your measurements with the 25-kilometer-square selection, as a control measure against which you can check your work.

5 Make sure that your 1605-pixel-square selection is still active. If you accidentally deselected the selection, reselect the map inset by clicking with the Rectangular Marquee tool at the top-left intersection of the guides.

6 Choose Analysis > Record Measurements. The Measurement Log panel appears at the bottom of the image window.

7 View the columns of data in the Measurement Log panel, using the scroll bar at the bottom of the panel if you need to. Note that the Area measurement is 625.000000 and Scale Units are kilometers—exactly what they should be.

ANIMATION	MEASUREMENT LOG								
Record Measurements									
	Scale Units	Scale Factor	Count	Area	Perimeter	Circularity	Height	Width	Gray Value (
0001	Kilometers	64.200000	1	625.000000	100.000000	0.785398	25.000000	25.000000	

You can customize the Measurement Log columns, sort data within columns, and export data from the log to a spreadsheet file.

8   In the Measurement Log, Ctrl-click (Windows) or Command-click (Mac OS) to select the Circularity, Integrated Density, and four Gray Value columns. You can reorder any column heading by clicking its name and dragging it to the right or left.

You can easily reorder the columns so that they display information in the best order for you. Just as easily, you can control which parameters, or data points, are calculated and shown.

9   Choose Analysis > Select Data Points > Custom. Scroll down to the Selections area, and deselect all of the Gray Value options and the Integrated Density option. You won't use these options, so you don't need to record them.
Click OK.

You won't do this now, but you can save these settings as presets for future projects. You can even create multiple measurement scale presets. However, only one scale can be used in a document at a time.

10   Control-click (Windows) or Command-click (Mac OS) to select the Circularity, Integrated Density, and four Gray Value columns in the Measurement Log. Click the Delete button in the upper-right corner of the panel to remove them. You won't need them for this lesson. Click Yes in the confirmation dialog box.

11   Choose File > Save to save your work so far.

Measuring irregular shapes

Now you'll calculate the area of an irregular shape, the water inside the 25-kilometer square area, but outside the breakers. As you measure, the Measurement Log tracks this data.

1 Choose Select > Deselect so that nothing is selected.

2 Select the Quick Selection tool (✎) in the Tools panel, and select Sample All Layers in the options bar.

3 Select one of the three black water areas. The Add To Selection option is automatically selected in the options bar.

4 Click each of the other two black areas to select them.

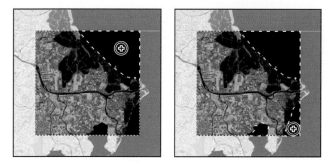

5 In the Measurement Log panel, click Record Measurements. Photoshop Extended records the area of all three individual selections plus the total of the three selected areas.

▶ **Tip:** Alternatively, you could choose Analysis > Record Measurements.

6 Look at the results in the Measurement Log panel. You can drag the top bar of the Measurement Log panel up to expand it. The log details each of the three selections for the water area as a line item; the top item, indicated by a Count of 3, totals the three measurements.

	Document	Source	Scale	Scale Units	Scale Factor	Count	Area	Height
0001	13Working.psd	Selection	Custom (1605 pi...	Kilometers	64.200000	1	625.000000	25.000000
0002	13Working.psd	Selection	Custom (1605 pi...	Kilometers	64.200000	3	134.460312	24.984424
0003	13Working.psd	Selection	Custom (1605 pi...	Kilometers	64.200000		104.892470	11.993769
0004	13Working.psd	Selection	Custom (1605 pi...	Kilometers	64.200000		19.781931	8.224299
0005	13Working.psd	Selection	Custom (1605 pi...	Kilometers	64.200000		9.785910	3.115265

ANIMATION | **MEASUREMENT LOG**

Record Measurements

Your measurements here and in the remaining procedures may vary from those we recorded, depending on the accuracy of your selection.

7 Choose Select > Deselect to deselect the selection of the three seas.

Measuring lines

Measuring lines with the Measurement tool in Photoshop Extended is similar to measuring with the Ruler tool in the Tools panel.

1   Choose Analysis > Ruler Tool.

2   Position the tool pointer at the end of the river on the left side of the map, just within the selection, and drag a line to the right end of the river at the boundary of the selected area.

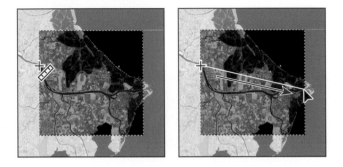

3   In the Measurement Log, click Record Measurements. The distance appears as a Length of about 25 kilometers and an Angle of –13 degrees in the log. This is the length of the river "as the crow flies."

Exporting measurements

You can export selected measurements as a tab-delimited file that can be opened in a spreadsheet application, such as Microsoft Excel. You can then use the spread-sheet application to perform further calculations on your data. You'll use the data you've recorded so far later in this lesson.

1   Return to the Measurement Log panel.

2   Shift-click the measurements to select all of the items in the list. You can also choose to select only some of the items.

3   Choose Export Selected (✋) from the Measurement Log panel menu.

4   In the Save dialog box, rename the file **13_inland_seas**, navigate to the Lesson13 folder, and click Save.

Measuring a cross-section

Now you'll add a little dimension and color. In this part of the lesson, you'll import a three-dimensional graphic that represents a cross-section view of the coastline. Then you'll measure the cross-section in two and three dimensions.

1   Switch to Bridge, navigate to the Lesson13 folder, and double-click the Cross-section.psd thumbnail to open the file in Photoshop.

2   Click the 13Working.psd tab to make the image active. You'll increase its canvas size to create a black area to its right.

3   Choose Image > Canvas Size. Set the width to **3700** pixels. Click the lower-left corner of the proxy so that the additional space will be added on the right. For Canvas Extension Color, choose Black. Click OK.

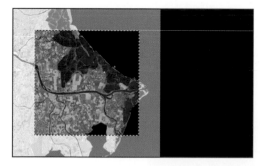

A black area about 1/3 the width of the image window is added to the right of the image.

4   Choose View > Show > Guides to hide the guides. Select the Border layer in the Layers panel.

5   Click the Arrange Documents button (▦) in the application bar, and choose a 2 Up option so that both the Cross-section.psd and Working.psd files are visible. Click the Cross-section.psd tab to make the file active.

You'll reposition the cross-section in the upper quadrant of the map, aligning its section letters to the map's section letters.

6 Select the Move Tool (⯐) in the Tools panel, and drag the illustration onto the 13Working.psd image. Position the illustration as shown in the following figure, so that the gold bar labeled Section overlaps the letters "A" and "B" in the upper-right quadrant of the map.

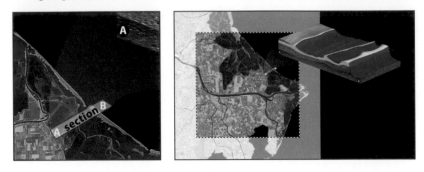

For design aesthetics, the three-dimensional rectangular cross-section is rotated relative to its two-dimensional representation, the gold bar.

If you were to fit the 3D cross-section into the 2D gold bar of the map like a puzzle piece, you would rotate the cross-section towards the top-left corner of the map by about 90 degrees, matching the letter "A" on the cross-section to that on the map. (The gold semitransparency swath represents this rotation.)

You'll make several measurements of the cross-section, starting with the length of its 2D representation.

7 Close the Cross-section.psd file without saving any changes to it.

8 Choose Analysis > Ruler Tool.

9 Using the Ruler tool, click a corner of the gold bar labeled Section, and drag the length of its side to measure the section's length.

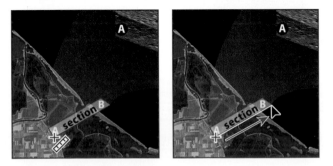

10 In the Measurement Log panel, click Record Measurements. Note the length: ours was 3.36 kilometers long.

You'll use this value in the next part of the lesson.

Circularity	Length	Angle
0.222550		
0.535211		
0.456779		
0.611665		
	25.570948	-13.132854
	3.360000	29.546512

Measuring in perspective using the Vanishing Point filter

Now you'll take some measurements of the cross-section itself, this time in three dimensions. The ability to measure in three dimensions is especially helpful for measuring topographic information from a similar map, an architectural CAD drawing—or any object in space whose dimensions you need to determine.

1 In the Layers panel, make sure that the Section layer is selected.

2 Choose Filter > Vanishing Point. The Vanishing Point dialog box appears, with the Create Plane tool selected.

You'll draw a plane on the front side of the cross-section.

3 Using the Create Plane tool (⌗), click the lower-left corner of the section to set the first anchor point. Then click the lower-right corner, the upper-right corner of the section, and then the upper-left corner to draw a plane on the side of the cross-section.

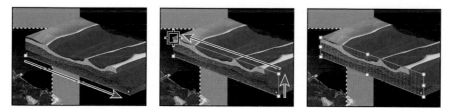

4 In the Vanishing Point dialog box, select the Measure tool.

5 Position the pointer over the left-bottom edge of the cross-section. Make sure that your pointer is over the grid (a cross with a ruler icon will appear). Click the left-bottom edge of the cross-section to set the first measuring point. Then, drag to the right-bottom edge.

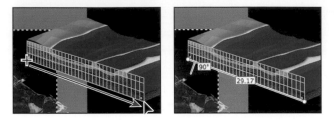

6 In the Length box at the top of the window, enter **3.36** or the value you ascertained in the previous procedure, when you measured the cross-section with the Ruler tool. This is the length in kilometers of the section.

Now you'll measure the depth of the section by measuring vertically along the left edge of the cross-section.

7 Drag again along the bottom edge of the cross section. A readout appears of the length of the cross-section (3.36) and the angle (90 degrees).

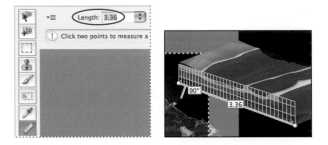

8 Using the Measure tool, click the top-left edge, and then drag downward to the bottom-left edge. The length and angle of the vertical line appear in the window, based on the length you entered in Step 6. The line shows the depth of the cross-section, 0.3 (kilometer) in our measurement.

9 Note the section depth value (0.3 kilometer in our measurement). You'll use this value later.

10 Click OK in the Vanishing Point dialog box to close it.

With your measurements done, you're ready to add the data to the infographic.

Adding a legend

You'll complete the infographic by creating a legend for it, using the measurements you've taken.

1   Switch to Bridge. Navigate to the Lesson13 folder, and double-click the Legend.psd file to open it.

2   Click the Arrange Documents button in the application bar, and choose a 2 Up layout. Make sure the Legend.psd file is active. Then, from the Layers panel, drag the Legend Group layer group onto the 13Working.psd image. Close the Legend.psd file without saving any changes.

3   Zoom out so that you can see the entire 13Working.psd image.

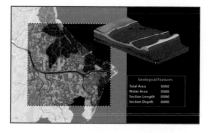

4   Using the Move tool (✛), position the Legend artwork in the lower third of the black background on right.

5   If you have a spreadsheet application, such as Excel, start the application. Navigate to the Lesson13 folder, and double-click to open the 13_Inland_Seas.txt file.

6   In Photoshop, select the Type tool (T) in the Tools panel.

7   Refer either to the measurements displayed in the spreadsheet file, 13_Inland_Seas, or to the values you noted earlier. Many of the values are in the Measurement Log panel. Select the "0000" next to each entry, and type the correct information into the legend table. Our measurements are below. You can substitute your own if they differ:

   • For Total Area, enter **625 km2**.

   • For Water Area, enter **134 km2**.

   • For Section Length, enter **3.36 km**.

   • For Section Depth, enter **0.3 km**.

8   Choose File > Save to save your work.

Creating a slide show

Your infographic is complete. After so much measuring and precise design work, it's time to create a slide show to show off your beautiful graphic to your colleagues.

1 Switch to Bridge, and navigate to the Lesson13 folder. Drag the 13Working.psd file into the Maps folder.

2 Double-click the Maps folder to display its contents. Shift-click the five Map_ Section files to select them, and then Control-click (Windows) or Command-click (Mac OS) the 13Working.psd file to add it to the slide show.

3 Choose View > Slideshow Options. You'll set up your slide show to dissolve from one image into the next, starting with the infographic you created.

4 In the Slideshow Options dialog box, select Scaled To Fit for the When Presenting, Show Slides option; for Transition, choose Dissolve. Leave the other options as they are.

5 Click Play to play slide show. To stop the slide show, press the Esc key on your keyboard.

You can repeat the slide show by choosing View > Slideshow. To flip through the images, press the Right Arrow key on your keyboard; to move backwards through the images, press the Left Arrow key.

You've successfully created an infographic with accurate measurements. Now you're ready to try out your measuring skills on other images in your portfolio.

Review questions

1 What is metadata? How do you add it to a Photoshop file?

2 How do you measure an object in Photoshop Extended with the Measurement tool?

3 What's the difference between the Ruler tool and the Measurement feature?

4 How do you measure in three dimensions?

5 How can you play a slide show of your work?

Review answers

1 Metadata is standardized information about a file, including the author's name, file resolution, color space, copyright, and keywords applied to a file. You can add metadata in the Metadata panel in Adobe Bridge.

2 To measure an object in Photoshop Extended, first set a measurement scale (Analysis > Set Measurement Scale); then, make a selection or use the Ruler tool to measure two points; and then click Record Measurements in the Measurement Log panel or choose Analysis > Record Measurements.

3 The Ruler tool in Photoshop lets you calculate the distance between any two points in the workspace. The Measurement feature in Photoshop Extended measures any area defined with the Ruler tool or with a selection tool, including irregular areas selected with the lasso, Quick Selection, or Magic Wand tools. You can also compute the height, width, area, and perimeter; or track measurements of one image or multiple images. Measurement data is recorded in the Measurement Log panel, where you can sort the data or export it to a spreadsheet file.

4 You can measure in three dimensions by applying the Vanishing Point filter, creating a grid, and then using its Measure tool to measure distances along the grid.

5 To play a slide show of your work, use Adobe Bridge. Select thumbnails of the images to include in the slide show, choose View > Slideshow Options to set display options, and then click Play to run the show. Once you've set slide show options, you can choose View > Slideshow to play it again.

14 PRODUCING AND PRINTING CONSISTENT COLOR

Lesson overview

In this lesson, you'll learn how to do the following:

- Define RGB, grayscale, and CMYK color spaces for displaying, editing, and printing images.

- Prepare an image for printing on a PostScript CMYK printer.

- Proof an image for printing.

- Save an image as a CMYK EPS file.

- Create and print a four-color separation.

- Understand how images are prepared for printing on presses.

 This lesson will take less than an hour to complete. Copy the Lesson14 folder onto your hard drive if you haven't already done so. As you work on this lesson, you'll preserve the start files. If you need to restore the start files, copy them from the *Adobe Photoshop CS4 Classroom in a Book* CD.

To produce consistent color, you define the color space in which to edit and display RGB images, and in which to edit, display, and print CMYK images. This helps ensure a close match between onscreen and printed colors.

About color management

Colors on a monitor are displayed using combinations of red, green, and blue light (called RGB), while printed colors are typically created using a combination of four ink colors—cyan, magenta, yellow, and black (called CMYK). These four inks are called *process colors* because they are the standard inks used in the four-color printing process.

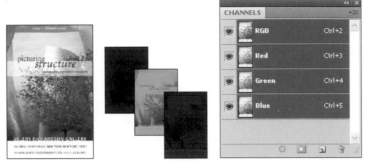

RGB image with red, green, and blue channels

CMYK image with cyan, magenta, yellow, and black channels

Because the RGB and CMYK color models use different methods to display colors, each reproduces a different *gamut*, or range of colors. For example, RGB uses light to produce color, so its gamut includes neon colors, such as those you'd see in a neon sign. In contrast, printing inks excel at reproducing certain colors that can lie outside the RGB gamut, such as some pastels and pure black.

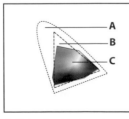

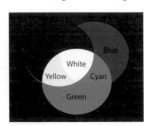

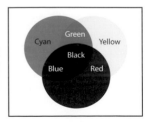

A. Natural color gamut
B. RGB color gamut
C. CMYK color gamut

RGB color model

CMYK color model

But not all RGB and CMYK gamuts are alike. Each monitor and printer model differs, and so each displays a slightly different gamut. For example, one brand of monitor may produce slightly brighter blues than another. The *color space* for a device is defined by the gamut it can reproduce.

RGB model

A large percentage of the visible spectrum can be represented by mixing red, green, and blue (RGB) colored light in various proportions and intensities. Where the colors overlap, they create cyan, magenta, yellow, and white.

Because the RGB colors combine to create white, they are also called *additive* colors. Adding all colors together creates white—that is, all light is transmitted back to the eye. Additive colors are used for lighting, video, and monitors. Your monitor, for example, creates color by emitting light through red, green, and blue phosphors.

CMYK model

The CMYK model is based on the light-absorbing quality of ink printed on paper. As white light strikes translucent inks, part of the spectrum is absorbed while other parts are reflected back to your eyes.

In theory, pure cyan (C), magenta (M), and yellow (Y) pigments should combine to absorb all color and produce black. For this reason, these colors are called *subtractive* colors. Because all printing inks contain some impurities, these three inks actually produce a muddy brown and must be combined with black (K) ink to produce a true black. (K is used instead of B to avoid confusion with blue.) Combining these inks to reproduce color is called four-color process printing.

The color management system in Photoshop uses International Color Consortium (ICC)-compliant color profiles to convert colors from one color space into another. A color profile is a description of a device's color space, such as the CMYK color space of a particular printer. You specify which profiles to use to accurately proof and print your images. Once you've selected the profiles, Photoshop can embed them into your image files, so that Photoshop and other applications can accurately manage color for the image.

For information on embedding color profiles, see Photoshop Help.

Before you begin working with color management, you should calibrate your monitor. If your monitor does not display colors accurately, color adjustments you make based on the image you see on your monitor may not be accurate. For information about calibrating your monitor, see Photoshop Help.

Getting started

First, start Photoshop and restore its default preferences.

1 Start Photoshop and then immediately hold down Ctrl+Alt+Shift (Windows) or Command+Option+Shift (Mac OS) to restore the default preferences. (See "Restoring default preferences" on page 4.)

2 When prompted, click Yes to confirm that you want to reset preferences.

Specifying color-management settings

In the first part of this lesson, you'll learn how to set up a color-managed workflow in Photoshop. Most of the color-management controls you need are in the Color Settings dialog box.

By default, Photoshop is set up for RGB as part of a digital workflow. If you are preparing artwork for print production, however, you'll want to change the settings to be more appropriate for images that will be printed on paper rather than displayed on a screen.

You'll begin this lesson by creating customized color settings.

1 Choose Edit > Color Settings to open the Color Settings dialog box.

The bottom of the dialog box interactively describes each option.

2 Move the pointer over each part of the dialog box, including the names of areas (such as Working Spaces), the menu names, and the menu options. As you move the pointer, Photoshop displays information about each item. When you've finished, return the options to their defaults.

Now, you'll choose a set of options designed for a print workflow, rather than an online workflow.

3 Choose Settings > North America Prepress 2. The working spaces and color-management policy options change for a prepress workflow. Then, click OK.

Proofing an image

You'll select a proof profile so that you can view a close onscreen representation of what an image will look like when printed. An accurate proof profile lets you proof on the screen (*soft-proof*) for printed output.

1 Click the Launch Bridge button (![Br]) in the application bar. In Bridge, navigate to the Lessons/Lesson14 folder, and double-click the 14Start.tif file. Click OK if you see an embedded profile warning.

An RGB image of a scanned poster opens.

2 Choose File > Save As. Rename the file **14Working**, keep the TIFF format selected, and click Save. Click OK in the TIFF Options dialog box.

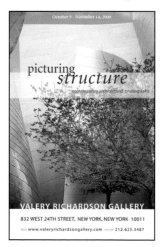

Before soft-proofing or printing this image, you'll set up a proof profile. A proof profile (also called a *proof setup*) defines how the document is going to be printed, and adjusts the onscreen appearance accordingly. Photoshop provides a variety of settings that can help you proof images for different uses, including print and display on the web. For this lesson, you'll create a custom proof setup. You can then save the settings for use on other images that will be output the same way.

3   Choose View > Proof Setup > Custom. The Customize Proof Condition dialog box opens. Make sure Preview is selected.

4   From the Device To Simulate menu, choose a profile that represents the final output device, such as that for the printer you'll use to print the image. If you don't have a specific printer, the profile Working CMYK–U.S. Web Coated (SWOP) v2 is generally a good choice.

5   Make sure that Preserve Numbers is *not* selected.

● **Note:** This option is not available when the U.S. Web Coated (SWOP) v2 profile is selected.

The Preserve Numbers option simulates how colors will appear without being converted to the output device color space.

6   From the Rendering Intent menu, choose Relative Colorimetric.

A rendering intent determines how the color is converted from one color space to another. Relative Colorimetric, which preserves color relationships without sacrificing color accuracy, is the standard rendering intent for printing in North America and Europe.

7   If it's available for the profile you chose, select Simulate Black Ink. Then deselect it, and select Simulate Paper Color; notice that selecting this option automatically selects Simulate Black Ink. Then click OK.

Notice that the image appears to lose contrast. Paper Color simulates the dingy white of real paper, according to the proof profile. Black Ink simulates the dark gray that actually prints to most printers, instead of solid black. Not all profiles support these options.

▶ **Tip:** To display the document with and without the proof settings, choose View > Proof Colors.

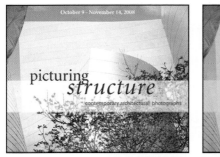

Normal image   Image with Paper Color and
                                Black Ink options selected

Identifying out-of-gamut colors

Most scanned photographs contain RGB colors within the CMYK gamut, so changing the image to CMYK mode converts all the colors with relatively little substitution. Images that are created or altered digitally, however, often contain RGB colors that are outside the CMYK gamut—for example, neon-colored logos and lights.

Before you convert an image from RGB to CMYK, you can preview the CMYK color values while still in RGB mode.

1 Choose View > Gamut Warning to see out-of-gamut colors. Adobe Photoshop builds a color-conversion table and displays a neutral gray in the image window where the colors are out of gamut.

Because the gray can be hard to spot in the image, you'll convert it to a more visible gamut-warning color.

2 Choose Edit > Preferences > Transparency And Gamut (Windows) or Photoshop > Preferences > Transparency And Gamut (Mac OS).

3 Click the color sample in the Gamut Warning area at the bottom of the dialog box. Select a vivid color, such as purple or bright green, and click OK.

4 Click OK again to close the Transparency And Gamut dialog box. The bright, new color you chose appears instead of the neutral gray as the gamut warning color.

5 Choose View > Gamut Warning to turn off the preview of out-of-gamut colors.

Photoshop will automatically correct these out-of-gamut colors when you save the file in Photoshop EPS format later in this lesson. Photoshop EPS format changes the RGB image to CMYK, adjusting the RGB colors as needed to bring them into the CMYK color gamut.

Adjusting an image and printing a proof

The next step in preparing an image for output is to make any color and tonal adjustments that are necessary. In this exercise, you'll add some tonal and color adjustments to correct an off-color scan of the original poster.

So that you can compare the image before and after making corrections, you'll start by making a copy.

1 Choose Image > Duplicate and click OK to duplicate the image.

2 Click the Arrange Documents button in the application bar, and select a 2 Up layout so you can compare the images as you work.

You'll adjust the hue and saturation of the image to move all colors into gamut.

3 Select 14Working.tif (the original image).

4 Click the Hue/Saturation button in the Adjustments panel to create a Hue/
Saturation adjustment layer. Then do the following:

- Drag the Hue slider until the colors, especially the tops of the buildings, look
  more neutral. (We used +15.)

- Drag the Saturation slider until the intensity of the colors looks more realistic
  (we used -65).

- Leave the Lightness setting at the default value (0).

5 Choose View > Gamut Warning. You have removed most of the out-of-gamut
colors from the image. Choose View > Gamut Warning again to deselect it.

6 With 14Working.tif still selected, choose File > Print.

7 In the Print dialog box, do the following:

- Choose your printer from the Printer menu.

- Choose Color Management from the pop-up
  menu at the top of the right column.

- Select Proof to select your proof profile.

- For Color Handling, choose Printer Manages
  Colors

- For Proof Setup, choose Working CMYK.

- If you have a color PostScript printer, click
  Print to print the image, and compare the
  color with the onscreen version. Otherwise,
  click Cancel.

Saving the image as a CMYK EPS file

You'll save the image as an EPS file in CMYK format.

1   With 14Working.tif still selected, choose File > Save As.

2   In the Save As dialog box, do the following:

- Choose Photoshop EPS from the Format dialog box.

- Under Color, select Use Proof Setup. Don't worry about the warning icon; you'll save a copy.

- Accept the filename 14Working.eps, and click Save.

> **Note:** These settings cause the image to be automatically converted from RGB to CMYK when it is saved in the Photoshop Encapsulated PostScript (EPS) format.

3   Click OK in the EPS Options dialog box that appears.

4   Save and then close the 14Working.tif and 14Working copy.tif files.

5   Choose File > Open, navigate to the Lessons/Lesson14 folder, and double-click the 14Working.eps file.

Notice in the image file's title bar that 14Working.eps is a CMYK file.

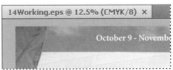

Printing

When you're ready to print your image, use the following guidelines for best results:

- Print a *color composite*, often called a *color comp*, to proof your image. A color composite is a single print that combines the red, green, and blue channels of an RGB image (or the cyan, magenta, yellow, and black channels of a CMYK image). This indicates what the final printed image will look like.

- Set the parameters for the halftone screen.

- Print separations to make sure the image separates correctly.

- Print to film or plate.

Specifying halftone screens

To specify the halftone screen when you print an image, use the Screen option in the Print dialog box. The results of using a halftone screen appear only in the printed copy; you cannot see the halftone screen on your computer screen.

When you print color separations, Photoshop prints a separate sheet, or *plate*, for each ink. For a CMYK image, it prints four plates, one for each process color. Each screen contains halftone information for the respective channel, including screen frequency, screen angle, and dot shape.

The *screen frequency* controls the density of dots on the screen. Since the dots are arranged in lines on the screen, the common measurement for screen frequency is lines per inch (lpi). The higher the screen frequency, the finer the image produced (depending on the line-screen capability of the printer). Magazines, for example, tend to use fine screens of 133 lpi and higher, because they are usually printed on coated paper and on high-quality presses. Newspapers, which are usually printed on lower-quality paper, tend to use lower screen frequencies, such as 85 lpi.

The *screen angle* used to create halftones of grayscale images is generally 45 degrees. For best results with color separations, select the Auto option in the Halftone Screen dialog box (which is accessible through the Print dialog box, as you'll see in a minute). You can also specify an angle for each of the color screens. Setting the screens at different angles ensures that the dots placed by the four plates blend to look like continuous color and do not produce moiré patterns.

Diamond-shaped dots are the most commonly used in halftone screens. In Photoshop, however, you can also choose round, elliptical, linear, square, and cross-shaped dots.

In this exercise, you'll adjust the halftone screens for the poster image, and then print the color separations.

1 With the 14Working.eps image open from the previous exercise, choose File > Print.

2 At the top of the right column of options, choose Output from the pop-up menu.

3 Click Screen at the bottom of the dialog box. (Screen is available only if you've selected a PostScript printer.)

● **Note:** By default, an image prints using the halftone screen settings of the output device or of the software from which you output the image. You usually don't need to specify halftone screen settings unless you want to override the default settings. Always consult your prepress partner before specifying halftone screen options.

4 In the Halftone Screen dialog box, do the following:

- Deselect Use Printer's Default Screen.

- Select each option in the Ink menu to see the Frequency, Angle, and Shape information for each color channel.

- Choose Cyan from the Ink menu, and then choose Ellipse from the Shape menu.

- Select each of the Magenta, Yellow, and Black inks from the Ink menu again, and notice that Ellipse is selected for each.

- Click OK to close the Halftone Screen dialog box.

By default, Photoshop prints any document as a composite image. To print this file as separations, you need to explicitly instruct Photoshop in the Print dialog box.

5 In the Print dialog box, do the following:

- Choose Color Management from the pop-up menu at the top of the right column.

- Select Document.

- Choose Separations from the Color Handling menu.

- Click Print.

6 Choose File > Close, and don't save the changes.

This completes your introduction to printing and producing consistent color using Adobe Photoshop. For more information about color management, printing options, and color separations, see Photoshop Help.

Review questions

1 What steps should you follow to reproduce color accurately?

2 What is a gamut?

3 What is a color profile?

4 What are color separations?

Review answers

1 Calibrate your monitor, and then use the Color Settings dialog box to specify which color spaces to use. For example, you can specify which RGB color space to use for online images, and which CMYK color space to use for images that will be printed. You can then proof the image, check for out-of-gamut colors, adjust colors as needed, and—for printed images—create color separations.

2 A gamut is the range of colors that can be reproduced by a color model or device. For example, the RGB and CMYK color models have different gamuts, as do any two RGB scanners.

3 A color profile is a description of a device's color space, such as the CMYK color space of a particular printer. Applications such as Photoshop can interpret color profiles in an image to maintain consistent color across different applications, platforms, and devices.

4 Color separations are separate plates for each ink used in a document. Often, you'll print color separations for the cyan, magenta, yellow, and black (CMYK) inks.

INDEX

SYMBOLS

2D layers, merging onto 3D layers 373
3D
    cross-sections 372
    design 394
    measuring in 419
    shapes 364
    workspace 365
3D Axis 380
3D features 364–391
3D files, importing 374
3D glasses, rendering for 389
3D layers
    adding spot lights 379–389
    animating 385–389
    creating 3D postcards 383–384
    creating from imported files 374–375
    manipulating with the 3D Axis 380
    merging 375
    merging 2D layers onto 373
    overview 366
    painting on 382
    resizing 375
    text in 382
3D Orbit tool 366, 367
3D panel 369–371
3D Pan tool 368, 383
3D postcards, creating 383–384
3D Roll tool 368
3D Rotate tool 366, 367, 369, 383
3D Scale tool 368, 375
3D shape presets 364
3D shapes, creating from layers 364
3D tools
    overview 44
    using 366

A

actions 319–327
    batch-playing 324–325
    creating new 321
    creating new set 321
    naming 321
    overview 319
    playing 323
    recording 321
Actions panel 321–327
    Play button 323
Add A Pixel Mask button 140
adding
    borders 317, 410
    canvas 51, 157, 316
Add To Path Area option 246
Add To Selection option 97
adjustment layers 21
    Color Balance 56
    creating 282–283
    Hue/Saturation 161–162
    Levels 282–284
    overview 282
adjustments
    Invert 86
    Levels 150
Adobe Authorized Training Centers 7
Adobe Bridge 393, 394–406
    adding favorites 136
    Content panel 402
    creating a slide show in 354
    customizing views 395–399
    enlarging panels 398
    enlarging previews 397
    Folders panel 395
    installing 3
    Keywords panel 401
    labeling images 402–403
    Loupe tool 397
    Metadata panel 397, 399
    opening files 13–14
    organizing assets 398–401
    overview 394
    panels 395
    Preview panel 396
    searching assets 398–401
    slide show 422
    stacking related images 402–404
Adobe Camera Raw
    adjusting white balance in 179
    Basic panel 181

dialog box 178
Open Object button 187
saving files in 188
synchronizing settings across
  images 184
workflow 179
Adobe Certification program 6
Adobe Dreamweaver 359
Adobe Illustrator
animating files from 342
editing Photoshop Smart Objects
  in 266
Glyphs panel 229
previewing files 396
Adobe InDesign 73
Adobe Photoshop CS4
installing 3
new features 2–3
plugins 6
resources 5
starting 4
Adobe Photoshop CS4 Classroom in
  a Book
copying lesson files 4–5
installing lesson files 4
prerequisites 3
Adobe Photoshop CS4 Extended 2,
  393, 412
3D features 364–391
Adobe Photoshop CS4 Product
  Support Center 6
Adobe Photoshop Lightroom 206
Adobe TV 6
Adobe Updater 39
aligning
layers 130
selections 299
slices 338–339
text 230
alpha channels 136
defined 169
loading as selection 153
overview 141
anchor points 243, 244
animated GIF files 342–348
animating
3D layers 385–389
layer styles 346
Animation panel 385
creating animations 342–349
play options 348
animations
creating 342–349
exporting 386–389
file format 342

previewing 345
tweening to create 344, 346
anti-aliasing 94
application frame, in Mac OS 12
Apply Layer comp box 129
architectural CAD drawings 419
Arrange Documents button 63
arrow keys
nudging selections with 83–84
Shift key with 83
Auto-Align Layers 130, 204
Auto Color command 54–55
Auto Contrast command 55
Auto Correction vs Auto Color 54
automatic commands
color adjustments 53–54
manual vs. 63–64
automating tasks 319–327
auto slices 336
hiding 340

B

background
color 254
removing 158
background layer 106
converting to regular layer 108
erasing 111
overview 108
badges, on slices 336, 337
barrel distortion 199
Baseline Shift 230
Basic panel (in Camera Raw) 181
Batch command 324
Bevel and Emboss layer style 279
bitmap images
overview 240
vector graphics vs. 240–241
Black Matte option (Refine Edges) 98
black point 181
_blank Target option 340
blending modes
applying to layers 115
overview 114
Blending Options dialog box 411
borders
adding 111, 126, 317, 407–412
dashed line 410–412
discarding 53
Bridge. See Adobe Bridge
Brightness slider (in Camera Raw)
  181
Brushes panel 28, 310

Brush tool, setting options 27–28,
  138
buttons, website 338

C

calibration, monitor 427
camera lens flaws, correcting
  199–201
Camera Raw. See Adobe Camera Raw
camera raw images. See Adobe
  Camera Raw
cameras supported by Adobe
  Camera Raw 177
creating 177
file formats for saving 188
histogram 183
opening 177–178
overview 177
proprietary 174
saving 185–186
sharpening 183
white balance and exposure
  adjustment 179–180
cameras, in 3D layers 366
canvas
adding 51, 157–158, 316, 417
rotating 263
Canvas Size dialog box 157, 316
center point, selecting from 84
channel masks 149
defined 169
layer masks vs. 151
channels
adjusting individual 149
applying filters to individual 303
copying 149
correcting noise in 192
displaying individual 139
displaying in respective color 148
editing in 149
hiding 148
hiding and showing 139
identifying selections with 149
naming 153
overview 136
printing size 287
turning off 148
viewing 147–148
Channels panel 136. See
  also channels
channel information 139
loading selections 153
mask display 151

Character panel 33, 118, 220, 223–224, 225, 228
checkerboard
    pattern 259–261
    transparency indicator 111
chromatic aberration 199
Chrome filter 303
Classroom in a Book 1
clipping layers 166–167, 271–272
    creating 162
    indicator 167
clipping masks 27
    creating 217–219
    defined 169, 215
    indicator 219
    shortcut 219
Clone Stamp tool 64–66, 67
cloning, and blending 197
closed paths 241, 245
CMYK color mode
    converting RGB images to 431
    filters 153
CMYK color model 427
    defined 426
    gamut 426
color
    additive 427
    adjusting overall 55
    blending 67, 69
    boosting 406–407
    brightening 406–407
    default text 217
    editing masks and 147, 154
    inverting 86, 278
    managed workflow 428–429
    matching across images 318–320
    out-of-gamut 431
    previewing CMYK values in RGB
        mode 431
    replacing 59–61
    selecting by 78
    setting background 254
    setting default 254
    setting foreground 254
    softening edge transitions 94
    swapping foreground and
        background 254
Color Balance adjustment layer 56
color casts, removing 54, 56
color comp 434
color corrections
    skin tones 319
    washed out images 407–408
colorizing 161–162
color management 428–429
    selecting when printing 433

color modes
    changing 72
    retouching for intended 48
Color panel 33
color profiles 427
Color Range dialog box 158
color settings
    restoring 5
    saving 5
Color Settings dialog box 428–429
color space 427
    device profile 427
combining images
    montage 295
    panorama 324–329
Commit Any Current Edits button
    125
Commit Transform button 261
Community Help 6
compression settings 353
context menus
    annotations 231
    browser 359
    layers 233
    overview 31–32
    Smart Objects 278
    type 222, 226
    web browser 332
continuous-tone images 353
contrast 57–60
Convert To Smart Objects command
    233
copying
    and anti-aliasing 94
    and transforming 87
    at same resolution 88
    channels 149
    Classroom in a Book lesson files
        4–5
    commands 88
    images 127, 287, 432
    images, and centering 110
    in perspective 281–282
    layers 109–111
    selections 86
    settings in Camera Raw 184
    text 227
Copy Merged command 88
corner points 244, 246
Create Plane tool 197, 273, 419
Crop And Straighten Photos
    command 102
cropping
    adjusting crop area 95
    and straightening automatically
        102

images 52–54, 295–296
    using other image dimensions 51
cropping shield 52
Crop tool 52, 295
    adding canvas with 51
cross-sections, 3D 372
curved paths 244, 246–247
Curves panel 20–21
customizing
    keyboard shortcuts 35, 276
    workspaces 34
Custom Shape tool 259
Cutout filter 303
cutouts 256–257

D

dashed lines, in a border 410–412
Default Foreground And Background
    Colors button 254
defaults
    resetting 4, 10
    resetting colors 26
depth of field, adding 202
desaturating 308–309
deselecting 18, 81
    paths 258
details, defining 184
Direct Selection tool 244, 256, 266
discretionary ligatures 229
Dismiss Target Path button 255
displaying layers 110
distortions, correcting 199–202
DNG file format 174, 177, 188
docking panels 32
document profiles 406
document size, displaying 127, 287,
    404–405
Dodge tool 61
Drag The Mesh tool 377
drop shadows 100–101, 123, 167
    layer style 219, 315
Duplicate Selected Frame button
    342, 343
duplicating images 432

E

edges
    sharpening 193–194
    softening 97–98
editing
    individual channels 149
    nondestructive 147
    quick masks 139–142
    shapes 256

editing images
    adjusting highlights and shadows
        189–191
    correcting distortions 199–201
    in perspective 196–200
    reducing noise 191–193
    removing red eye 190–191
    sharpening edges 193
Edit Plane tool 274
effects
    copying 347
    moving 167
    tweening 346
Elliptical Marquee tool 17, 78
    anti-aliasing and feathering 94
    centering selection 84
    circular selections with 82
EPS file format 434
Eraser tool 96
exporting
    animations 386–389
    HTML pages 349–351
Eyedropper tool 168
eye icon, in the Layers panel 107

F

Favorites panel, in Bridge 13
Feather command 94
feathering 94, 197
file formats
    animation 342
    from Camera Raw 188
    image quality and 295
    three dimensional 2
    transferring images between
        applications and platforms
        188
    type 229
file information 404
files
    reverting to unchanged version
        21
    saving 21, 127–130
file size
    compressing for web 353
    flattened vs. unflattened 127
    printing 287
    reducing 127, 287–289
    with channels and layers 287
Fill Pixels option 259
fill properties, shape layer 255
film functionality 394
Filter Gallery 153, 156
    overview 304

filters 303–306
    adding clouds with 117
    applying to masks 153
    improving performance 303
    overview 305
    shortcuts 305
Fit On Screen command 85
flattening layers 127–130, 287–288
    stamping and 288
    white fill replaces transparency
        287
focus, adjusting 202
fonts
    alternates 229
    selecting 216, 224–225
foreground color 254
four-color printing 72–73, 426
fractions 229
frames
    new based on previous 343
    repositioning 344
    tweening 346
Freeform Pen tool 241
freehand selections 90–91
Fuzziness slider 60

G

gamma 57
gamut 426
    colors outside of 431–432
Gamut Warning 431–432
Geometry Options menu 246
GIF, animated 342
GIF compression 349, 350
Glass filter 154, 303
gradient masks 154–155
Gradient Overlay layer style 302
gradient picker 120
gradients
    applying to mask 154–155
    listing by name 120
Gradient tool 120
grid, perspective 274
grouping images (in Bridge).
    See stacking images
guides 227, 234
    adding 160, 215, 297, 408
    deleting 408
    displaying 234
    for creating slices 341
    overview 297
    Smart Guides 299

H

Halftone Screen dialog box 435, 436
halftone screen settings 435–436
hand-coloring selections 306
Hand tool 93
Healing Brush tool 67–68
    setting options 68
    Spot Healing Brush tool vs. 66
Heal option 197
hiding
    all layers but one 148
    channels 148
    layers 110
highlights
    adjusting 189–191
    manually adjusting tonal range
        57–60
    Shadow/Highlight command
        55–56
high-resolution images 49
    filters and 303
Histogram panel 57–59
histograms
    in Camera Raw 183
    interpreting 406
History panel
    changing number of states 31
    clearing actions 321
    undoing multiple actions 28–31
Horizontal Type tool 118, 216, 223,
    225
    setting options 220
HTML pages
    exporting 349–351
    naming 339
hue
    adjusting for printing 432
    replacing in image 59–61
Hue/Saturation adjustment layer
    161, 407
hypertext links 334
    adding 339, 340, 341
    defined 334

I

illustrations with type 353
images
    adding canvas to 157–158
    centering and copying 217
    continuous-tone 353
    copying 127
    cropping 295
    determining scan resolution 50
    duplicating 432

images *(continued)*
    fitting on-screen 93
    fitting to screen 19
    flattening 128–130, 287
    labeling in Bridge 402–403
    matching color schemes 318–320
    optimizing for web 349–351, 353
    rating 402–403
    resizing for web 186
    resolution 49–50
    searching in Bridge 398–400
    sharpening 183
    size and resolution 49–50
    solid-color 353
    technical 394
    viewing image dimensions
        404–405
    washed out 407–408
Image Size command 88
image window 12, 15, 16–17
    fitting image to 85
    scrolling 22
importing
    3D files 374–375
    Illustrator artwork 277–278
    layers from other files 272–273
    Smart Objects 277–278
infinite lights, in 3D layers 370–371
infographics 393, 407–423
    legends 421–422
Inverse command 19
Invert command 86
inverting masks 142, 164

J

JPEG compression 349, 350
JPEG file format
    camera raw images and 177
    image degradation and 195, 295
justifying type 228

K

keyboard shortcuts
    creating 35–37, 276–277
    customizing 276
    duplicating 86
    filters 305
    loading selections 153
    Move tool 82
Keyboard Shortcuts And Menus
        dialog box 35–37
keyframes, in animation 385
keywords, searching images by 398,
        401–402

L

labeling images 402–403
Lasso tool 69, 78, 90–91
    closing selection 91
lasso tools 90–91
    anti-aliasing and feathering 94
layer comps 284–286
    adding 284
    overview 129
    viewing different 285
layer effects 279
    copying 101
    removing 101
layer groups 286–287
    clipping 166
    copying 163
    flattening 288–289
    merging 288
layer masks
    adding 155
    defined 169
    selection indicator 156
    shape layer 255
    turning on and off 147
    unlinking 147, 152
layers
    3D shapes from 364
    adding 117–118
    adjustment 282–284
    aligning 130
    as animation frames 342
    background 108
    blending modes 114–115
    clipping 271–272
    converting to background 108
    copying 88, 109–111
    copying and centering 110, 113,
        115, 224, 228, 229, 233
    copying and merging 88
    creating by copying 250
    deleting 248
    deleting hidden 264
    effects 119–122, 121–124
    erasing 111–113
    flattening 127
    flattening visible 128
    grouping 163
    grouping by content 285–287
    grouping into Smart Object
        232–233
    hiding 107, 110
    hiding all but selected 111, 148
    linking 116–118, 222
    locking 107
    matching colors 319
    merging 72, 232–233, 272,
        287–288
    merging 3D layers 375
    merging groups 288–289
    merging visible 127
    moving between documents 159
    opacity 114
    overview 106
    printing size 287
    rasterizing 278
    rearranging 112–114
    removing pixels from 111–113
    renaming 109
    resizing 116–118
    selecting contents 273
    shape 254, 255
    showing 110
    slices from 340
    stamping 288–289
    switching between combinations
        of 284
    template 253, 264
    thumbnails, hiding and resizing
        107
    transforming 116
    transparency 114–115
    tweening 346
    type 118
    unlinking from layer mask 147,
        152
    warping 232–233, 234–235
Layers panel
    animating with 342–349
    deleting hidden layers 264
    overview 107–108
    Quick Mask mode indicator 138
    shape layers 255, 258
    vector mask 258
layer styles
    adding 279
    adding to type 219
    animating 346–348
    applying 119–122, 121–124
    copying to other layers 315
    Drop Shadow 315
    Gradient Overlay 302
    Outer Glow 347
    overview 119, 121
    Pattern Overlay 411
Layer Via Copy command 250
legends, map 421–422
Lens Correction filter 199–201
Levels
    adjusting channel 150
    adjustment layer 57, 282, 282–
        283, 406

Lighting Effects filter 303
lightness
    adjusting 61
    adjusting for printing 433
    replacing color 59–61
lights, in 3D layers
    adjusting 370–371, 378
    changing the color of 371
    overview 366
    spot lights 379–389
linear gradients 117–119
line art 353
lines, measuring 416
linking
    layers 222
    masks to layers 147
Load Path As Selection option 249
low-resolution images 49

M

Mac OS, differences in work area 11
Magic Wand tool 78, 248
    anti-aliasing 94
    combining with other tools
        88–89
Magnetic Lasso tool 78, 92–93
    anti-aliasing and feathering 94
Magnetic Pen tool 241
magnification 15
magnifying glass. *See* Zoom tool
Make Selection dialog box 250
Make Work Path From Selection
    option 249
maps, in 3D layers 366
maps, measuring 419
marquee tools 78
Mask Edge button 145
masks
    applying filters to 153
    color values for editing 136, 147
    inverting 142, 164
    loading as selection 151–153
    moving contents 165
    of delicate edges 158–161
    overview 136
    replacing colors in 59
    terminology 169
    type 166–168
    unlinking from layer 152
Masks panel 140, 142, 145, 147, 164
    sliders in 147
Match Color dialog box 318
materials, in 3D layers 366
Measurement Log panel 412, 415
    deleting data points 414

exporting data 416
    presets 414
Measurement tool, setting scale 412
measuring objects 412–418
    control value 413
    exporting data 416
    irregular 415–417
    lines 416
    presets 413
    setting scale 412–413
Merge Layers command 233
Merge Visible command 128, 288
merging
    2D layers onto 3D layers 373
    3D layers 375
    images 130, 202
    layers 72, 127, 288
meshes, in 3D layers 366
    merging into the same 3D layer
        375
metadata
    adding to images in Bridge 400
    searching images by 398–400
Metadata panel (in Bridge) 397, 399
midtones 57
mistakes, correcting 26–33
mobile authoring 48
Mode command 72
monitor calibration 427
monitor resolution 49–50
montages, assembling 295–303
Move tool 24, 251
    moving selections 80
    scissors icon 85
moving
    panels 32
    selections 80–81

N

navigation buttons, website 338–340
    previewing function 337
Navigator panel 22
New Layer Based Slice command
    340
New Layer From 3D File command
    374
No Image slices 341
noise, reducing 191–193
nondestructive filters 312

O

objMesh component 376
online galleries 354
opacity

animating 344–345
    layer 114–115
Open Object button (in Camera
    Raw) 187
open paths 241, 245
OpenType file format 214, 229
optimizing images 353
options bar
    compared to panels 34–35
    overview 23–24
    setting type options in 23
Outer Glow layer style 347
out-of-gamut color 431–432
output resolution, determining 49

P

page layout, preparing images for
    72–73
painting
    blending strokes 197
    on 3D layers 382
    with Spot Healing Brush tool
        66–67
painting effects 306, 310
panels
    compared to options bar 34
    expanding and collapsing 33–34
    floating 253
    overview 32–33
    undocking 33
    working with 24–26
panoramas, creating 324–328
Paper Color option 431
paper, simulating white 431
Paragraph panel 33, 228
paragraph type 216
    adding to 229
    designing 226–228
Paste Into command 88
pasting
    and anti-aliasing 94
    at same resolution 88
    commands 88
    in perspective 275, 279, 281–282
    text 228
Patch tool 69–70
paths 241–242
    closing 245, 247
    converting smooth points to
        corner 246
    converting to selections 248–249,
        249–251
    deselecting 255–256, 258
    drawing curved 244
    drawing straight 244

paths *(continued)*
    guidelines for drawing 243
    naming 249
    saving 245, 247
path segments 244
Path Selection tool 255, 256
Paths panel 245, 246
    deselecting paths 255
    vector mask 256
Pattern Overlay layer style 411
patterns
    creating 259–261
    dashed line 411–413
PDF image gallery 207
PDF slide show 207
Pencil tool 241
Pen tool 254
    as selection tool 243
    drawing paths 243–247
    keyboard shortcut 241
    overview 241–242, 244
    setting options 245–246
perspective
    adding 273–276
    adding to type 278–280
    editing images in 196–200
    measuring in 419–421
    pasting in 275
    plane 278
photo correction
    adjusting contrast 57–60
    automatic 53–54, 71–72
    automatic vs. manual 63
    cropping and straightening 52–54
    removing color cast 56
    replacing colors 59–61
    resolution and size 49–50
    retouching strategy 48
    saturation 59–61
    straightening and cropping 52–54
    tonal range 57–60
    unsharp masking 71–72
Photomerge dialog box 325
Photoshop. *See* Adobe Photoshop
Photoshop EPS file format 432
Photoshop file format 295
Photoshop Help 6
Photoshop Raw file format 177
    camera raw format vs. 177
pincushion distortion 199
pixels
    blending 197
    defined 10, 49, 240
    image and monitor 49–50

Place command 277
placing files 277–278
    Adobe Illustrator text 261–262
    resizing 280
plug-ins 10
point type 216
    distorting 225–226
    paragraphs vs. 226
Polygonal Lasso tool 78, 280
    anti-aliasing and feathering 94
Polygon tool 256
portfolio, creating 207–209
PostScript fonts 214, 229
pound sign (#) 337
preferences
    gamut-warning color 431
    restoring default 4
    units and rulers 408
Preserve Numbers option 430
Preview panel (in Bridge) 396
Print dialog box 433, 436
Printer Manages Colors option 433
printing color 425–437
    adjusting tone and color 432–434
    CMYK model and 426–427
    guidelines 434
    identifying out-of-gamut color 431–432
    proof 432
    proofing images on screen 429–432
    resolution 49
    saving image as separations 434
    specifying halftone screens 435–436
printing inks, simulating 431
process colors 48, 426
Proof Colors command 431
proofing images 429–432
proof profiles 430
    selecting 433
proof setup 430
prototyping 214, 270
PSD format 188
    camera raw images and 177
Purge command 303

Q

Quick Mask mode 138
quick masks 136
    creating 137–140
    editing 139–142
    painting color 138
Quick Selection tool 78, 79–80

R

Radius slider, Unsharp Mask filter 71
RAM 406
    filters and 303, 305
raster images, overview 240
Rasterize Layer command 278
rasterizing
    Smart Objects 278
    vector masks 147
rating images 402–403
Record Measurements command 415
Rectangular Marquee tool 78, 89
Red Eye tool 190–191
Reduce Noise filter 191–193
Refine Edge 69, 94, 96–98
Refine Mask dialog box 145
removing backgrounds 158
Render Video dialog box 387
Replace Color command 59–61
resizing
    3D layers 375
    layers 116
    panels 33
resolution 49–50
retouching/repairing
    auto-mending 69–70
    by blending pixels 67–68
    by cloning 64–66
    overview 48
    removing blemishes 66–67
    setting correct resolution 49–50
RGB color mode
    converting image to CMYK 431
    filters 154
RGB color model 426–428, 427
    described 427
    gamut 426
Ripple filter 303
rollovers
    defined 332
    from slices 338, 358–359
Roll The Mesh tool 377
Rotate Light tool 370, 378
Rotate Mesh tool 377
Rotate View tool 263
rotating 92, 164, 252
    the canvas 263
ruler guides 215, 297
rulers 216
    displaying 253, 297
    hiding 164
    setting unit of measure 297, 407

S

Sample Aligned option 65
saturation
    adjusting with Sponge tool 62
    replacing in image 59–61
Saturation slider (in Camera Raw)
    181
Save For Web And Devices dialog
    box 349–350, 353
saving
    image as separations 434
    optimized images 353
Scale Mesh tool 377
scale, setting for measurements 412
scaling 87, 218
    layers 116
scan resolution 50
scene, 3D 375
scratch sizes 406
screen angle 435
Screen blending mode 347
screen frequency 435
scrubbing 24, 223
searching images 398
selecting
    freehand and lines 88–89
    from center point 84–85
    high-contrast edges 92–93
    inverse selection 89–90
    layer contents 273
    layers 111
    overview 78
    slices 336
    text 125
selections
    blending 197
    by color 78, 96–101
    circle 85
    constraining 19
    converting to paths 248–249
    copying 88
    copying to another image
        250–251
    deactivating 18
    duplicating 86
    elliptical 81–89
    expanding 98
    feathering existing 94
    fine-tuning edges 97–98
    fixed size 407–408
    freehand 78
    from masks 151–153
    geometric 78
    hiding edges 84
    indentifying with channel 149

indication 18
inverting 19, 409
loading using shortcuts 153
making intricate 158–161
measuring 412
moving 18, 19, 80–81, 82, 85–86
moving border 82
moving incrementally 83
precise 249
rotating 91–92
saving on separate layers 99–100
showing edges 84
softening 94
subtracting from 89, 250
subtracting from while loading
    309
selection tools 78–79
    Pen tool 243
_self Target option 339
separations
    printing 435–437
    saving image as 434
shaders, in 3D layers 366
Shadow/Highlight adjustment
    189–191
Shadow/Highlight command 55–56
shadows
    adjusting 189–191, 406
    adjusting manually 57–60
shape layers 255
    subtracting shapes 256–257
    tool option 254
shapes
    custom 259–262
    editing 256
    measuring 415–417
    subtracting from 257
sharpening images
    in Camera Raw 193
    using the Smart Sharpen filter
        193
    using the Unsharp Mask filter 71
shortcuts, customizing 35, 276
Show Extras button 297
Show/Hide Visibility column 110
Show Transform Controls option
    262
sidecar XMP files 184
Single Column Marquee tool 78
Single Row Marquee tool 78
skin tones, correcting 319
Slice Options dialog box 337
slices 336–343
    aligning 338–339
    creating buttons from 338
    creating for rollovers 358–359

defined 334
dividing 341
layer-based 340–341
methods for creating 341
naming 339
optimizing for web 349
selecting 336
selection indicator 337
symbols 336, 337
targeting 339
unlinking from layer 341
Slice Select tool 336, 349
Slice tool 338
slide shows 354, 422–423
Smart Filters 312–315
Smart Guides 299
Smart Objects
    automatic update on editing 261,
        266
    editability 232
    editing 236, 308
    filtering and painting 278
    grouping layers into 232–233
    layer thumbnail 261
    linking vector masks to 262
    overview 261
    placing 277
    rasterizing 278
    Smart Filters and 312
    warping 234–235
Smart Sharpen filter 193
smooth points 244, 246
snapping, guides 297
soft-proofing 429–432
solid-color images 353
Spatter filter 303
spell checking 222
Sponge tool 62
Spot Healing Brush tool 66–67, 67
spot lights, adding to 3D layers
    379–389
Sprayed Strokes filter 303
spreadsheet applications 421
    exporting data to 416
stacking images 402–404
stacking order
    changing in layer sets 286
    changing layer 112–114
stacks, opening 404
Stained Glass filter 303
stamping layers 288–289
Standard mode 137
starting Photoshop 10
status bar 15, 405
    choosing options from 127

straightening images 52–54
Stroke dialog box 410
stroking 410
Subtract From Shape Area option 257
swashes 229
Swatches panel 25–26
swatches, selecting 25
Switch Foreground And Background Colors button 254
synchronizing settings in Camera Raw 184

T

Target option 339
technical images 394
temperature, image 179
template layers 253
    deleting 264
text. *See also* type
    3D 382
    adding 216, 227–228, 299–303
    coloring 24–26
    copying 227
    creating 118–119
    default color 217
    deselecting 25
    editing imported 277
    moving 24, 119
    pasting 228
    placing from Adobe Illustrator 261–262
    selecting 125
textures, in 3D layers 366
three-dimensional. *See* 3D
Threshold slider, Unsharp Mask filter 71
thumbnails
    layer 107
    layer mask 147
    shape layer 255, 258
    Smart Object 261
TIFF (Tagged Image File Format) 73, 429
    camera raw images and 177
    overview 188
tint, defined 179
Toggle Lights button 370, 378
tonal range
    adjusting automatically 54
    adjusting manually 57–60
tools
    constraining 18–19
    HTML creation 334
    keyboard shortcuts for 241

overview 40
    selecting hidden 17–18
    selection 78–79
    using 14–20
Tools panel
    compared to other panels 34–35
    double-column view 15
    overview 40
    selecting and using tools from 14–20
tool tips, displaying 15
topographic information 419
tracking 222, 224, 228
transformations
    bounding box 87
    freeform 116–117, 252–253, 279
transforming
    in perspective 279
    layers 116–118
    Smart Objects 262
transparency
    adjusting 114–115
    indicating 111
    in masks 154
    in web-optimized images 353
    removed on flattening 272
Transparency And Gamut dialog box 431
TrueType fonts 229
Tween dialog box 345
tweening frames 342, 344–346
    with copied effect 347
type. *See also* text
    aligning 216
    as design element 220–223
    centering 230
    clipping mask 215
    clipping mask with 217–219
    coloring 168, 221
    creating 168, 216–217
    formatting controls 223–224
    glyphs 229
    justifying 228
    masking with 166–168
    overview 214
    paragraphs 226–228
    previewing 223–224
    recoloring 280
    resizing 214
    resolution independent 214
    selecting 228, 231
    setting options 216, 227, 231
    styles 224
    swashes 229
    tricks 222
    true fractions 229

vertical 230–231
    warping 225–226
typefaces
    formats 214
    selecting 216, 223–224
type layers 118
    creating new 222
    moving with mask layer 222
    selecting contents 222
    updating 242
Type tool 23–24

U

undocking panels 33
Undo command 28
undoing actions 26–33
Unsharp Mask filter 71–72
updates for the Photoshop CS4 application 39
user forums 6
user slices 336
USM (unsharp masking) 71–72
U.S. Web Coated (SWOP) v2 profile 430

V

Vanishing Point filter 196–200, 273–276
    applied to Smart Object 278–279
    defining grid 196–198
    editing objects with 197
    measuring in 419–421
vector graphics 10
    bitmap images vs. 240
    drawing shapes 252–254
    overview 240
    subtracting shapes from 256–257
vector masks 255
    converting to layer mask 147
    defined 169
    selecting 256
    selection indication 258
    unlinking from layer 147
vertical type 230–231
Vertical Type tool 230
video functionality 394
vignetting 199

W

warping
    layers 232–233, 234–235
    type 225–226, 236

web content
    color mode 48
    optimizing images for 349–351,
        353
Web Design workspace 334–335
web galleries 354
white balance, adjusting 179–180
White Balance tool (in Camera Raw)
    179–180
white point 181
widget, 3D Axis 380
Windows, differences in work area
    11
work area 10 45
    differences between Mac OS and
        Windows 11
workflows
    color-managed 428–429
    prepress 429
Working CMYK - U.S. Web Coated
    (SWOP) v2 profile 430
Work Path
    naming 249
    overview 245
    saving 247
workspaces
    Adobe Bridge 395–399
    Advanced 3D 365
    customizing 34–38, 334
    default 11
    preset 34–35
    saving 38

X

XMP files 184

Z

Zoomify feature 333, 353
zooming out 82
Zoom tool 15–18

Production Notes

The *Adobe Photoshop CS4 Classroom in a Book* was created electronically using Adobe InDesign CS3. Art was produced using Adobe InDesign, Adobe Illustrator, and Adobe Photoshop. The Myriad Pro and Warnock Pro OpenType families of typefaces were used throughout this book.

References to company names in the lessons are for demonstration purposes only and are not intended to refer to any actual organization or person.

Images

Photographic images and illustrations are intended for use with the tutorials.

Lesson 4 Pineapple and flower photography © Image Source, www.imagesource.com

Typefaces used

Adobe Myriad Pro and Adobe Warnock Pro are used throughout the lessons. For more information about OpenType and Adobe fonts, visit www.adobe.com/type/opentype/.

Team credits

The following individuals contributed to the development of this edition of the *Adobe Photoshop CS4 Classroom in a Book*:

Project Manager: Elaine Gruenke

Technical Writer: Brie Gyncild

Technical Editor: Zorana Gee

Compositor: Lisa Fridsma

Copyeditor and Proofreader: Karen Seriguchi

Indexer: Brie Gyncild

Cover design: Eddie Yuen

Interior design: Mimi Heft

Art Director: Andrew Faulkner

Designers: Elaine Gruenke, Keely Reyes

Design Assistant: Sam Graves

Adobe Press Editor: Victor Gavenda

Adobe Press Production Editor: Hilal Sala

Adobe Press Project Editor: Connie Jeung-Mills

Contributors

Jay Graham—began his career designing and building custom homes. He has been a professional photographer for more than 22 years, with clients in the advertising, architectural, editorial, and travel industries. He contributed the "Pro Photo Workflow" tips in Lesson 6.
http://jaygraham.com

Arne Hurty—is an award-winning technical illustrator and designer who composed the scientific illustration for Lesson 13.
http://www.baycreative.com

Tyler Munson—lent his design and art direction to Lessons 3 and 14. With his San Francisco design and branding firm, munsonDesign, Tyler has created programs for clients that include Gap, Palm, Oracle, and music producer Paul Oakenfold.
http://www.munsondesign.com

Lee Unkrich—has directed major films for Pixar. His photographs appear in Lessons 5 and 9 of this book.

The fastest, easiest, most comprehensive way to learn
Adobe® Creative Suite® 4

Classroom in a Book®, the best-selling series of hands-on software training books, helps you learn the features of Adobe software quickly and easily.

The **Classroom in a Book** series offers what no other book or training program does—an official training series from Adobe Systems, developed with the support of Adobe product experts.

To see a complete list of our Adobe® Creative Suite® 4 titles go to www.peachpit.com/adobecs4